Energy Investing
DeMYSTiFieD®

Energy Investing
DeMYSTiFieD®

Davis W. Edwards

New York   Chicago   San Francisco   Athens   London   Madrid   Mexico City
Milan   New Delhi   Singapore   Sydney   Toronto

1 2 3 4 5 6 7 8 9 0 DOC/DOC 1 9 8 7 6 5 4 3

ISBN   978-0-07-181274-0
MHID   0-07-181274-1

e-ISBN   978-0-07-181275-7
e-MHID   0-07-181275-X

Library of Congress Cataloging-in-Publication Data

Edwards, Davis W.
  Energy investing demystified / by Davis Edwards.
    pages cm.
  Includes index.
  ISBN-13: 978-0-07-181274-0 (alk. paper)
  ISBN-10: 0-07-181274-1 (alk. paper)
  1. Energy industries.   2. Investments.   I. Title.
  HD9502.A2E34 2010
  332.6—dc23   2013008350

McGraw-Hill Education books are available at special quantity discounts to use as premiums and sales promotions, or for use in corporate training programs. To contact a special sales representative, please visit the Contact Us page at www.mhprofessional.com.

This book is printed on acid-free paper.

This book is dedicated to my children,
Spencer and Brianna. Hopefully, they will enjoy the
written word as much as they enjoy science and math.

This book is also dedicated to my wife, Angela,
who has taken care of everything while I spent time writing.

About the Author

Davis W. Edwards, FRM, ERP, is a senior manager in Deloitte & Touche's National Securities Pricing Center managing energy derivatives valuation. Prior to joining Deloitte, he was division director of credit risk at Macquarie Bank and senior managing director on the statistical arbitrage trading desk at Bear Stearns. He is a regular speaker on the topic of financial modeling and mathematics applied to real-world problems. He is the author of the book, "Energy Trading and Investing," and the director of the Houston chapter of the Global Association of Risk Professionals.

Contents

Introduction

Energy products have become some of the most heavily traded commodities in the world following deregulation in the gas, oil, and electricity industries in the late 20th century. Prior to deregulation, prices were set by governments or other regulatory agencies. Along with slowing innovation and reducing efficiency, this limited private investments in these industries. As these markets were deregulated, opportunities for small investors multiplied. Currently, there are an abundance of trading and investing opportunities in the energy markets.

Deregulation has not ended government involvement in the energy industry. It merely changed how this involvement is manifested. The energy industry remains one of the most highly regulated industries in the world. Regulations exist at the international, national, and local levels. In many cases, these regulations have conflicting goals. For example, affordable energy has fueled human progress for the past century, eliminating poverty and improving living conditions for many people. However, this has come at the price of increased pollution and the risk of global warming. This can lead to diverging energy policies at different levels of government.

CHAPTER OBJECTIVES

After completing this chapter, the student should have an understanding of

- Investing
- The role of regulation of energy markets

How to Use this Book

This book is intended to be both a reference manual and a training course. It is patterned after training courses given to traders and professional investors by energy companies, hedge funds, and investment banks when they first start working on a trading desk. The purpose of this book is to give the reader the same level of knowledge as a professional trader or energy investor might possess on these topics. After reading this book, the reader should have a solid understanding of the products, infrastructure, and industries that make up the energy market.

To first time investors, it might seem odd that this book spends so much time explaining the details of the financial markets that can help someone become a good investor. Initially, it might seem unfair that someone armed with a how-to book should be competing for investment opportunities with MBAs and PhDs from top schools, educated and provided with the best data that money can buy. However, it can be done—and done successfully.

One key is to do your own work. By the time a broker is calling about investment opportunities, there probably isn't a lot of opportunity left. Hundreds of thousands of other smart people have had the chance to look at the opportunity first. Easy profit opportunities disappear pretty quickly, and what gets left over is not always that appealing. Knowing about what is actually going on in the industry allows you to understand trends when they start forming. It dramatically increases the chance of finding a good opportunity early.

However, that's only part of the investing story. What tends to get missed in investing is the concept of risk. Trading isn't always about finding good opportunities. Largely, it's a matter of avoiding bad opportunities. If an investor can avoid losing money, most of the other outcomes look pretty good. The better an investor is able to avoid large losses, the more likely they are to be successful in the long run. The key to avoiding investment disasters lies in understanding the details of the industry

Investing is the commitment of money to an endeavor with the goal of making a profit. This can be done directly by speculating on future price movements through the purchase of futures, swaps, forwards, and options. Investing can also be done indirectly through purchasing stocks and bonds issued by companies involved in the energy markets.

- **Stocks (Equity Investments).** An investment that makes the investor a partial owner in a company.
- **Bonds (Fixed Income Investments).** An investment that involves loaning money in return for interest payments.
- **Options, Futures, Swaps, and Forwards.** A direct investment to buy or sell a commodity in the future. Commonly, these investments are liquidated prior to delivery.

This book is divided into two major sections. The first section describes the physical side of the energy industry—the products and businesses that define the energy industry. The second section gives an overview of the financial products that allow investors to invest in the energy industry. The material and the questions in this book are similar to the material and questions that need to be understood by professional traders who work on a trading desk or at a hedge fund.

Energy Prices

Energy prices are different than the price of most other financial commodities. One reason is that energy is an essential resource to most people—almost everyone uses some type of energy product every day. When shortages occur, or prices start to skyrocket, governments have a strong incentive to stabilize the market. Compared to other financial markets, some characteristics of the energy market are price spikes and mean reversion.

- **Price Spikes.** Because energy is so heavily used, even a small mismatch between supply and demand can lead to a price spike. Deregulated markets are set up so that when there is too little supply to meet everyone's needs, prices will rise until someone willingly decides to cut back on their purchases.

- **Mean Reversion.** Energy prices can snap back to their pre-spike equilibrium levels as quickly as they can spike upwards. In the financial industry, this is called *mean reversion*. For example, during an August heat wave, the unwillingness of consumers to forego air conditioning might cause electricity prices to skyrocket. However, as soon as the outdoor temperature drops to comfortable levels overnight, consumer demand for the electricity can disappear and electricity prices return to where they were prior to the heat wave.

When a government exerts control over a market, they aren't looking to protect the interests of investors. In many cases, they do just the opposite—they transfer money from investors to consumers. Understanding the motivations of governments is the first step to understanding the energy market.

Industry Regulation

Because energy is a necessary commodity for many people, the energy industry is one of the most regulated industries in the world. This regulation occurs at all levels of government. At a national level, concerns of political independence, economic stability, and climate change often dominate debates. At local and regional levels, pollution, reliability, and affordability of power become important to members of these communities. In many cases, it is difficult to distinguish between politics and energy industry regulation.

The shifting balance between government energy priorities is a source of investing opportunities as well as a source of investing risk. Policy changes are a source of opportunity because they create a constant uncertainty in the energy market. However, regulation is also a source of risk since regulators are typically going to look after the needs of consumers rather than investors.

To create an energy policy, governments have to balance the needs of many constituents. Some major concerns include:

- **Policy Independence.** By withholding or restricting energy supplies, governments can seek to influence or control policy decisions in other areas. In other cases, governments will look to protect themselves from being influenced.

- **Economic Security.** Energy resources are not evenly distributed around the world. Some parts of the world have a surplus that can be sold to other countries. Over time, the transferring of enough money out of one area and sending it to another area will damage the economy that is exporting money and importing energy.

- **Affordable Energy.** Access to affordable energy like electricity and gasoline is one of the primary methods that governments can use to reduce poverty and improve quality of life for constituents. Cheap energy makes for happy consumers, and happy consumers make for a stable government.

- **Clean Environment.** Low cost sources of electricity can release substantial amounts of pollution. Dangerous conditions caused by pollution and unsafe facilities can be a threat to constituents of a community.

Energy Independence

When a country controls its own energy supplies, it is less exposed to the political and economic risks associated with being dependent on supplies from another country. For example, in 2009, Russia shut down many of the natural gas pipelines supplying Germany and Eastern Europe with sources of heating during an extremely cold winter. News articles at the time linked the shutdown to Russia reacting to political criticism from Europe regarding Russia's actions in Belarus and Ukraine.

Relying on the lowest cost, nonpolluting imported energy resources may expose a country to political pressure from a variety of sources. For example, pipelines are a convenient way to transport energy but are vulnerable to damage and hard to defend during conflicts. In the example of Germany, the country was looking to phase out nuclear power units that were unpopular with German consumers. The German government had to balance a risk (imported natural gas from Russia) with a goal (reducing dependence on nuclear power).

Affordable Power

Affluent countries and affluent special interest groups place a much lower value on eliminating poverty than those governments trying to cope with widespread poverty. Affluent communities, like California in the United States, tend to focus on building renewable power, eliminating pollution, and other projects that will raise energy prices. Most of the consumers in that region can afford higher costs. However, a large number of countries like China, India, and most of Africa are fighting a war on poverty. Providing low cost, reliable power is part of an effort to reduce poverty. High energy prices would undermine the goal of eliminating poverty. As a result, the relative importance of cheap power compared to eliminating pollution varies dramatically by area.

Reliability

The economy of industrialized countries is often reliant on a steady supply of energy in the form of electricity and transportation fuel. This need often has to be balanced against consumer activism aimed at eliminating certain technologies.

For example, in the mid-1960s, the population of Long Island, NY was growing quickly and needed additional power units. Long Island is a heavily populated island running east–west from the boroughs of Brooklyn and Queens to rural farmland 120 miles east of New York City. As with all islands, transmission of electricity from the mainland is difficult. It is also difficult to transport large amounts of fuel necessary for conventional power plants. When the Long Island Lighting Co. (LILCO) decided to build a nuclear generation unit on the eastern side of the island near Shoreham, it encountered massive community opposition. The criticism of the nuclear plant eventually led to its abandonment. This led to extremely high power prices and heavier use of conventional facilities, many of which were highly inefficient.

DISCUSSION QUESTIONS

Policy Decision 1: "…and stay out!"

A consumer group is advocating the use of imported natural gas as an affordable, low-pollution way to become less reliant on highly polluting coal. The natural gas comes from a region whose political ideology is very different from your views and you are concerned that the source region will use the fuel to blackmail your region. How much policy interference is acceptable in exchange for cheap, reliable power?

Would you be willing to give up in exchange for less pollution:

- Women (Men) having (losing) the right to vote?
- Legalize (Outlaw) abortion?
- Outlaw (Legalize) drugs or alcohol?
- Outlaw (Legalize) handguns?
- Adoption of some religion other than your own as a state religion?

Policy Decision 2: "It's all about the children"

A consumer advocacy group is advocating severe cuts in carbon dioxide emissions to diminish the risk of global warming and improve the lives of people a century from now. The higher costs of energy will damage the economy and lead to unemployment.

What kind of consequences need to be avoided in order to justify increased poverty today?

- If future generations are already likely to be twice as well off as we are today, should we push 30% of people into poverty to make future generations 10% more affluent than that baseline?
- If future generations are already likely to be twice as well off as we are today, should we push 10% of people today into poverty today to make future generations 50% more affluent than that baseline?
- Should we do nothing for the future unless they are likely to have worse lives than we have today?

Policy Decision 3: "Dollars and Sense"

The high costs of doing business within a state have led to a large number of companies relocating to less expensive areas. While not the sole cause of the high costs, electricity costs for the region are substantially higher than nearby areas. The high costs of power are directly related to environmental regulations passed by the community.

- Would you personally be willing to give up your job and take a less profitable employment in exchange for clean, nonpolluting power?
- If the relocating businesses will just build polluting generation and factories in their new areas, is it still worthwhile to pay higher prices and suffer the loss of jobs in your area?
- Is forcing companies to relocate the best option? Would less restrictive local policies that keep more companies in the regulated community reduce overall pollution more than having them relocate to a community with no environmental regulations?

Energy Investing
DeMYSTiFieD®

Part I

The Energy Markets

Chapter 1

Petroleum, Refined Products, and Biofuels

This chapter introduces fossil fuels and discusses the relationship between solid, liquid, and gaseous fuels. It then goes on to focus on one type of fuel (liquid fuels). The next chapter discusses fuels that exist in gas and solid forms at standard temperature and pressure.

Over 90% of the world's energy is supplied by fossil and biofuels. These fuels are composed of hydrocarbon molecules that produce heat when combined in a chemical reaction with oxygen. The length and structure of the molecules determine the property of each fuel. The shortest molecules, called *natural gases*, exist as gases at standard temperature and pressure conditions. The mid-length molecules exist as liquids. These are called *petroleum* products. The longest chains are solids and called *coal*.

CHAPTER OBJECTIVES

After completing this chapter, the student should have an understanding of

- The major types of fuels
- Oil and gas exploration and drilling
- Types of crude oil

- Crude oil transport
- Petroleum refining
- Refined products like diesel, gasoline, and jet fuel

Hydrocarbon Fuels

Almost all fuels used to produce energy are composed of hydrogen and carbon. In chemistry classes, they would be called *hydrocarbons*. The principle difference between different types of fuels is the length of the carbon–carbon chains. Very short chains of carbon exist as gases, longer ones as liquids, and the longest of all as solids. Hydrocarbons release energy when their carbon and hydrogen bonds are broken and combined with oxygen in the process of combustion. In other words, hydrocarbons are fuels that release energy when burned. Hydrocarbon fuels exist as solids, liquids, and gases (see Figure 1-1).

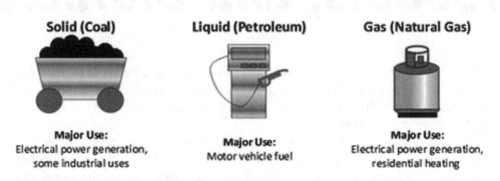

Solid (Coal)

Major Use:
Electrical power generation, some industrial uses

Liquid (Petroleum)

Major Use:
Motor vehicle fuel

Gas (Natural Gas)

Major Use:
Electrical power generation, residential heating

FIGURE 1-1 • Hydrocarbon Fuels Exist as Solids, Liquids, and Gases

Small hydrocarbon molecules—those that have one, two, three, or four carbon atoms—exist as a gas under standard conditions. The smallest hydrocarbon (methane, chemical formula CH_4) is called *natural gas. Longer gaseous* molecules are collectively called *natural gas liquids* or *liquefied petroleum gas.*[1] Even longer molecules—those with five to approximately sixty carbon atoms—exist as liquids under standard conditions. These are collectively called *petroleum.*[2] The shorter chain liquids flow readily and can easily vaporize into gas. Longer chains are very viscous and may need to be heated before they flow easily. Once molecules get very large, they no longer turn into liquids under any normal conditions. These solid fuels are called "coal." There are many varieties of coal which vary in hardness and composition.

Viscosity

Viscosity is a measure of resistance. A low viscosity liquid is commonly described as *thin* and flows easily. When compared to the spectrum of petroleum products, gasoline and water are examples of low viscosity liquids. A high viscosity liquid is commonly described as *thick* and does not flow easily. Maple syrup or molasses are examples of high viscosity liquids.

The relative value of each fuel is affected by a large number of factors. Fuels with a high energy density (heat content) and that are easy to use, transport, and store are the most valuable. For example, vehicular fuels, like gasoline (petrol), diesel, and jet fuel tend to have high energy density (see Table 1-1). Lighter fuels, like propane and butane, may be equally easy to use but have less energy content than gasoline. Heavier fuels, like Bunker Fuel (Fuel Oil No. 6) are typically more difficult to use than gasoline. As a result, these fuels are typically less expensive than common vehicular fuels.

Approximate heat content of various fuels		
Name		Units
Crude Oil	5.800	MMBTU/BBL
Jet Fuel (Jet-A)	5.670	MMBTU/BBL
Gasoline	5.150	MMBTU/BBL
Diesel (No.2 Fuel Oil)	5.825	MMBTU/BBL
Bunker Fuel (No. 6 Fuel Oil)	6.287	MMBTU/BBL
Ethane	3.082	MMBTU/BBL
Ethane-Propane Mixture (70 percent-30 percent)	3.308	MMBTU/BBL
Propane (C3)	3.836	MMBTU/BBL
Isobutane (IC4)	3.974	MMBTU/BBL
Butane-Propane Mixture (60 percent-40 percent)	4.130	MMBTU/BBL
Butane (NC4)	4.326	MMBTU/BBL
Natural Gasoline (C5+)	4.620	MMBTU/BBL
Natural Gas (Dry)	1024	BTU/cf^3
Natural Gas (Wet)	1101	BTU/cf^3

TABLE 1-1 • Heat Content of Fuels

Source: Energy Information Agency, Annual Energy Outlook 2011, appendices.

Even more difficult to use, and less expensive, is a solid fuel like coal. While it would be possible to burn any of these fuels for energy, some fuels are easier than others to use, and are correspondingly more valuable.

The relative value of fuels affects prices throughout the fossil fuel value chain. For example, when fossils fuels are removed from the ground, they exist as a mixture of fuels and unwanted substances that must be separated from one another. The value of that mixture is heavily dependent on the components and the effort necessary to remove pollutants. Raw fuel has to be *refined* into usable products. For a variety of reasons, this is typically done at a refinery or a processing plant located a long distance from the oil well or coal mine. There is typically one distribution system to get raw materials (like crude oil) to the refinery or processing plant, and a separate distribution system to get the refined products (like gasoline) to consumers.

Exploration & Production

Energy investing starts with exploration and production. While it's possible to produce renewable energy, the easiest and most cost effective way to meet consumer demand for energy is often to use existing fossil fuel sources. This requires identifying the location of potential resources and extracting them from the ground.

During this process, energy companies typically do not want to purchase land. Instead, they will usually lease the land or purchase the mineral rights for a piece of property. This allows them to extract the fuel from the ground and then move on to the next field. The owners of the land get paid royalties (usually a percentage of the profit). Exploration involves both finding potential reserves and negotiating contracts with the owners of the mineral rights.

In the U.S., the rights to oil and gas located under the surface are often owned by private individuals. In most other regions, fossil fuel resources are owned by the government of the host country. Regardless of who owns the land, exploration companies must typically get licenses to explore for new resources and other licenses to develop the resources for production.

The Landman

Landman is a term that refers to both men and women who assist oil and gas exploration companies in the negotiation of titles and leases to property. A landman is responsible for contacting land owners who might be interested in selling mineral rights and negotiating the necessary contracts.

There are several types of contracts that may be signed for the production of oil and gas reserves. Energy exploration and production is a speculative activity. It involves the risk that development costs will not be recovered because too little fuel is extracted or because commodity prices have fallen. In addition, there are a variety of specialized skills needed to make exploration projects run smoothly. A variety of contracts can be used depending on the interest and ability of the participants to take on the risk of development and the task of selling the fuel after it is extracted from the ground.

- **Tax and Royalty.** The exploration company gives the owner of the oil and gas rights a percentage of the profit that it obtains for selling fuel. Typically, the exploration company will pay an upfront licensing fee and percentage of the gross profits. In this type of contract, the exploration company takes on all of the risk of developing resources. A typical contract will give the land owner one-eighth of the gross profits.

  For example, if a well produces 10,000 barrels of oil at an $80 average price, the land owner will get (1/8th) (10,000 barrels) ($80/barrel) = $100,000 royalty payment.

- **Production Sharing.** The exploration company gives the owner a percentage of the fossil fuels that are produced. In this type of contract, the exploration company takes on the risk of developing fossil fuel reserves, and passes on a portion of the output to the owner who must arrange to sell or use the output.

- **Service Contract.** With a service contract, the oil company acts as a contractor. The oil company is paid a fee to produce oil and gas rather than taking ownership of the crude oil. This involves relatively little risk for the exploration and production company with most of the costs being paid by the land owner.

Traditional Wells

Fossil fuels are formed when decaying organic material is trapped in an area where it can't disperse. When material is trapped underground, it is placed under tremendous heat and pressure. Over millions of years, this heat and pressure splits the organic material into shorter hydrocarbon chains. These short hydrocarbon chains (fossil fuels) are typically less dense than the surrounding rock and start to rise to the surface. If they hit an impermeable layer of rock, the hydrocarbon fuels may pool underground and become trapped. When a hole in the impermeable rock is drilled by an exploration company, the fuel continues its journey to the surface (see Figure 1-2).

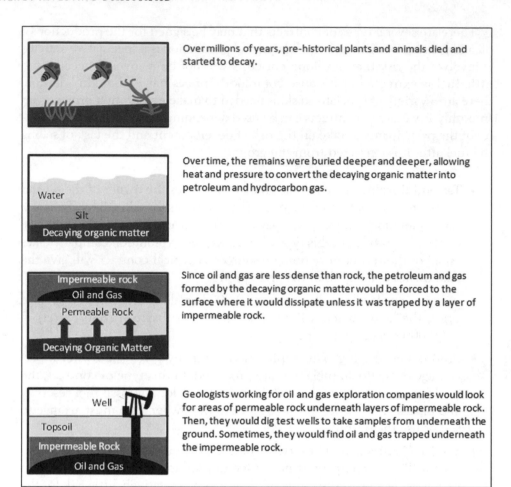

Over millions of years, pre-historical plants and animals died and started to decay.

Over time, the remains were buried deeper and deeper, allowing heat and pressure to convert the decaying organic matter into petroleum and hydrocarbon gas.

Since oil and gas are less dense than rock, the petroleum and gas formed by the decaying organic matter would be forced to the surface where it would dissipate unless it was trapped by a layer of impermeable rock.

Geologists working for oil and gas exploration companies would look for areas of permeable rock underneath layers of impermeable rock. Then, they would dig test wells to take samples from underneath the ground. Sometimes, they would find oil and gas trapped underneath the impermeable rock.

FIGURE 1-2 • Formation of Traditional Oil and Gas Resources

There are three density related mechanisms that force the *migration* of oil and gas to the surface. When hydrocarbons are broken into smaller pieces by heat and pressure, the newly matured hydrocarbons take up more space because smaller hydrocarbons are less dense than larger hydrocarbons. First, this raises the pressure in the location where this occurs and pushes the hydrocarbons out of the area. Second, oil and gas (and almost all other liquids and gases) expand when they get hot. Temperatures deep in the earth are higher than at the surface and this further increases the pressure when the hydrocarbons are forced downwards. As a result, the primary way to relieve this overpressure is to force the hydrocarbons upwards. Finally, because oil and gas are lighter than the surrounding rock and water, buoyancy will also force oil and gas upwards.

Key Concept

Formation of Oil and Gas

- Oil and gas are formed from decaying organic matter.
- Hydrocarbons are lighter than precursor organic matter, rock, and water. Oil and gas are forced to the surface by overpressure, heat, and buoyancy.
- Some oil and gas will be trapped underneath impermeable rock layers, forming pools that can be recovered by drilling.

A large portion of oil and gas formed in this way will make its way to the surface where it will eventually dissipate into the atmosphere. The portions that get trapped are the oil and gas resources known as *fossil fuel*. Historically, oil and gas exploration focused on finding geological layers of rock that could trap hydrocarbons and drilling test wells to determine if any fossil fuels were trapped underneath. Modern technology has revolutionized that process. Geologists now use seismic waves to create three-dimensional underground maps using computers to interpret and collate test results. This is a much more effective way of looking for liquids and gas trapped underground.

In many cases, because the oil and gas are under substantial pressure underground, they will flow to the surface with little effort on behalf of the oil driller. In some cases, water can be pumped into the well to increase the underground pressure and force oil to flow out.

Oil Sands (Heavy Oil)

With traditional oil wells, the gas needs to flow from underground to the surface. However, this prevents the usage of heavy crude oil reserves because heavy crude oil does not flow well. Heavy crude is extremely viscous and ranges from the consistency of molasses to a solid at room temperature. If heavy oil deposits are located close to the surface, they can be removed by strip mining. Otherwise, high temperature steam has to be injected underground to convert the heavy oil into a liquid that is suitable for extraction.

Removing heavy oil from the ground is often destructive to the environment and requires immense amounts of energy and water. The petroleum produced by oil sands is less desirable than traditional sources of fuel. However, heavy oil deposits are much more abundant than traditional oil deposits.

Oil Sands

Heavy oil is much more abundant than traditional oil resources but presents a variety of technological, economic, and environmental challenges for producers.

- Heavy oil production requires an immense amount of both energy and water to produce sufficient steam to extract it from the ground.
- The inability to obtain a sufficient supply of water is commonly the limiting factor in the economic production of heavy oil.
- The heavy crude processing requires expensive, complex refineries to convert oil sands into gasoline or diesel fuel.

Shale Gas (Hydraulic Fracking)

In a conventional well, hydrocarbons, stored in a layer of porous, permeable rock are trapped underneath an impermeable layer of rock. A porous rock has large cavities that contain hydrocarbons. Permeable rock has small cracks that allow gas to move between sections of the rock. A porous, permeable rock has cavities and cracks connecting a majority of the cavities to one another (see Figure 1-3).

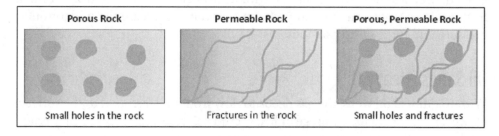

FIGURE 1-3 • Porous, Permeable Rocks

In some cases, organic matter may become trapped inside the cavities within porous, impermeable rock. In these cases, if the rock surrounding the hydrocarbons can be fractured, the hydrocarbons can be extracted. The most common way to create fractures in rock is to inject water or similar hydraulic fluid into a rock formation and then use the liquid to propagate compression waves caused by explosions deep into the formation. This process is known as *hydraulic fracturing*, or *fracking*. It has been proven commercially viable at removing hydrocarbons from shale rock formations.

The water used in this process can often be recovered and reused multiple times after it has been treated to remove pollution. Pollution is typically not due to the natural gas and lighter hydrocarbons that are being removed. Light hydrocarbons are nontoxic and already exist in the atmosphere. However, fracking has the potential to release anything that has been trapped in the shale layer. If heavy metals or other pollution are trapped in the shale, those can dissolve into the fracking liquid. These pollutants must be removed before they are allowed to contaminate drinking water.

Key Concept

Fracking (Hydraulic Fracturing)

Hydraulic fracturing is used to convert porous rock containing hydrocarbons into porous, permeable rock by creating small fractures in the rock formation.

- Fracking, and shale gas production, are relatively new technologies.
- Shale gas produced by fracking can be produced at low cost and uses resources that were previously not viable sources of fossil fuel.

Shale Oil (Shale Rock Processing)

Another way to extract hydrocarbons from porous, but impermeable, rock is to use traditional mining techniques and then crush the rock in a processing plant. Technology for producing fuel in this manner has been around for over 200 years; however, it is rarely economically viable. This process differs from shale gas extraction because, with shale rock processing, shale is removed from the ground prior to processing.

Key Concept

Shale Oil

Although they share similar names, *shale oil* and *shale gas* production involve two different processes. Shale oil processing involves standard mining techniques and processing of the rock outside the ground. Shale gas uses hydraulic fracturing and does not remove rock from the ground.

- Shale oil technology has existed for hundreds of years.
- Shale oil production is not usually economically viable.

Shale oil involves traditional mining and crushing shale rocks after they have been removed from the ground.

Deepwater Drilling

Deepwater drilling involves exploration and production of oil and gas resources which are located more than 500 feet (150 meters) underwater. Drilling for fossil fuels deep underwater provides a wide variety of technological challenges. Due to the high pressure, it is very difficult for humans to survive and work while deep underwater. As a result, humans typically have to work remotely from floating platforms above water. This places an increased burden on remote monitoring.

The risk of catastrophic equipment failure is also much higher. Deepwater drilling places a much higher stress on well components than traditional drilling. For example, gas bubbling out of crude oil is more likely to occur when drilling in deep water due to the pressure difference between the top and bottom of the pipe. A liquid will be forced to move given enough pressure. However, if a gas bubble becomes trapped, the pressure may continue to build until it destroys the pipe. Longer pipes have more surface area where a weak spot can occur. This problem is further compounded if shorter pipes are welded together to form a longer pipe or if the pipe needs to bend somewhere along the line because this creates a place for gas bubbles to form.

Key Concept

Deepwater Drilling

Substantial fossil fuel deposits are located offshore. They are considerably harder and more expensive to access than traditional deposits.

- Deepwater drilling involves drilling at depths exceeding 500 feet (150 meters).
- The risk of oil spills and equipment failure is much higher for deepwater production when compared to traditional oil production.

The production of deepwater oil resources is very sensitive to crude oil markets. High prices make deepwater production profitable, while lower prices make deepwater production unprofitable.

Oil and Gas Reserves[3]

The actual amount of crude oil trapped underground is generally not known until a well is fully exhausted. As a result, crude oil reserves (the amount of oil remaining in a field) are typically described in terms of probability of it being extracted. For example, P90 refers to a 90% to 100% chance of recovery. P50 refers to 50% to 100% chance of recovery. P10 refers to a 10% to 100% chance of recovery (see Figure 1-4).

Typically, P90 reserves are much smaller than P50 and P10 reserves. For any given well, the distributions will not necessarily be normally distributed. However,

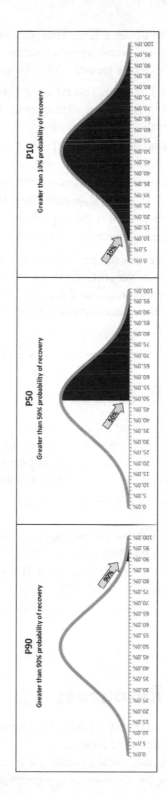

FIGURE 1-4 • P10, P50, and P90

13

when reserves are calculated over a large enough number of samples, a normal distribution becomes a much better approximation of reality. Another way to categorize reserves is by the terms *proven*, *probable*, and *possible* reserves.

- **Proven Reserves (1P).** Proven reserves are generally defined as having a 90% certainty of being produced with current technology and under current economic and political conditions.
- **Proven and Probable Reserves (2P).** Probable reserves are generally defined as having a 50% to 90% probability of being produced with current technology and under current economic and political conditions.
- **Proven, Probably, and Possible Reserves (3P).** Probable reserves are generally defined as having a 10% to 50% probability of being produced with current technology and under current economic and political conditions.

Related to the term *oil and gas reserves* is the term *oil and gas resources*. Oil and gas resources refer to the total volume of hydrocarbons present in a field regardless of whether they can be extracted or if it is profitable to do so. This term, and its associated meaning, is much less commonly used than the term reserves.

Key Concept

Oil and Gas Reserves

Oil reserves are described based on the probability that oil can be recovered under current conditions (current prices, current technology, current government policies, etc.). If current conditions change, perhaps due to a new invention or a change in market prices, the size of oil and gas reserves will change.

- **P90.** A 90% and higher chance of recovery. This is also known as 1P (*Proven Reserves*).
- **P50.** A 50% and higher chance of recovery. This is known as 2P because it covers *Proven and Probable* Reserves.
- **P10.** A 10% and higher chance of recovery. This is known as 3P because it covers *Proven, Probable, and Possible* Reserves.

Key Concept

Oil and Gas Resources

Oil and gas resources is the term that refers to the total volume of fuel present in a gas or oil field irrespective of whether the technology exists to remove it or whether it would be economically profitable to do so.

Another complication when comparing the oil and gas wells to one another is that each field will contain a different mix of natural gas, natural gas liquids, and crude oil. Either the ratio between gas and oil production can be reported, or the output can be converted into a single unit. The gas–oil ratio is commonly reported in cubic feet (ft^3) of gas per barrel (BBL) of crude oil. For the purpose of calculating reserves, fossil fuels are typically represented as a single number called the *Barrel of Oil Equivalent* (BOE). Any nonliquid hydrocarbon, like natural gas, needs to be converted into these alternate units. The heating value of the crude oil and natural gas, measured in Btus or Joules, is typically used to make the conversion.

Key Concept

Gas–Oil Ratio

The gas–oil ratio is the ratio of gas (commonly in cubic feet, ft^3) to crude oil (usually in barrels, BBL). This ratio can be constructed using a variety of units. The term *oil well* refers to a well which primarily produces crude oil. The term *gas well* refers to a well that primarily produces gas.[4]

- **Oil Well.** Gas–oil ratio less than 100,000 ft^3/BBL
- **Gas Well.** Gas–oil ratio greater than 100,000 ft^3/BBL

Key Concept

Barrel of Oil Equivalent (BOE)

BOE is used to describe the reserves existing in an oil and gas field as a single number. The thermal energy (heating value) of the crude oil and gas in a field is used to make the conversion between volume of gas and barrels of oil equivalent.[5]

- One BOE is approximately equal to 5,300 − 6100 ft^3 of wet natural gas.
- Global oil reserves are often reported in billions of BOEs (BBOE).

Crude Oil

In its natural state, crude oil is a mixture of different fossil fuels found underground where decaying plant life became trapped under a layer of nonporous rock. After millions of years, heat and pressure converted the decaying plant life into hydrocarbons. The mixture of hydrocarbons in these underground reservoirs can vary widely. For example, when it is first extracted from the ground, crude oil often contains gas that has to be siphoned off and particulates that need to be filtered out.

Because of this nonuniform nature, crude oil is dangerous to use directly out of the ground. Lighter portions of it can form explosive vapors that spark very easily, while heavier portions may not flow easily or ignite smoothly. As a result, crude oil is usually separated into components that are more uniform in composition. For example, gasoline, diesel fuel, and jet fuel are all examples of portions of crude oil. Collectively, these portions are called *petroleum products*. After crude oil is distilled, each product has its own name with widely accepted specifications for its use. The broader term *petroleum* refers to crude oil and all of its liquids components.

Crude oil is the single most traded commodity in the world. As a result, its political and economic influence is extremely large. This influence has led to a high level of government involvement in the industry and the crude oil market is subject to intense international scrutiny. Crude oil is often viewed as a benchmark for the energy and commodity sectors and can have a disproportionate influence on other commodity prices because of its size and the awareness surrounding this market.

Often, crude oil will be referred to as *sweet* or *sour*. These terms describe the sulfur content of crude oil. Sulfur is a major pollutant, which along with smelling bad, is a major source of acid rain. During combustion, as with carbon and hydrogen, sulfur also combines with oxygen. In the presence of water (another byproduct of combustion), sulfur oxides can form sulfuric acid. Crude oil with less than 0.5% sulfur is considered "sweet." Crude oil with a sulfur content of more than 0.5% is typically classified as "sour."

Key Concept

Describing Crude Oil

- **Sweet** crude has less than 0.5% Sulfur.
- **Sour** crude has more than 0.5% Sulfur.

   Sweet crude is more valuable than sour crude. It is commonly about 5% more valuable.

The terms *light* and *heavy* are also used to describe crude oils. These terms describe the average density of crude oil. In general, since lighter products (like jet fuel and gasoline) are more valuable than the heavier products (like heavy fuel oil and asphalt), lighter crude oils will be more valuable than heavier crude oils. This is an approximation, since the actual mixture of components that make up the crude oil will determine its actual value. It is possible that crude oils of the same average density will have different prices.

West Texas Intermediate and Brent Futures Contracts

The two most important crude oil financial products are the West Texas Inter-mediate (WTI) and Brent Crude futures contracts. Both of these financial con-tracts are based on light sweet crude oils near major refining regions. WTI is the major benchmark for crude oil located in the interior of North America and Brent Crude is the benchmark for Atlantic ship-borne crude oil.

Density of petroleum products is classified by *API gravity*. The American Petroleum Institute (API) gravity[6] is a measure of how heavy a crude oil is rela-tive to a similar volume of water. Higher API gravities are associated with lower density liquids. Liquids with an API gravity higher than 10 degrees will float on water, while liquids with lower API gravity will sink. *Light crude* generally has an API gravity of 38 degrees or more, and *heavy crude* an API gravity of 22 degrees or less. Crude with API gravity between 22 and 38 degrees is gener-ally referred to as medium crude. Crude oils with an API gravity above 45 are referred to as *condensate*. In general, light crudes are the most valuable. Heavier crudes contain a lower proportion of gasoline and Diesel than lighter crudes. Compared to light crude, condensate has a large portion of short molecular chain components that exist as gas at room temperature.

API and the Value of Crude Oil

Crude oil with a higher API gravity (lighter crude oil) is more valuable than heavier crude until approximately 45 API gravity, when the carbon chains become shorter and less valuable (see Table 1-2).

API Gravity	Name	Relative Value
< 10	Bitumen	Lowest Value
10-22	Heavy Crude	Low Value
22-38	Medium Crude	High Value
38-45	Light Crude	Highest Value

TABLE 1-2 • Crude Types

To an energy investor, the density of crude oil is important because in some parts of the world, like Europe, crude oil is typically traded by weight (metric tons, abbreviated *MT* or *tonnes*). In other parts of the world, like the U.S., crude oil is traded by volume (barrels, abbreviated *BBL*). The denser a substance, the smaller the volume required for a given amount of weight. This means that conversion between units becomes an obstacle to investors. Some common unit conversions:

- Forty-two gallons per barrel
- Approximately 7.5 BBL of light crude per metric ton

Degree API	Specific Gravity	Conversions		
		(lb/US gal)	BBL / MT	
8	1.0143	8.4573	6.2066	
9	1.0071	8.3971	6.2511	
10	1.0000	8.3378	6.2955	
15	0.9659	8.0532	6.5180	Bachaquero 17
20	0.9340	7.7875	6.7405	Maya
25	0.9042	7.5386	6.9629	Vasconia
30	0.8762	7.3053	7.1854	WTS, Arab Light, Dubai, Urals
35	0.8498	7.0859	7.4078	Azeri Light, Bonny Light, Bach Ho, Kirkuk
40	0.8251	6.8793	7.6303	WTI, Brent
45	0.8017	6.6844	7.8527	
50	0.7796	6.5003	8.0752	
55	0.7587	6.3260	8.2977	
58	0.7467	6.2259	8.4311	

TABLE 1-3 • Crude Oil Volume/Weight Conversions

To convert from an arbitrary API gravity to a density, it is first necessary to calculate the specific gravity of the substance SG = (API + 131.5) / 141.5. Then, it is necessary to calculate the ratio of that specific gravity to the specific gravity of water. Finally, that ratio can be multiplied by the density of water to calculate the density of the substance.

BBL per MT = 890.82 / (API + 131.5) for a given API Gravity[7]

Another unique feature of the crude oil market is the importance of the futures contracts on setting the price for physical contracts. In many commodity markets, there is an active *spot* market[8] that helps determine the price of physical commodities. However, in the crude market, due to the delay in taking crude out of the ground and having it arrive at the refinery, most price discovery comes from futures trading markets rather than set in a spot auction. When physical crude oil transactions are priced, they are usually marked to the *prompt month* futures contract. The prompt month futures contract is the next futures contract to settle.

Futures contracts typically cease trading a week or two before the start of the delivery month. For example, The NYMEX WTI contract settles about approximately two-thirds of the way through the month prior to delivery. In cases where greater precision is required, the contract specifications can be obtained from the exchange. In those specifications, the terms of the contract will be spelled out in detail. This will look something like the following:

> *Trading in the current delivery month shall cease on the third business day prior to the twenty-fifth calendar day of the month preceding the delivery month. If the twenty-fifth calendar day of the month is a non-business day, trading shall cease on the third business day prior to the last business day preceding the twenty-fifth calendar day. In the event that the official Exchange holiday schedule changes subsequent to the listing of a Crude Oil futures, the originally listed expiration date shall remain in effect. In the event that the originally listed expiration day is declared a holiday, expiration will move to the business day immediately prior.[9]*

If the price of a physical delivery contract is set by the average price of the prompt future over each business day, that means that the price will be set by the next month futures for approximately two-thirds of the month and the second month futures for the last third of the month. For example, if a physical contract whose price is linked to the prompt contract settles in August, for two-thirds of the month, prices will be determined by the September futures contract. At that point, the September contract will expire, and the October contract will become the prompt contract.

Petroleum Transportation

Once crude oil is extracted from the ground, it needs to be transported to a refinery to separate the components of the crude oil into marketable products. In most cases, crude oil is transported by pipeline to a port facility, loaded onto a transport ship, and sent to a refinery for processing. The international trade in crude oil is the largest market in the world measured in both volume and value. In contrast, the international market for refined products like gasoline and diesel fuel is comprised of much smaller regional markets.

Key Concept

Free On Board Price

The most common price quoted for physical crude oil is the *free on board* price at the point of origin. This is the price of crude oil aboard ship after export taxes have been paid. This price *does not* reflect the cost associated with transporting the crude oil to its destination.

There are a variety of reasons that the international market focuses on crude oil rather than refined products. First, refineries can cost billions of dollars to build and can have an expected lifespan of 50 years or longer. A refinery will outlive almost any single oil field. Second, oil fields are often located in remote areas of the world. It is harder to find a trained work force in a remote area than outside a major city which has multiple refineries. Third, local refineries can better optimize their output to meet local demands and local regulations. Finally, safety for both workers and investors is a consideration. Crude oil is often produced in undeveloped, dangerous parts of the world. A refinery is a multi-billion dollar investment that is best placed in a safe location where it is unlikely to be damaged by violence or nationalized by an unfriendly government.

The maximum size of the ships used to transport crude oil is usually limited by some physical constraint like the water depth at docking facilities or the size of a canal that the ships might pass through. Larger ships are more cost effective at transporting crude oil, provided that they can follow the same route and dock at the same facility as smaller ships. However, smaller ships are often used in order to utilize canals or dock at existing terminals. Canals can dramatically reduce the length of a trip and the largest ships may require specialized terminals in order to accommodate their size (see Figure 1-5).

Petroleum Refining

When it comes out of the ground, crude oil is a mixture of many substances. Refineries separate raw crude oil into its constituent components and break heavier components into lighter ones. This process starts with fractional distillation. It is often followed up by additional processes to extract more value from the crude oil. The simplest refineries separate crude oil into its components. More complex refineries perform additional steps to break down the largest crude oil molecules into smaller, more valuable, molecules.

Capacity Millions BBL	Length	Beam	Draft	Description
Coastal Tanker 0.3	205m	29m	16m	Less than 50,000 DWT, mainly used for transportation of refined products (gasoline, gasoil).
Panamax (LR1) 0.5	230m	32m	13m	Between 60,000 to 80,000 DWT. This is the maximum size vessel that can traverse the Panama Canal prior to its 2014 expansion
Aframax (LR2) 0.75	245m	42m	14m	Between 80,000 and 120,000 DWT (typically 80,000 DWT). AFRA = American Freight Rate Association.
Suezmax 1.0	285 m	45 m	16.5 m	Tankers between 125,000 and 180,000 DWT and capable of traversing the Suez Canal without offloading any cargo.
VLCC 2.0	350 m	55 m	22 m	Very Large Crude Carrier. 150,000 to 300,000 DWT. Can be accommodated by the expanded dimensions of the Suez Canal. Flexibility to use many terminals since many can accommodate their draft.
ULCC 3.3	415 m	63 m	30 m	Ultra Large Crude Carrier. 300,000 DWT to 550,000 DWT. Used for long-haul crude oil routes from Persian Gulf to Europe or East Asia (around South Africa or through Strait of Malacca). Because of their immense size, ULCC ships require custom built terminals.

Deadweight Tonnage (DWT). DWT is a measure of ship carrying capacity. It measures the number of metric tonnes of cargo, stores, and fuel that can be transported.

FIGURE 1-5 • Types of Crude Oil Cargo Vessels

The simplest way to separate crude oil is through a process known as *fractional distillation*. In this process, crude oil is placed into a long cylindrical container called a *distillation column*. The heavier portions of crude oil sink to the bottom, allowing the lighter portions to be siphoned off of the top. Distillation can be sped up by heating the crude. Not only does this make the crude oil flow better, but by controlling the temperature, specific hydrocarbons will boil off one at a time and can be removed by a vacuum pump. Different hydrocarbon chains will have progressively higher boiling points based on the length of the carbon chains. This isn't a perfect process, but each fraction that is siphoned off can be distilled several times to get it progressively more purified (see Figure 1-6).

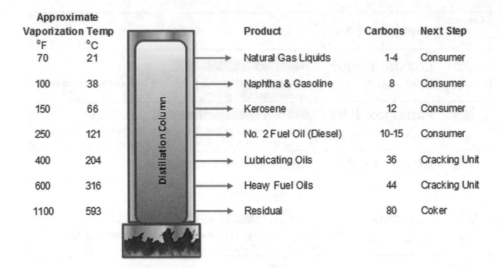

Approximate Vaporization Temp		Product	Carbons	Next Step
°F	°C			
70	21	Natural Gas Liquids	1-4	Consumer
100	38	Naphtha & Gasoline	8	Consumer
150	66	Kerosene	12	Consumer
250	121	No. 2 Fuel Oil (Diesel)	10-15	Consumer
400	204	Lubricating Oils	36	Cracking Unit
600	316	Heavy Fuel Oils	44	Cracking Unit
1100	593	Residual	80	Coker

FIGURE 1-6 • A Distillation Column Separates Liquids by Carefully Heating a Mixture

Key Concept

Refining Uses Large Amounts of Energy

Refining requires a massive quantity of energy. Gasoline, diesel, and jet fuel may all be boiled several times at an extremely high temperature before being used by consumers.

Another way to improve the quality of a refinery's output is to send the heavier components through additional steps that break down the less valuable longer carbon chain heavy products into lighter, more valuable products. This adds to the cost of a refinery, but allows it to utilize heavier crude oil much more efficiently.

Once the most valuable components are siphoned off, a large amount of heavier crude oil remains in the distillation column. This is often referred to as *vacuum tower bottoms or atmospheric tower bottoms* depending on the configuration of the distillation column. The heaviest portions at the bottom of a tower are called *slop*. With the proper equipment, these products can be further broken down into valuable components. Otherwise, they can be sold off to another refinery with that equipment.

Refineries are often described by their complexity:

- **Topping.** A topping refinery separates crude into constituent petroleum products by distillation. It produces a low octane grade of gasoline-like product, called *naphtha*, but doesn't have the equipment necessary to produce gasoline. It is uncommon for these refineries to process heavier crude oils.
- **Hydroskimming.** A hydroskimming refinery adds reforming equipment, necessary to produce gasoline from naphtha, to the distillation column. Although a hydroskimming refinery is more complex than a topping refinery, it still lacks equipment to handle heavier crudes and is considered a simple refinery. As a result, hydroskimming refineries are only cost effective when used to refine lighter crude oils.
- **Cracking.** A cracking refinery adds vacuum distillation and catalytic cracking equipment to a hydroskimming facility. The cracking unit increases the amount of light oil produced by a refinery by breaking the longer carbon chain heavier products into smaller chain lighter products. A cracking refinery is a medium-complexity refinery that is marginally profitable when refining heavier crude oils.
- **Coking.** A coking refinery adds another step to the refining process—a *delayed coking process*—which further breaks down heavier products. A delayed coking process converts the vacuum residue into higher value products. A refinery with a coker is considered to be a complex refinery and is usually able to profitably refine heavy crude oils.

While more expensive to construct, more complex refineries have greater flexibility to process a wide variety of crude oils. They also tend to have the larger, more stable profit margins. This is because it is easier to optimize the product mix of complex refineries since they have the option to use low-cost heavier crudes while still producing a large quantity of high-cost finished products.

Key Concept

Relative Value of Refineries

Simple refineries (topping, hydroskimming) are substantially less profitable than complex refineries (those with coking and cracking units). Light crude prices are bid up because they are easy to refine into desirable products. However, there is less competition for heavy crude. This results in lower heavy crude prices. As a result, refineries that can use heavy crudes tend to have much better profit margins than those that can't use heavy crudes.

Refined Petroleum Products (gasoline, diesel, and jet-fuel)

The output products from a refinery are collectively called *refined petroleum products*. The most important of these is *gasoline* (also called *petrol*). Gasoline is a motor fuel that is used in most internal combustion vehicles. Other important products are diesel fuel, jet fuel, and heavy fuel oil. Because a refinery will break down heavier crude into lower density products, a 42 gallon barrel of crude oil will produce approximately 45 gallons of refined products (see Figure 1-7).

Approximate Mix of Products Made from 42 U.S. Gallon Barrel of Crude Oil

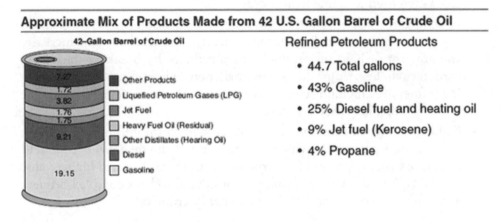

42–Gallon Barrel of Crude Oil

7.27
1.72
3.82
1.76
1.75
9.21
19.15

■ Other Products
□ Liquefied Petroleum Gases (LPG)
■ Jet Fuel
□ Heavy Fuel Oil (Residual)
■ Other Distillates (Hearing Oil)
■ Diesel
□ Gasoline

Refined Petroleum Products

• 44.7 Total gallons

• 43% Gasoline

• 25% Diesel fuel and heating oil

• 9% Jet fuel (Kerosene)

• 4% Propane

FIGURE 1-7 • Barrel Breakdown by Gallons
Source: Energy Information Agency, October 2008

One way to estimate the profitability of refining is to look at the price differential between the finished products from a refinery and the cost of the crude oil. Since a refinery produces approximately twice as much gasoline as diesel fuel, and those are two of the most valuable products, a 3-2-1 crack spread is a common proxy for refinery profitability. In a 3-2-1 crack spread, 3 barrels of crude oil is assumed to produce 2 barrels of gasoline and 1 barrel of No.2 Diesel Fuel (see Figure 1-8).

The formulation for any commonly traded fuels will be publically available and is determined by historical convention, local regulations, or international standards.

Fuel oils are described with a number between 1 and 6 that indicates the weight and viscosity of the oil. Many of these products are no longer in active use. This classification system was originally developed during the early refining period and has changed somewhat over time. The viscosity, boiling point, and

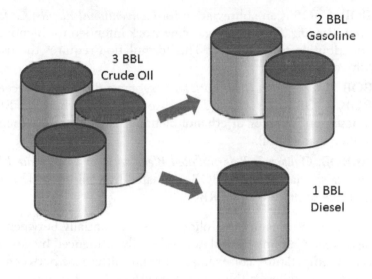

FIGURE 1-8 · A 3-2-1 Crack Spread

carbon chain length of the fuel oils increase as the numbers increase. The heaviest oil (No. 6 Fuel Oil) has to be heated to get it to flow. Prices are typically highest for the low numbered fuels and decrease as the fuel number increases. Some of the more common refined products are:

- **Naphtha.** Naphtha is a light, low octane fuel that can be converted into higher octane gasoline. It mainly consists of molecules with 5 and 6 carbon atoms, and is a major component of natural gas *condensate*. It is similar, but slightly less valuable, than blendstock gasoline.

- **Gasoline (Petrol).** Gasoline is the most common vehicular fuel for internal combustion engines. It is commonly called *gas* in the United States and *petrol* in England. Gasoline is composed of a mixture of hydrocarbons that are 5–9 carbons long. The formulation of gasoline is highly regulated and varies widely because of local regulations. In wholesale markets, it is most commonly sold as blendstock that can be mixed with additives like ethanol to meet local regulations.

  o **Straight run.** A low octane gasoline distilled directly from crude oil. Historically, this was the most common form of gasoline. The low octane rating of straight run gasoline requires additives (traditionally lead) to raise the octane level sufficiently high to prevent engine knocking. Regulations to reduce lead in gasoline have caused straight run to be superseded by later formulations.

o **CBOB.** CBOB is an abbreviation for *Conventional Blendstock for Oxygenate Blending*. This is base gasoline stock intended for blending prior to distribution to consumers. This formulation requires the use of an additive, MTBE.[10]

o **RBOB.** *Reformulated Blendstock for Oxygenate Blending*. A successor to CBOB, RBOB is the standard blendstock in areas where MTBE usage is phased out in favor of ethanol blending. This is more expensive to produce than CBOB.

o **CARBOB.** *California Reformulated Blendstock for Oxygenate Blending*. This is a special form of RBOB mandated by California. This is more expensive to produce than RBOB.

The formulation of consumer gasoline varies substantially between regions and by time of year. Gasoline formulation is heavily influenced by government regulations and temperature. For example, a major difference between winter- and summer-grade gasoline is the vapor pressure needed for proper combustion. In cold weather, the summer formulation of gasoline will have a lower vapor pressure and might not combust properly. As a result, cold weather requires a higher vapor pressure. However, in the summer, higher vapor pressure means that gasoline evaporates more easily. This contributes to ground-level ozone and smog. Because of that, governmental regulations often require seasonal formulations for gasoline.

Key Concept

Octane Rating

Grades of gasoline are typically differentiated by an *octane rating* that indicates the quality or predictability of ignition. Engines designed to use higher octane gasoline can be built with tighter specifications, which can lead to improved performance. There is little benefit to using a higher octane gasoline in an engine designed for a lower octane formulation.

For consumer gasoline, in addition to octane rating, refiners will often use different additives to differentiate different grades of gasoline. For example, premium gasoline might be higher octane and have an additive to reduce engine deposits when compared to a nonpremium gasoline.

- **Number 1 Fuel Oil (Kerosene).** Kerosene is the next lightest fuel after naphtha and gasoline. This fuel oil is rarely traded and has largely been superseded by jet fuel in either the Jet-A or Jet-A1 formulations.

  o **Jet Fuel.** The three most common jet fuels are Jet A, Jet A-1, and Jet B. All of these fuels are formulated to meet standardized international specifications. Jet A is the primary specification for jet fuel used in the United States, while Jet A-1 is used in the rest of the world. The primary difference is that Jet A has a higher freezing point and Jet A-1 has an anti-static additive. Jet B is much less commonly traded, and is used in extreme cold-weather conditions.

- **No. 2 Fuel Oil (Diesel, Gas Oil, Heating Oil).** No. 2 Fuel Oil is commonly described as *diesel fuel* when used as a vehicular fuel and *heating oil* when used to provide heating. All No.2 Fuel Oils are chemically similar. Diesel fuel typically has a higher cetane[11] rating and lower sulfur percentage than heating oil. Historically, this fuel was also called *Bunker A*, although this term is not currently in common usage.

  o Some formulations of No. 2 Fuel Oil have higher sulfur contents than other formulations. Higher-sulfur content No.2 Fuel Oil may be referred to as *heating oil, off-road diesel*, or *red diesel*. To differentiate high and low sulfur fuels to consumers, high sulfur No.2 Fuel Oil gets dyed red. The red color makes it clear that the product cannot legally be used as highway diesel. However, it can be used for farm equipment and home heating.

Key Concept

Cetane Rating

Similar to octane rating for gasoline, the cetane number of diesel fuel measures the quality of combustion during compression ignition.

- **No. 3 Fuel Oil.** This grade was merged into the number 2 specification and is rarely found in the financial markets.
- **No.4 Fuel Oil.** No. 4 Fuel Oil is sometimes called "residual fuel oil." It is used as heating oil where a preheater is not available. This fuel oil is rarely traded in financial markets.
- **No. 5 Fuel Oil (Navy Special).** No. 5 Fuel Oil is a heavy fuel oil that requires preheating to 170–220 °F (77–104 °C) before being used as a fuel. Historically, this fuel has also been known as *Navy Special* or *Bunker B*.
- **No. 6 Fuel Oil (Bunker Fuel).** No. 6 Fuel Oil is a high-viscosity residual oil requiring preheating to 220–260 °F (104–127 °C). This is the most commonly traded heavy fuel oil. Historically, it was called *Bunker* C. In practice, the term *bunker fuel* now refers to No.6 Fuel Oil. This fuel is commonly used as fuel for large ships due to its low cost and the ability to control its temperature aboard ship.

Names of Refined Products

A single product name may refer to several different products with slightly different formulations. Names are usually consistent within a narrow industry, but are often reused in a different manner by a related industry.

Refined petroleum products are traded in different units. In the U.S., trading may occur in either barrels or gallons. In other parts of the world, trading may be done by volume (liters) or by weight (metric tons). Since each product will have a different density, it is necessary to use a product specific conversion when translating between volume and weight measurements (see Table 1-5).[12]

Product	Specific Gravity	Barrels per Metric Ton	Liters per Metric Ton
Gasoline	0.74	8.5	1351
Kerosene (Jet Fuel)	0.81	7.8	1240
No. 2 Diesel (Gas Oil, Heating Oil)	0.84	7.5	1192
No. 6 Fuel Oil (Fuel Oil, Bunker Fuel)	0.94	6.7	1065
Pure Water	1.00	6.3	1000

TABLE 1-5 · Approximate Petroleum Product Volume / Weight Conversions

Units of Traded Products

Refined products are often quoted in units like gallons or liters that are familiar to consumers.

- There are 42 gallons per barrel.
- Volumes to weight conversions are product specific.
- Prices may be traded in a variety of units. For example, petroleum products may be traded in U.S. cents ($USC) rather than dollars ($USD).

Biofuels (Ethanol, Biodiesel)

Biofuels are transportation fuels, like ethanol and biodiesel, which are made from renewable organic materials. The process for creating biofuels is a man-made process similar to the process that forms fossil fuels in nature. Technology is used to convert organic material into vehicular fuels. These fuels are usually blended with the petroleum fuels like gasoline and diesel fuel. With specially designed engines, biofuels can also be used on their own. Ethanol and biodiesel are usually more expensive than the fossil fuels, since it is necessary to grow crops before processing and only a small portion of each plant can be used for fuel. However, biofuels tend to be very clean-burning because their feedstocks can be grown in controlled conditions.

Ethanol

Ethanol is an alcohol-based fuel distilled from the sugar found in grains such as corn or sugar cane. The process for creating this fuel is very similar to the process for making alcoholic beverages. In the U.S., most ethanol is distilled from corn. In other parts of the world, like Brazil, ethanol is also distilled from sugar cane. Ethanol contains less energy per unit of volume than gasoline and is more corrosive. Regional legislation determines how much ethanol (if any) is added to gasoline. For example, in the two largest ethanol producing countries, the United States and Brazil, nearly all gasoline contains some ethanol. The most common formulation in the U.S. is 10% ethanol and 90% gasoline.

Most gasoline engines can use E10 (gasoline with 10% ethanol), but higher percentages of ethanol often require specially built *flex fuel* engines. Ethanol can degrade rubber seals and gaskets in engines that haven't been designed to use higher percentages of ethanol. Because of this, the schedule to phase in different formulations of ethanol can be spread over many years to allow for enough new cars to be equipped to handle the new formulation.

- **E10.** E10 is a consumer gasoline that contains 10% ethanol. As of 2012, this was the most common blend used in the United States.
- **E25.** E25 is a consumer gasoline that contains 25% ethanol. As of 2012, this was the most common formulation of gasoline used in Brazil. Due to the corrosive nature of ethanol, engines have to be specially built to use this type of fuel.
- **E85.** E85 is an alternative fuel that contains up to 85% ethanol by volume. Vehicles that use E85 are specially named as flexible fuel vehicles (FFV). These vehicles require engines specifically designed to handle high percentages of ethanol in their fuel.

Key Concept

Ethanol

Ethanol is alcohol—the same ingredient that is in alcoholic beverages. After it is produced, it is *denatured* to make it undrinkable.

- Ethanol is produced from food crops, and regulations concerning the amount of ethanol required for gasoline blending can have a direct impact on food costs.
- The E## terminology describes how much ethanol is in a fuel as a percent of the total volume. For example, E10 is 10% ethanol by volume.
- Ethanol contains less energy than gasoline. An engine will burn more ethanol than gasoline to do the same amount of work.

Biodiesel

Biodiesel is a fuel made from vegetable oils that can be used in compression ignition (diesel) engines with little or no modification. Biodiesel is safe, biodegradable, and produces similar or lower amounts of pollution than petroleum-based diesel fuel. Like ethanol, using vegetable oil as a vehicle fuel can compete with its use as a food product. However, unlike ethanol, some of the primary vegetable oils used for biodiesel, like soybean oil, can be produced from animal feed production byproducts and cooking waste.

Biodiesel has chemical characteristics nearly identical to petroleum-based diesel fuel. Because of that, mixtures of 20% or less biodiesel can be used as a direct substitute for diesel fuel with no engine modifications. Biodiesel can also be blended with petroleum diesel in any percentage without suffering any significant loss of fuel economy. However, because biodiesel is a stronger solvent than petroleum diesel, a very high percentage of biodiesel in fuel may require specialized engines.

- **B2–B5.** B2 refers to a 2% biodiesel/98% diesel blend by volume. Similarly, B5 refers to 5% biodiesel/95% diesel blend. Low-percentage biodiesel blends like B2 through B5 are popular fuels in the trucking industry because biodiesel has excellent lubricating properties. As a result, these blends can improve engine performance and lengthen the lifespan of engines.

- **B100.** B100 is pure biodiesel. Pure biodiesel is a solvent which can loosen and dissolve sediments in storage tanks. It may also cause rubber and other components to fail in older vehicles.

Biodiesel

Biodiesel is diesel fuel made from renewable sources.

- Biodiesel is nearly identical to petroleum-based diesel fuel.
- The B## terminology describes how much biodiesel is in a fuel as a percent of the total volume. For example, B5 is 5% biodiesel by volume.

QUIZ

1. **What is not a disadvantage of a ULCC (Ultra Large Crude Carrier) relative to smaller vessels?**
   A. ULCC ships are too large to traverse canals.
   B. For the same distance traveled, ULCC transport is more expensive per unit of fuel transported.
   C. ULCC ships require specialized docking facilities.
   D. ULCC ships are limited in their ability to enter shallow coastal waters.

   Correct Answer: B

   Explanation: As long as they can follow the same route, transport costs are smaller on a per-unit basis when larger ships are used to transport crude oil.

2. **What is the best definition of a hydroskimming facility?**
   A. A refinery built to maximize production of gasoline.
   B. A refinery that contains specialized equipment like a coking unit and a catalytic cracker to break down heavy distillates.
   C. A simple refinery that produces naphtha but is unable to produce gasoline.
   D. A simple refinery that produces a large amount of residual fuel oil relative to its gasoline and diesel production.

   Correct Answer: D

   Explanation: Answer D correctly describes a hydroskimming facility. It is a simple refinery which can produce gasoline but lacks the specialized equipment necessary to break down heavy distillates.

3. **Which statement about ethanol is *not* true?**
   A. Ethanol has a higher octane than gasoline.
   B. For the same volume, ethanol contains less energy than gasoline.
   C. Ethanol is typically made from parts of plants that can't be used as food.
   D. Ethanol is corrosive and can damage engine parts if not diluted or used in an engine specially designed to use ethanol as a fuel.

   Correct Answer: C

   Explanation: Ethanol is typically made from the same parts of plants that get used for food. Because it is made from food, one criticism of ethanol production is that ethanol tends to make staple foodstuffs like corn and sugar more expensive. All of the other answers are correct.

4. **What term would be used to describe crude oil with 2.1% sulfur content?**
   A. Sweet
   B. Sour
   C. Light
   D. Heavy

   Correct Answer: B

   Explanation: Crude oil with a sulfur content of more than 0.5% sulfur is typically classified as sour, while oil with less than 0.5% sulfur is considered sweet. There is some variation in the border between sweet and sour, but 2.1% is well into the sour range. The terms light and heavy refer to density of oil rather than its sulfur content.

5. **Which term refers to the process of separating a mixture into its components by boiling it and then condensing the resulting vapor?**
   A. Distillation
   B. Catalytic conversion
   C. Catalytic cracking
   D. Vacuum cleaning

   Correct Answer: A

   Explanation: Distillation is the process of separating a mixture into its components by boiling it and then condensing the resulting vapor. Distillation may be called *vacuum distillation* if it is done in a vacuum, but not *vacuum cleaning*.

6. **Of the choices given, what is typically the most valuable type of fuel?**
   A. Gaseous fuels
   B. Low viscosity liquid fuels
   C. High viscosity liquid fuels
   D. Solid fuels

   Correct Answer: B

   Explanation: Low viscosity liquid fuels are typically the most valuable type of fuel due to their high energy density and engineering properties.

7. **Anthony, an analyst at an auditing firm, needs to mark a December physical crude oil contract to market. The floating price of the contract is specified as an average of the prompt WTI contract price plus $0.15. The expiration of the January WTI contract is exactly two-thirds of the way through the month. Using the quoted prices for WTI futures, calculate the mark price of the physical crude oil contract.**

WTI Contract Price	
Nov contract price	$95/BBL
Dec contract price	$96/BBL
Jan contract price	$97/BBL
Feb contract price	$98/BBL

   A. $96.15/BBL
   B. $97.15/BBL
   C. $97.33/BBL
   D. $97.48/BBL

   Correct Answer: D

   Explanation: The correct answer is D. Since the contract is based on the prompt future price, it is necessary to calculate the price from the January and February contracts. For two-thirds of December, the January contract is the prompt contract (the December contract closed in November). For the last one-third of the month, the February contract is the prompt contract. (2/3) * Jan + (1/3) * Feb + $0.15 = $97.48.

8. **Fossil fuels are primarily composed of what common elements?**
   A. Carbon and hydrogen
   B. Carbon and oxygen
   C. Hydrogen and oxygen
   D. Oxygen and nitrogen

Correct Answer: A

Explanation: Fossil fuels are hydrocarbons. Hydrocarbons are composed of chains of carbon and hydrogen.

9. **Why would a heavy crude oil, like Mexico's Maya Crude, be cheaper than lighter crude oils like Arab Light Crude?**
   A. Heavy crudes like Maya Crude are more difficult to transport.
   B. The supply of untapped Maya Crude reserves is larger than the supply of Arab Light reserves.
   C. Middle Eastern crude oil is higher quality than crudes from other parts of the world.
   D. Refineries need specialized equipment to process heavy crude oils that is very expensive.

Correct Answer: D

Explanation: Heavy crudes need specialized equipment, like cracking and coking units, to be fully processed. This equipment is extremely expensive and is not installed at every refinery. The other answers are mostly misdirection. Middle Eastern crude oil is typically not considered a premium crude. Heavier crude is no more or less difficult to transport than light crude, and an untapped supply of crude has limited effect on current market prices.

10. **Which is the largest trading market by value of commodity traded?**
    A. Gasoline
    B. Crude oil
    C. Gold
    D. Electricity

Correct Answer: B

Explanation: The crude oil market is the largest trading market in the world whether it is measured by value (for example, in U.S. dollars of product traded) or by quantity of commodity traded (either weight or volume).

Chapter 2

Natural Gas, Natural Gas Liquids, and Coal

Solid and gaseous hydrocarbon fuels are commonly used for heating or to generate electricity. Compared to liquid petroleum products, these fuels are less desirable as a vehicular fuel. However, because these fuels tend to be more abundant and lower cost than liquid fuels, these fuels tend to be heavily used for other purposes.

CHAPTER OBJECTIVES

After completing this chapter, the student should have an understanding of

- Natural Gas
- Liquefied Natural Gas (LNG)
- Natural Gas transportation
- Natural Gas storage
- Natural Gas Liquids (NGLS) / Liquefied Propane Gas (LPG)
- Coal

Natural Gas

Natural gas is a nonrenewable fossil fuel used to provide heat and generate electricity. It is primarily composed of *methane*, a relatively common, colorless, odorless, non-corrosive, nontoxic gas that is already present in small quantities in the atmosphere. When found underground, most pollutants in natural gas can be removed without complex equipment. As a result, natural gas has a reputation as a cost-effective, clean-burning fuel. Its major limitation is that it is a gas. In gaseous form, natural gas must be kept in airtight containers so that it won't dissipate and is generally distributed by pipeline rather than liquefied or compressed.

Key Concept

Why Does Natural Gas Smell Bad?

Because natural gas is colorless, odorless, and tasteless, an odorant like mercaptan is typically added before distribution. This gives natural gas a distinct unpleasant odor (it smells like rotten eggs). This added smell serves as a safety measure by allowing gas to be detected by smell when a leak occurs.

Natural gas is primarily composed of methane (CH_4) but often contains small amounts of heavier hydrocarbon gases like ethane (C_2H_6), propane (C_3H_8), and butane (C_4H_{10}). In its natural form, natural gas is commonly mixed with atmospheric gases like nitrogen and carbon dioxide. Because the composition of natural gas varies so widely, it is commonly traded in units of heat energy like British thermal units (Btu) or joules (J) rather than in units of volume (like cubic feet). However, it is still important to know the relationship between natural gas energy content and volume since storage containers are often sized by volume.

In the United States, natural gas is traded in British thermal units (Btu). In locations that have adopted the metric system, it is traded in joules. For wholesale markets, the most common units are MMBTU (millions of Btu) and Mega joules (MJ, millions of joules). Stored natural gas is often handled in volume units (billions of cubic feet). Consumers might use still other units (see Table 2-1). For example, in North America, consumer gas is sold in *therms*. A therm is 100,000 Btu, or one-tenth of an MMBtu.

From Units		To Units	
Quantity	Unit	Quantity	Units
1	MMBTU	1.056	GJ (Gigajoule)
1	MMBTU	1,055.87	MJ (Megajoule)
1	MMBTU	1,000,000	BTU
1	MMBTU	10	Therms
1	MMBTU	1	Dcf (Dekatherm)
1	Bcf (Billion cubic feet)	1,024,000	MMBTU
1	MT of Oil Equivalent	39.65	MMBTU
1	BBL of Oil Equivalent (BOE)	5.25	MMBTU (Wet Gas)
1	BBL of Oil Equivalent (BOE)	5.65	MMBTU (Dry Gas)

TABLE 2-1 • Common Natural Gas Conversion Factors

Natural Gas Concepts

Natural gas is commonly traded by its heat content rather than volume or weight. This is important to investors, since different hydrocarbon gases have different heat contents per unit of volume.

- Raw natural gas usually has a heat content of between 900 and 1200 Btu per cubic foot
- Pure natural gas, also known as methane, has approximately 1024 Btu per cubic foot

Natural gas can be found underground as a fossil fuel or created from a variety of chemical processes. When underground, natural gas might be found dissolved in crude oil, trapped within rock formations, or reside alongside coal deposits. When natural gas is dissolved in crude oil, it is called *associated gas*. Associated gas is dangerous to oil drillers because it bubbles out of crude oil when the crude oil is brought to the surface. The resulting high pressure of the gas can lead to equipment failure if the gas is allowed to pool in a bend or near a weak spot in a pipe.

The constituents of every batch of raw natural gas are different. In general, the lightest and most abundant gas is methane (which is normally called *natural gas*). The heavier gases are called *natural gas liquids*. To distinguish whether natural gas contains primarily methane or a mix of heavier gases, the terms *dry* and *wet* gas are used. *Dry natural gas* is primarily methane—this is what gets delivered to consumers. *Wet natural gas* contains substantial quantities of heavier hydrocarbons. These have to be removed before the gas can be sold to customers. The terms *natural gas liquids* (NGLs) and *liquefied petroleum gas* (LPGs) refer to these heavier gases.

Key Concept

Wet and Dry Natural Gas

Wet and *dry* are terms that refer to the presence of heavier hydrocarbons in natural gas. Even though it can't be used without processing, *wet natural gas* tends to be slightly more valuable than *dry natural gas* due to the presence of less common, but more valuable, gases like propane and butane.

- **Dry Gas.** Dry natural gas is primarily composed of methane (the lightest hydrocarbon.)
- **Wet Gas.** Wet natural gas contains a large percentage of heavier hydrocarbons like propane and butane.

As the simplest fossil fuel, natural gas is very plentiful. It also contains fewer pollutants than most other fossil fuels. The extremely low boiling point of methane makes it easy to remove pollution. If a mixture containing methane is cooled, other substances will turn into liquids before methane. This allows methane to be siphoned off and purified relatively easily. However, the extremely low temperature liquefaction point of natural gas also limits how it can be transported and stored.

Natural Gas Transportation

Natural gas is most commonly transported through pipelines. Some of these pipelines are transcontinental in length, while others span a single town. Pipelines are an efficient way to transport gas. Pipelines operate by pressure differentials. When a compressor creates a high pressure zone at one end of a pipe, and a vacuum is created at the other end, suction will pull the gas through the pipe. As long as gas is continually pushed into one end of the pipe (*injected*) and removed from the other end (*withdrawn*), gas can be cost effectively moved long distances. Pipelines typically involve large upfront costs and relatively low per-unit costs.

Key Concept

Natural Gas Pipelines

Natural gas is commonly transported by pipelines. These pipelines are limited to land and require constant pressure in the pipeline to ensure a smooth flow of gas. Because of the need to create a vacuum that will suction the gas over transcontinental distances, natural gas pipelines can't shut down and restart quickly. As a result, natural gas pipelines typically need to run full time.

- **Injection.** The process of placing gas into a pipeline
- **Withdrawal.** The process of removing gas from a pipeline

There are two major types of natural gas pipelines. *Transportation pipelines* involve the long distance transportation of natural gas. *Distribution pipelines* are concerned with delivering gas to end users. Distribution pipelines tend to be more complex than transportation pipelines. With a distribution pipeline, the pipeline operator has to maintain a network of connections to a large number of consumers. In contrast, a transportation pipeline might have one or two branches. The complexity of delivery pipelines comes at a cost. It often costs as much to deliver gas the last mile from a citygate to a consumer as it costs to move the gas across the country.

Pipelines often interconnect with one another. The intersection of two or more transportation pipelines is called a *hub*. The connection between transportation pipelines and a distribution pipeline is called a *citygate*. Both hubs and citygates are common delivery locations for natural gas contracts. Consumers of natural gas are often called the *burner tip*. Historically, a burner tip was an actual piece of equipment. However, burner tips are no longer used and the term now refers to a consumer.

Key Concept

Henry Hub Futures Contract

Hubs and citygates are often the delivery locations specified in natural gas contracts. For example, the natural gas futures contract traded on the NYMEX (New York Mercantile Exchange) is the most important natural gas contract in North America. The underlying commodity for this contract is natural gas delivered at the Henry Hub, which is located near the Louisiana Gulf Coast at the interconnection of 13 pipelines. Most natural gas forward prices in North America—and most electricity ones too—are heavily based on this contract.

Pipelines typically have a variety of locations where gas can be injected or removed from the system. A point where someone injects gas into a pipeline is called a *receipt point*. This is where the pipeline receives the gas. A point where someone takes gas out of the pipeline is called a *delivery point*. The names are based on the pipeline's obligation, rather than the obligations of the purchaser of the transportation contract.

It would be very unusual for a transportation customer to receive the same molecules of gas that they placed into the system. All of the gas placed into a pipeline gets comingled, and it is very common for the owner of a gas transportation contract to be allowed to inject gas at one point while simultaneously removing it at a distant location.

Key Concept

Natural Gas Transportation

A variety of terms are used to indicate types of and locations on a pipeline.

- **Transportation Pipeline.** A natural gas pipeline primarily concerned with long distance transportation.
- **Distribution Pipeline.** A natural gas pipeline primarily concerned with distributing gas to consumers.
- **Receipt Point.** A receipt point is a location where gas is placed into the pipeline (where the pipeline receives the gas).
- **Delivery Point.** A delivery point is a location where natural gas is removed from a pipeline (where the pipeline delivers the gas).
- **Hub.** A hub is an interconnection between two transmission pipelines. Storage facilities are commonly located at hubs.
- **Citygate.** A citygate is an interconnection between a transportation pipeline and a distribution pipeline.
- **Burner Tip.** A term referring to a consumer of natural gas.

Contracts for natural gas transportation can be *firm* or *interruptible*. A firm contract guarantees that the necessary pipeline capacity will be available to transport the natural gas. An interruptible contract will allow transportation whenever customers with firm transportation contracts are not using their full capacity. There are a wide variety of terms used in transportation contracts.

- **Reservation Charge.** The reservation charge is a fixed monthly charge paid to the pipeline to reserve transportation capacity.
- **Commodity Charge.** A commodity charge is the variable cost for transportation. This charge is usually quoted per unit of gas to be transported.

- **ACA (Annual Cost Adjustment) Charges.** The ACA is a small charge that adjusts transportation costs for inflation.

- **GRI (Gas Research Institute) Charges.** For U.S. pipelines, the GRI charge is a small fixed charge used to fund a nonprofit industry group, the Gas Research Institute.

- **Fuel Usage.** Fuel usage describes the amount of natural gas lost in transportation. This lost gas is commonly used as payment in kind to provide power to the compressors responsible for moving the gas.

- **Receipt Adder.** A receipt adder is a fixed price adjustment used to determine the price at the receipt point relative to the price of a nearby benchmark.

- **Delivery Adder.** A delivery adder is a fixed price adjustment used to determine the price at the delivery point relative to the price of a nearby benchmark.

- **Volume.** The quantity of natural gas that can be transported.

Interruptible transport can be obtained from a pipeline on an as-available basis at a price negotiated with the pipeline. When firm transportation customers are not utilizing their reserved capacity, interruptible transportation customers can use the pipeline. The value of interruptible transportation depends on someone else not maximizing their own economic profit.[1] From an investment standpoint, utilizing interruptible transport requires in-depth knowledge of how a pipeline's firm customers conduct their business.

For anyone that needs to guarantee transportation, firm transportation agreements are a way to contractually guarantee space is available. Many natural gas pipelines are regulated utilities,[2] which need to provide open access to all market participants (on a first-come basis) and use the same regulated pricing structure for all customers. For regulated utilities, the fee structure charged by the pipeline, called a *tariff*, will be listed in a public document which can be obtained from either the pipeline company or the regulating agency. This will look something like Figure 2-1.

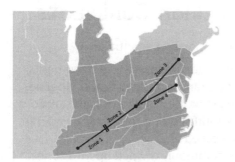

From Zone	To Zone	Reservation Charge ($/MMBTU)	Commodity Charge ($/MMBTU)	Fuel % Winter	Fuel % Summer
1	2	$0.13	$0.0150	0.21%	0.24%
1	3	$0.27	$0.0350	0.21%	0.24%
1	4	$0.22	$0.0250	0.21%	0.24%
2	3	$0.14	$0.0200	0.21%	0.24%
2	4	$0.09	$0.0250	0.21%	0.24%

Notes:
All charges are per MMBTU per day

FIGURE 2-1 · Pipeline Map and Tariff Schedule

The units of trading written into each tariff will often vary from pipeline to pipeline. For example, some tariffs will list reservation charges as a monthly charge, while others will quote a daily charge. Similarly, the cost per quantity may be quoted by either volume or heat content. It is commonly necessary to convert prices from two different pipelines into comparable units before comparing them. Using the example tariff in Figure 2-1:

Sample Question 1. Calculate the monthly reservation cost of firm natural gas transportation between Zone 1 and Zone 3 for 10,000 MMBtu /day. Assume the month has 30 days.

Answer. $81,000. This is calculated by multiplying the volume (10,000 MMBtu/day) times the daily reservation charge ($0.27/MMBtu /day) times the number of days in the month (30).

(10,000 MMBtu) * ($0.27 / MMBtu days) * (30 days) = $81,000

Sample Question 2. Calculate the amount of gas that would need to be injected into Zone 1 during the summer to receive 10,000 MMBtu of gas at Zone 4.

Answer. 10,024 MMBtu. Gas will be lost transporting it between Zone 1 and Zone 4. If 10,000 units need to be received at Zone 4, there must be a large amount of gas inserted at Zone 1. Since 0.24% of the gas is lost, the quantity at Zone 1 is $(1/(1-0.024\%)$ * (quantity needed at Zone 4).

(10,024 MMBtu at Zone 1) = (10,000 MMBtu at Zone 4) / (1−0.24%)

Not all pipelines are separated into zones. In some cases, there is a fixed cost to transport natural gas anywhere on a pipeline. The cost for transporting natural gas on these pipelines is called a *postage stamp* rate.

Key Concept

Natural Gas Transportation Contracts

A variety of terms are used in natural gas transportation contracts.

- **Tariff.** Pipeline rates are commonly public documents. These documents, called tariffs, describe the charges used to transport gas over the pipeline. Tariffs can usually be found on the pipeline or the regulator's web site. For example, in the United States, pipeline tariffs can be found on a Federal Energy Regulatory Commission web site called eFERC.
- **Zones.** Different areas on a pipeline are commonly divided up into zones.
- **Postage Stamp.** A postage stamp rate is the cost to transport gas on a pipeline having a single rate zone.

Liquefied Natural Gas (LNG)

Another way to transport natural gas is to convert it into a liquid and transport it on a ship. To liquefy natural gas, it is necessary to lower its temperature to –263°F (–160°C). As a liquid, natural gas is 1/610 of its gaseous volume. This makes transporting gas by ship feasible. The insulation needed to keep natural gas cold involves large scale operations, since small scale transportation is still not cost effective. The main limitation of LNG transportation is the large amount of fuel that needs to be consumed to cool and then reheat natural gas. There are three main steps in the LNG process: *liquefaction*, *transportation*, and *regasification*.

- **Liquefaction and Exporting.** To transport natural gas as a liquid, it is necessary to cool the natural gas to –263°F (–160°C). Liquefaction plants are responsible for that process. Liquefaction is a multistage process where sequential cooling units, called a *train*, progressively cool the natural gas. These plants are usually linked to producing regions by short-range pipelines and are responsible for separating out any natural gas liquids (NGLs), cooling the natural gas, and loading it into storage containers for transfer to specially designed tanker ships. A large amount of energy is expended during the liquefaction processes.

- **Transportation.** Once LNG is loaded aboard ship, specially designed tankers will transport the fuel to its destination. These ships have to be specifically designed to handle extremely cold liquids and keep them insulated. Even then, some of the liquid methane will convert back into a gas. As a result, a small percentage of the natural gas will be lost in transportation. Larger scale transports, faster travel time, and cryogenic cooling systems to refreeze the boiled-off gas can reduce these losses.

- **Regasification and Importing.** After transportation, natural gas must be converted back into a gas and processed to meet pipeline standards before it is delivered to customers. This is done at a regasification plant. This plant transfers the liquefied natural gas from the tanker ships and stores it in specially designed containers to keep the LNG at low temperature until it is ready to be warmed up. Although the technology to heat up the gas is fairly straightforward, a large amount of energy is lost in this process.

Key Concept

Liquefied Natural Gas (LNG)

Liquefied natural gas (LNG) is composed primarily of methane cooled to –263°F (–160°C), which allows natural gas to be transported by ship. Compared to pipelines, LNG transport is substantially more expensive. LNG is typically only economical when importing natural gas to areas without a locally available supply.

Natural Gas Storage

Before and after gas is transported, it must commonly be stored. Storage serves two purposes. First, storage allows gas to be stockpiled in areas where consumer demand can exceed a pipeline's capacity to deliver fuel. For example, in a cold winter, the consumer demand for natural gas (for heating) may exceed the capacity of the pipeline to bring in additional supplies of fuel. Storage will help a natural gas utility meet consumer demand. Second, it is necessary for pipeline operators to regulate the pressure on the pipeline. Gas moves from areas of high pressure to areas of low pressure. To keep the pipeline flowing, gas must constantly be injected into one side of the pipeline and withdrawn from the other side. Storage at both sides of a pipeline prevents short-term variations in either injections or withdrawals from shutting down the pipeline.

Natural gas is commonly stored in underground reservoirs (porous, permeable rock formations) similar to areas where it was originally removed from the ground. A large number of natural gas storage facilities were originally natural gas wells that have been refilled after being exhausted. Other storage facilities include salt caverns or underground aquifers. Dry natural gas is injected into the storage facility until it is at a relatively high pressure. It can then be removed by suction.

The speed at which gas can be injected and removed from the facility will depend on pressure. Higher pressures allow gas to be moved around more quickly, but may damage the rock formation. The higher the actual pressure of the facility, the easier it is to remove the gas, and the harder it is to inject more. At very low pressures, it is extremely difficult to remove gas from a facility but gas can easily be injected. Facilities that can operate under high pressures can switch between these states more readily and are much more valuable than facilities that can operate only at low pressures.

Because the ability to remove gas from a facility decreases as the pressure falls, there will be some gas that cannot be economically removed. The speed of removing the gas will be so slow as to make removal uneconomical. Gas that cannot be physically removed from a storage facility is called *unrecoverable gas*. In addition, higher pressures in the storage facility will push more gas into the walls. Facilities are rarely completely airtight, and if enough pressure is added, the gas will eventually reach a more permeable area and start to escape from the storage facility.

Storage facilities typically maintain a certain level of gas, called *base gas* or *cushion gas*, to keep the facility at sufficiently high pressure. Base gas is not removed from a storage facility during normal operations although a portion of it may be removed during extreme shortages. The quantity of gas used for withdrawals during normal conditions is called *working gas*. The relative level of base and working gas is a trade-off. Larger amounts of base gas keep the facility at a higher pressure and allow the remaining working gas to be removed more quickly. Smaller amount of base gas allow more gas to be removed, but the speed that the gas exits the facility will be lower.

Key Concept

Natural Gas Storage

Natural gas is typically stored in underground rock formations similar to the formations where natural gas was obtained. Facilities that can operate under high pressure allow gas to be injected and removed more quickly. Higher performance facilities are substantially more valuable than low performance facilities. The geology of the rock formation determines the maximum safe pressure of gas in the facility.

- **Unrecoverable gas.** Unrecoverable gas cannot be physically removed from the storage facility without damaging the facility.
- **Base or cushion gas.** Base gas is used to keep the storage facility at a desired pressure and is not removed during normal operations.
- **Working gas.** Working gas can be withdrawn or injected into the storage facility.

There are three primary types of underground storage facilities used for natural gas: depleted gas reservoirs, salt caverns, and aquifers. Depleted gas reservoirs are the cheapest type of storage facility. Salt caverns are the highest performance. Aquifers are the lowest performance and are only used when there is no alternative available. About 50 percent of the total capacity of depleted reservoirs needs to be reserved as a gas cushion. Only about 33 percent of the capacity of salt caverns needs to be reserved, while aquifers often have about 80 percent of their capacity reserved for base gas. Each of these three storage methods have their advantages and disadvantages.

- **Depleted Reservoirs.** Once a natural gas reservoir has been emptied, it can be refilled. Refilling a depleted reservoir can be a cost-effective method of creating a storage unit if the original pipes and equipment are still in place. While not all reservoirs are suitable for refilling, if one exists in the right area, it might be a good candidate to be converted into a storage facility. There are few environmental concerns with depleted reservoir storage, since natural gas had been stored in that location for millions of years. There is usually little need to inject gas into a depleted reservoir since it would already contain unrecoverable gas that couldn't be removed the first time it was used.

- **Salt Caverns.** Salt caverns are high performance natural gas storage facilities. They are more expensive to develop than depleted gas reservoirs. Salt caverns are often developed by dissolving underground salt deposits with water and reusing the resulting space for natural gas storage. The rock walls that remain after removing salt deposits tend to be very strong and impermeable (otherwise salt would have penetrated the wall). Salt facilities can often operate at twice the pressure of depleted reservoirs. Development costs for salt caverns are higher than for depleted reservoirs because a base level of unrecoverable gas has to be injected into the facility and new equipment has to be purchased.

- **Aquifers.** Aquifers are the least desirable and most expensive type of natural gas storage. These are only used when they have a large geographic advantage over other types of storage—they are in the right place and nothing else is available. These storage fields typically require a large amount of unrecoverable natural gas to be injected into the ground before they can be used. This is only economical when natural gas is extremely cheap. Aquifers are typically limited to very low pressures.

Alternative storage technology is generally not cost effective on a large scale. For example, storing enough natural gas to supply the city of Chicago for an entire winter is not possible using pressurized metal containers. Large, high pressure containers are a public safety risk. Aside from their flammable contents, the metal shards from a ruptured pressure container can be deadly. The risk goes up with the size of the container and the pressure of its contents. Similarly, liquefied natural gas typically requires too much energy to be stored, unless there are mitigating economic factors. Keeping a large supply of natural gas at –263°F (–160°C) might be feasible at a port facility if the natural gas arrives liquefied. However, it would be very difficult to get it cold if it was placed into a pipeline and transported cross-country at room temperature.

Key Concept

Types of Underground Storage

There are three main types of natural gas storage units.

- **Depleted Reservoirs.** A depleted reservoir is a natural gas storage unit created by reusing an existing depleted reservoir located in an advantageous location. It is reused by refilling it with natural gas. This is a low cost, medium performance storage unit.

- **Salt Caverns.** A salt cavern is a high cost, high performance facility that is created by dissolving a salt dome underneath the ground.
- **Aquifers.** Aquifers are high cost, low performance natural gas storage facilities that are only constructed when no reasonable alternative exists.

Natural Gas Liquids (NGLs) / Liquefied Propane Gases (LPGs)

Natural gas liquids (NGLs) are combustible gases heavier than methane (natural gas) but still light enough to exist in a gaseous state at standard temperature and pressure. These gases are commonly found dissolved in crude oil or natural gas. They are separated from natural gas at natural gas processing plants or from crude oil at refineries. *Liquefied petroleum gas* refers to a mixture of two of the heavier NGLs (propane and butane).

Compared to methane, heavier NGLs like propane and butane are much more easily liquefied by compression. These gases are approximately 270 times more compact as a liquid than as a gas. As a result, these gases are typically transported and stored in a liquid state. A typical use for these products is as a fuel for cooking (like a backyard grill). For example, liquefied propane can be stored in a pressurized container and easily converted to a gas when a valve is opened to release it.

NGLs can be referred to by their proper name or by the carbon content. When the carbon nomenclature is used, the number after a C indicates how many carbon atoms are in each molecule (see Table 2-2). Methane is rarely called C1, and is included to demonstrate the relationship of the heavier gases to methane.

Note: An isomer (iso-) has the same chemical formula but different structure than the "normal" version of the substance. Typically, "normal" is defined as the structure most commonly found in nature.

Abbreviation	Name	Boiling Point
C1	Methane (chemical formula CH_4, normally called *natural gas*)	-263°F (-160°C)
C2	Ethane (chemical formula C_2H_6)	-127°F (-89°C)
C3	Propane (chemical formula C_3H_8)	-43°F (-42°C)
IC4	iso-Butane (chemical formula $i-C_4H_{10}$)	16°F (-9°F)
NC4	normal Butane (chemical formula $n-C_4H_{10}$)	34°F (-1°C)
C5+	Pentanes and heavier hydrocarbons (anything heavier than Butane) — commonly referred to as *natural gasoline* or *condensate*.	97°F (36°C)

TABLE 2-2 · Natural Gas Liquids

Key Concept

C1 Natural Gas versus C5+ Natural Gasoline

Natural gas and *natural gasoline* are very different substances. *Natural gas (C1)* is composed of methane, the lightest hydrocarbon gas, while *natural gasoline (C5+)* is composed of heavier hydrocarbons and is very similar to low-octane petroleum called *naphtha*.

NGLs are seldom completely purified. As a result, there are several grades of fuel for each product specifying the required purity of the products. The two main grades of natural gas are *pipeline grade* and *fractionation grade*. Pipeline grade has to conform to the quality standards specified by pipeline companies in the "General Terms and Conditions (GTC)" section of their tariffs. These quality standards vary from pipeline to pipeline and depend on the design of the pipeline, interconnecting pipelines, and the intended consumer of the product. Some common clauses include:

- Btu content
- A minimum dew point temperature level (below which any vaporized gas liquid in the mix will tend to condense at pipeline pressure)
- Limits on pollutants and non-fuel gas
- Limits on particulate solids and liquids that could be detrimental to the pipeline or its ancillary operating equipment

These standards are necessary to prevent damage to a pipeline. Heavier NGLs have a higher Btu content than lighter NGLs. As a result, producers often have an economic incentive to increase the Btu content of fuel by including heavier products in a mix. However, these products are more likely to condense inside the pipeline and may be difficult to remove. Since pipelines are airtight, liquids will not evaporate once trapped in the pipeline. These liquids are often corrosive, and pipeline companies have to frequently monitor the dew point of gas being injected into their systems.

NGL Trading

When NGLs are traded, the contractual terms will specify the quality and required characteristics.

- Traded NGL products can be traded in units based on heat content (Btu or joules) or by volume (gallons or liters).
- *Pipeline grade* NGL products are usually 5% to 10% less expensive than *fractionation* grade NGL products. Fractionation grade products are less purified and contain a higher quantity of valuable heavy NGLs.
- Pipeline grade NGL products are typically named for the pipeline whose specifications determine their composition.

The steps required to create pipeline grade NGLs depends on the composition of raw material coming into the processing unit. Since the composition of raw materials varies substantially, there is a lot of variation among gas processing units. Some of the more common steps include:

1. **Gas/Oil Separation.** If NGLs or natural gas are mixed with crude oil, the two can be separated by alternately heating and cooling the mixture several times.
2. **Free Water and Condensate Separation.** Any remaining free water, condensate, or other liquids need to be drained off.
3. **Dehydration.** Water vapor is removed through dehydration.
4. **Contaminant Removal.** Hydrogen sulfide, carbon dioxide, helium, and oxygen are atmospheric gases that must be removed from NGLs. Sulfur is commonly removed through the use of amine solutions that absorb the sulfur compounds. Gases are typically separated by filter tubes that rely on gravity to pull heavier gases to the bottom tubes of the processing unit.
5. **Nitrogen Removal.** Nitrogen is commonly removed by either heating/cooling the gas or through the use of chemical solvents.
6. **Methane Separation.** Methane has a much lower boiling point than other NGLs, so it is commonly removed by cooling the NGLs until they turn into a liquid and then siphoning off the methane. This can also be done through several chemical processes.

7. **Fractionation.** The last stage of the process involves separating the NGLs into component gases. This can be done by heating up the liquefied gases, allowing them to boil off one at a time.

Key Concept

Heavier NGLS (Propane and Butane)

Heavier NGLs like propane and butane are more easily converted into liquids and stored in a pressurized container than lighter gases like methane and ethane. Either high pressure or low temperature can be used to convert a gas into a liquid. In the case of propane or butane, moderate pressure is sufficient to keep these substances as liquids at room temperature.

The terminology to describe natural gas and natural gas liquids is often confusing (see Table 2-3 and Table 2-4).

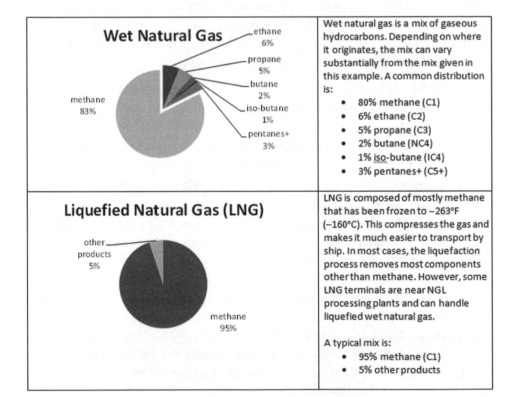

Wet Natural Gas

methane 83%
ethane 6%
propane 5%
butane 2%
iso-butane 1%
pentanes+ 3%

Wet natural gas is a mix of gaseous hydrocarbons. Depending on where it originates, the mix can vary substantially from the mix given in this example. A common distribution is:

- 80% methane (C1)
- 6% ethane (C2)
- 5% propane (C3)
- 2% butane (NC4)
- 1% iso-butane (IC4)
- 3% pentanes+ (C5+)

Liquefied Natural Gas (LNG)

other products 5%
methane 95%

LNG is composed of mostly methane that has been frozen to −263°F (−160°C). This compresses the gas and makes it much easier to transport by ship. In most cases, the liquefaction process removes most components other than methane. However, some LNG terminals are near NGL processing plants and can handle liquefied wet natural gas.

A typical mix is:

- 95% methane (C1)
- 5% other products

TABLE 2-3 • Wet and Liquefied Natural Gas

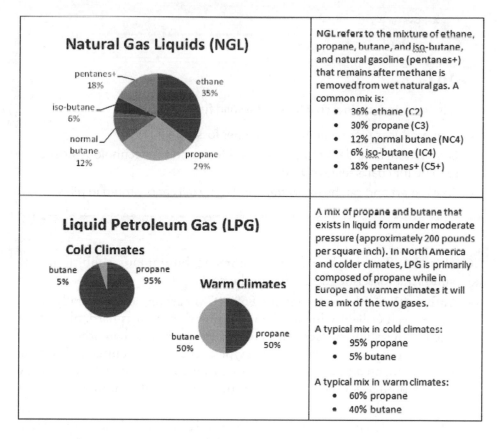

Natural Gas Liquids (NGL)

pentanes+ 18%
ethane 35%
iso-butane 6%
normal butane 12%
propane 29%

NGL refers to the mixture of ethane, propane, butane, and iso-butane, and natural gasoline (pentanes+) that remains after methane is removed from wet natural gas. A common mix is:

- 36% ethane (C2)
- 30% propane (C3)
- 12% normal butane (NC4)
- 6% iso-butane (IC4)
- 18% pentanes+ (C5+)

Liquid Petroleum Gas (LPG)

Cold Climates

butane 5%
propane 95%

Warm Climates

butane 50%
propane 50%

A mix of propane and butane that exists in liquid form under moderate pressure (approximately 200 pounds per square inch). In North America and colder climates, LPG is primarily composed of propane while in Europe and warmer climates it will be a mix of the two gases.

A typical mix in cold climates:
- 95% propane
- 5% butane

A typical mix in warm climates:
- 60% propane
- 40% butane

TABLE 2-4 • NGLs and LPGs

Coal

Coal is the term for a solid hydrocarbon fuel. It is a combustible black or brownish-black sedimentary rock composed of long carbon chains. In addition to carbon chains, coal also contains small rocks, dust particles, and other mineral deposits. It is difficult to separate the hydrocarbons in coal from all of the other substances prior to combustion. As a result, compared to other fossil fuels, burning coal typically releases high amounts of pollution.

The primary use of coal is to provide heat for steam turbines used to generate electricity. Coal is a cost-effective fuel because of its relative abundance, low mining costs, and ease of storage. Many countries have large coal deposits, including the United States, Russia, and China.

Key Concept

Coal

Coal is an abundant, low cost fuel. It is a solid fuel.

- Coal produces more pollution than other fossil fuels.
- Coal is more abundant than other fossil fuels and the technology needed to mine for coal is relatively simple.
- Coal is inert and can be easily transported by rail car or stored in piles.

Coal is classified into four grades (anthracite, bituminous, subbituminous, and lignite) that describe the quality of the coal.

- **Anthracite.** Anthracite contains 86%–97% carbon, and generally has a heating value slightly higher than bituminous coal. It is hard, black coal, often with a shiny surface. Anthracite is less polluting than other types of coal. However, it is a relatively rare type of coal and accounts for less than 1% of the global coal reserves. China currently accounts for most of the world's production of anthracite. In the United States, anthracite comes from western Pennsylvania.

- **Bituminous Coal.** Bituminous coal is a dense black or dark brown solid that often contains well-defined bands of bright and dull material. It contains between 45% and 86% carbon and is the most common type of coal. This coal often contains a tar-like fuel, *bitumen*, which gives this coal its name. Bituminous coal accounts for about half of U.S. coal production. In the United States, West Virginia, Kentucky, and Pennsylvania are the largest producers of bituminous coal.

- **Subbituminous Coal.** Subbituminous coal has a lower heating value than bituminous coal and contains between 35% and 45% carbon. Low carbon subbituminous coal is often dull, dark brown, and crumbles easily. Higher carbon subbituminous coal is black and much harder. Approximately half of the coal produced in the United States is sub-bituminous. In the United States, Wyoming is the leading source of subbituminous coal.

- **Lignite.** Lignite is the lowest grade of coal. It is an inferior coal with low energy content. It is sometimes referred to as "burnable dirt." Lignite contains 25%–35% carbon and produces a large amount of pollution when combusted. It is often very cheap and not worth transporting long distances. It is primarily used to generate power in generation units located adjacent to the mining area. Lignite accounts for about 7% of U.S. coal. In the United States, most lignite is mined in Texas and North Dakota.

Key Concept

Types of Coal

Coal is an abundant, low cost fuel. It is relatively easy to mine, transport, and store.

- **Anthracite.** Anthracite is a high quality coal that is the lowest pollution coal. However, it is relatively uncommon.
- **Bituminous and Subbituminous Coals.** Bituminous and subbituminous coals are the most common types of coal.
- **Lignite.** Lignite is inferior coal that produces high levels of pollution. It is very low cost, but not commonly traded or transported.

Coal Mining

There are two main types of coal mines: strip mines and underground mines.

Strip mines

Strip mining removes the soil and rock above coal deposits. It leaves an exposed coal *seam* that can easily be removed by construction equipment. This equipment is similar to regular construction equipment, but built on a much larger scale for use in mining. For example, the tires on a mining truck might be 12 feet high (approximately 4 meters tall), with the rest of the vehicle built to the same scale.

In cases where an extremely thick layer of coal exists close to the surface, a large amount of coal may be removed from a single mine. For example, in Wyoming's Powder River Basin, where coal deposits may run 70 feet deep, a few acres of land may produce millions of tons of coal. A related technique is mountaintop removal and valley-fill mining. With these techniques, tops of mountains are removed by a combination of explosives and mining equipment and deposited into nearby valleys.

Unless the areas are *reclaimed* after being strip mined, strip mining can be very destructive to the environment. Many surface mines have been reclaimed so well that it can be hard to tell that there was mining in the area. However, many areas have not been reclaimed. As a result, strip mining often has a reputation of being damaging to the environment.

Underground mines

Underground mines have less overall impact on the environment than surface mines. However, underground coal mining is a dangerous business. There are a variety of dangers inherent to coal mines ranging from methane leaks to explosions and collapsing tunnels.

Transportation

Once it has been mined, coal is often transported by railcar or barge to its destination. This affects how coal is traded. Largely because mining costs are so low, transportation costs can make up a large portion of the consumer cost of coal. The cheaper the coal, the less economical it is to ship over long distances. This is different than transporting liquids and gases. Liquid and gas pipelines typically have very low per-unit costs. There is a high up-front cost to build a gas or liquids pipeline, but low marginal costs for additional volume. In contrast, for coal, each additional unit costs approximately the same amount to transport as the first.

Key Concept

Coal-to-Liquids (CTL)

Much in the same way that coking units convert heavy petroleum products into lighter petroleum products, coal can also be converted into liquid petroleum through processing. The Fischer–Tropsch process is a series of chemical reactions developed in Germany during the 1920s to convert carbon monoxide and hydrogen into fuel. This technology has received intermittent investment attention. High startup costs and volatile crude oil prices have prevented large scale commercialization of the process.

QUIZ

1. **What term is used to describe a location where natural gas is injected into a pipeline?**
   A. Receipt point
   B. Delivery point
   C. Natural gas hub
   D. Citygate

   Correct Answer: A

   Explanation: A receipt point is a location where natural gas is injected into a pipeline. Natural gas hub and citygate are terms meant to confuse the reader as these are common receipt and delivery points. However, hubs and citygates don't need to be injection points—they could be only distribution locations.

2. **An LNG regasification plant must do the following to ensure quality of its output?**
   A. It must ensure its products are free of methane and other pollutants.
   B. It must ensure its products are consistent with natural gas pipeline specifications in the country of origin.
   C. It must ensure its products are consistent with natural gas regulations specified by the pipeline which will be used to transfer the LNG from the regasification terminal to consumers.
   D. All of the above.

   Correct Answer: C

   Explanation: The quality of the gas that comes from an LNG terminal must meet the specifications of the gas pipelines which will be used to transport the fuel to consumers. These specifications may vary by pipeline and country. Answer A is incorrect because natural gas is primarily composed of methane.

3. **What is the primary component of consumer-grade natural gas?**
   A. Propane
   B. Methane
   C. Butane
   D. Pentane

   Correct Answer: B

   Explanation: Consumer-grade natural gas is composed primarily of methane. Consumer-grade natural gas is also called dry natural gas.

4. **What is the main reason(s) that an emerging market country would consider coal as a primary fuel for electrical generation?**
   I. Coal is low cost.
   II. A large amount of coal is available locally and wouldn't have to be imported.
   III. The technology to mine and generate power from coal is readily available.

A. Only I
B. I and II
C. I and III
D. All of the above

Correct Answer: D

Explanation: Affordability, local supplies, and mature technology are all reasons that would be considered when determining whether to use coal or another fuel as the basis of an electrical grid.

5. **Which of the following statements regarding refined NGL transportation are correct?**
    A. Isobutane must be transported in a pressurized container because it will contaminate a pipeline.
    B. Natural gas liquids are commonly transported via pipelines.
    C. Natural gas liquids and liquefied natural gas are synonyms and use the same transportation technologies.
    D. Ethane/propane mixtures are seldom transported through pipelines.

Correct Answer: B

Explanation: NGLs are commonly transported through pipelines. Propane, butane, and isobutene are heavy enough that they may also be transported as liquids inside pressurized containers. LNG refers to liquefied natural gas that has been frozen to –263°F (–160°C).

6. **Organize the following type of natural gas storage facilities in order of least to most desirable performance characteristics:**
    A. Aquifer, salt cavern, depleted reservoir
    B. Salt cavern, depleted reservoir, aquifer
    C. Depleted reservoir, aquifer, salt cavern
    D. Aquifer, depleted reservoir, salt cavern

Correct Answer: D

Explanation: Aquifers have the least desirable performance characteristics, depleted reservoirs are in the middle, and salt caverns have the most desirable performance characteristics.

7. **What is the highest grade of coal?**
    A. Lignite
    B. Bituminous
    C. Anthracite
    D. Subbituminous

Correct Answer: C

Explanation: Anthracite is the correct answer. Other solid carbon substances exist along the coal spectrum. For example, when compressed, anthracite will turn into graphite and eventually diamond. However, these substances are not generally considered coal or a fuel.

8. **What is the term that describes a large volume of natural gas dissolved in underground crude oil reserves due to high pressure on the crude oil?**
   A. Associated gas
   B. Petroleum gas
   C. Swamp gas
   D. Working gas

   Correct Answer: A

   Explanation: Although natural gas is sometimes referred to as a petroleum gas, the gas dissolved in underground crude oil reserves is known as associated gas. Answers C and D are not related to the question.

9. **Natural gas typically has what level of heat content?**
   A. 600 to 900 Btu/ft³
   B. 900 to 1,200 Btu/ ft³
   C. 1,200 to 1,500 Btu/ ft³
   D. 1,500 to 1,800 Btu/ ft³

   Correct Answer: B

   Explanation: Most natural gas has a heat content that ranges between 900 and 1200 Btu per cubic foot. Associated gas (gas found in oil wells) will typically have a higher Btu content because the gas will contain some of the heavier components found in the crude oil. Gas with a high CO_2 content will have a lower Btu content.

10. **What term is commonly used as a synonym for an end user of natural gas?**
    A. Citygate
    B. Firm transportation buyer
    C. Interruptible transportation buyer
    D. Burner tip

    Correct Answer: D

    Explanation: The term burner tip refers to a consumer, or end user, of natural gas.

Chapter 3

Electricity

Electricity is an energy carrier that provides a convenient and efficient way to get energy to where it is needed. It is an essential part of modern life used for lighting, heating, cooling, and powering electronic appliances. The business of generating, transmitting, and distributing electricity forms one of the largest industries in the world and provides a wide variety of investment opportunities.

CHAPTER OBJECTIVES

After completing this chapter, the student should have an understanding of

- Electricity as a commodity
- Electrical generation
- Electrical transmission
- Alternative sources for electrical energy like solar, wind, and hydrogeneration
- Renewable energy certificates (REC)
- Capacity markets

Electricity

Electrical current, commonly referred to as electricity, is a way to transport energy. While it isn't a source of energy, electricity can distribute energy created in a central location to places where it is needed. Electricity provides a convenient way to power small motors and electronic devices. At its most basic, electrical current is created by electrons moving through a conductive wire. There are a number of ways to get electrons to move through a wire. For example, electricity can be produced by manipulating the relationship between electrical currents and magnetism. It can also be produced through a chemical reaction.

The two most important properties of electricity are *voltage* and *current*. Voltage is a measure of the potential energy contained in the electric current. Current is the actual flow of electrons over a wire. These two items are closely related. Voltage causes current, and current does the actual work. Using a simple example of a water pipe, voltage is similar to water pressure. Like voltage, pressure is a type of potential energy that doesn't do much until the water is allowed to flow. When a tap is opened, high pressure will force water to flow more quickly than low pressure. The speed of the water coming out of the tap will depend on the change in pressure. Electrical current, like flowing water, is capable of performing work.

Higher voltage lines allow energy to be transferred more efficiently. Less power is lost in the transmission process at higher voltages. However, higher voltages are more dangerous than lower voltages. High voltage lines also create more electromagnetic interference. As a result, the power grid is built around equipment that transforms electrical current to high voltages for long distance transportation, and then steps down to lower voltages for delivery to consumers.

Key Concept

Voltage and Current

Voltage is a potential to do work. Current is a flow of electrons that actually performs work. The relationship between the two can be manipulated to optimize an electrical current for a particular task.

- **Voltage.** Voltage describes the potential of electricity to do work and is commonly measured in volts. In addition, the higher the voltage, the less power is lost during transmission.
- **Current.** Current describes the flow of electrons and is commonly measured in amperes (amps). High electrical currents cause more power to be lost during transmission.

Other terms important to the electrical grid are *power* and *energy*. *Power* is a rate at which work is done. For example, being able to stack 500 bricks an hour is a measure of power. *Energy*, also called *work*, is power multiplied by time. For example, "a man stacks 500 bricks an hour for 8 hours" describes a quantity of work.

In the electrical industry, power is commonly measured in watts. A watt is the rate at which work can be performed when one ampere of power moves through a potential difference of one volt. Units of power are commonly used to describe generation units. For example, a power plant might be described as a 100MW unit. This describes the potential rate at which the plant can operate. Electricity is traded in units of energy. For example, electricity may be traded in units of megawatt-hour (MWh). A megawatt hour is 1,000 watts of power for the period of 1 hour. A megawatt-hour is a measure of work.

Key Concept

Power and Energy

Power is the rate at which work is performed. This is used to describe genera-tion units. Energy is a measure of work—an amount of power multiplied by some period of time. Electricity is bought and sold in units of energy.

- **Power.** Power is the rate at which work is done. Power is the combination of voltage and current and is measured in watts.

- **Energy (Work).** Energy is measured in units of rate of work multiplied by time. This is measured in units like megawatt-hours or joules.

Before electricity can be used, it must be transported to the location of the consumer. The two most common technologies for transporting electricity are alternating current (AC) and direct current (DC). Both methods have advantages and disad-vantages. With DC power, electrical current flows in one direc-tion around a circuit. This allows DC power to provide a steady supply of power. AC power alternates the direction of the cur-rent. Alternating the direction of the current allows the voltage (and current) of AC power to be easily increased or decreased on the power line. This allows AC power networks to step up voltage for long distance transport and then decrease voltage for residential delivery. It also allows AC power networks to ensure a constant voltage across the network. Direct current power is primarily used for point-to-point connections where manipulating voltage is less important.

When the voltage of AC power is graphed, it is a sine wave. The average amount of power to be transferred over the AC line is approximately 70% of the peak voltage. The average voltage is often called the Root Mean Square (RMS) value of the sine wave (the square root of the average of the square of the voltages). (See Figure 3-1.) To provide consistent AC power to consumers, three power lines with offset sine waves are usually run together.

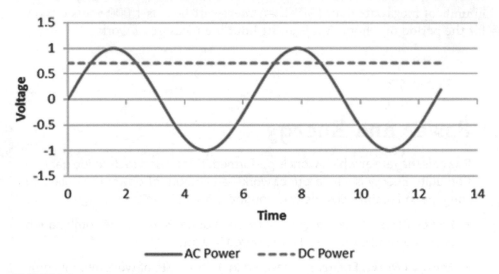

FIGURE 3-1 · AC and DC Power

Since AC power is a wave, it is important that all generation units produce electricity at exactly the same frequency. Otherwise, the power produced by each generator will cancel out energy produced by other generators. The need to synchronize generation units limits the ability of nonsynchronized power grids to import or export power from and to each other. Both technological (it's too hard to coordinate) and political (don't want someone else controlling the power grid) reasons can contribute to nonsynchronized power grids.

Key Concept

AC and DC Power

An electrical current can always move in the same direction (direct current) or alternate the direction of flow (alternating current).

- **AC Power.** Alternating current transmission is the most commonly used technology to transmit power on the power grid because of the ability to easily modify AC line voltage.

- **DC Power.** Direct current power is used for point-to-point transmission of power or where a constant voltage is desired. DC power can be used for long-distance transmission where there are no intermediate loads between source and destination.

- **Synchronization.** An engineering requirement that limits ability to transport power across power grids that don't line up their generation frequencies.

Some common units for power and energy:

- Btu   British thermal unit, a measure of energy
- MMBtu   A million Btu
- kW   Kilowatt, a measure of power
- MW   Megawatt, 1,000 kW, a measure of power
- MWh   Megawatt hours, a measure of energy
- J   Joules, a measure of energy
- MJ   Megajoules, 1,000 Joules, a measure of energy

The Power Grid

The power grid is a network of transmission lines that connects power producers and power consumers. It includes the power plants that produce energy, the consumers that use it, the power lines that carry it, and the substations and transformers that link power lines together. In order to work properly, the entire power grid needs to work together. For example, the amount of power entering the network has to be matched to the power being consumed. Additionally, the peaks and troughs in AC power have to line up or else they will cancel each other out. Finally, everyone can't be trying to transmit power over the same power line.

Key Concept

Synchronization

There are a large number of real-world issues that affect power transmission. Outages or changes to any part of a power grid will affect the rest of the grid. In addition, adjoining regions that don't coordinate their power grids with one another will be unable to transfer power between them. The most common solution is to centralize coordination of the power grid by giving authority to regional organizations. However, that limits the ability of local communities to make changes to the power grid.

Each power grid has a system operator responsible for keeping things working smoothly. For smaller power grids, a utility company may be in charge of the power grid. For larger grids that span larger areas, the grid operators may be called Independent Service Operators (ISOs) or Regional Transmission Organizations (RTOs). A *regulated* electricity market is a power grid where a utility company coordinates the grid as a government-sponsored monopoly. The monopoly utility will generally own all of the power lines and most of the generation units in its service area. A *deregulated* market is a power grid coordinated by an ISO or RTO. In deregulated markets, the ISO or RTO will not own the power lines or the generation units. However, the ISO/RTO will be responsible for coordinating and overseeing all of the generation and transmission in its service area.

Key Concept

Regulation

Both regulated and deregulated markets have similar amounts of government oversight. In a regulated market, the public utility commission (PUC) will typically determine wholesale power prices. In a deregulated market, wholesale power prices will be determined by the operating costs of the most expensive generation unit that is required to operate. The term **wholesale power** is used to distinguish it from other charges that might show up on a consumer's bill. The price paid by consumers is called the **retail price** of power, and typically contains charges for power (wholesale prices) plus local distribution charges and fees imposed by the utility.

- **Regulated Market.** A power grid coordinated by a utility that owns transmission and generation assets and operates as a government-sponsored monopoly.
- **Deregulated Market.** A power grid coordinated by an organization (usually called an *Independent System Operator* or a *Regional Transmission Organization*) that does not own transmission or generation assets.

The work of getting electricity to consumers is often broken into four components (see Figure 3-2). The first is *generation*, the work of creating electricity. The second is long distance transportation, called *transmission*. The third is *distribution*, which involves getting the power the last mile from the local substation to the consumer. The fourth and final step is *retail sales*, which involves billing and customer service. In regulated markets with a monopoly utility, the

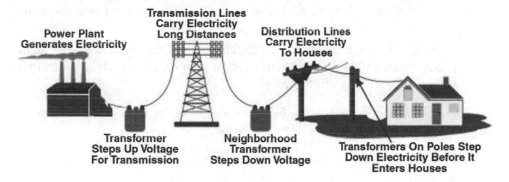

FIGURE 3-2 • The Power Grid
Source: National Energy Education Development Project

utility is typically responsible for all four jobs. In deregulated markets, it is common for these responsibilities to be split between multiple entities.

- **Generation.** Power plants that generate electricity.
- **Transmission.** Long distance transportation of power, typically at high voltages, with a relatively simple structure. Similar to the skeleton or major blood vessels of the human body.
- **Distribution.** Short distance transportation, typically at low voltages, at a neighborhood level, connecting every building to the grid, similar to capillaries in the human body.
- **Retail Sales.** Customer service and billing. In deregulated markets, the retail sales company is typically responsible for contracting with generators to ensure sufficient capacity is available to serve their customer base.

Generators create electrical power and place it onto the transmission system. A step-up transformer is used to convert the output of the generation unit into high-voltage AC power. It is then transmitted long distances over high voltage lines to minimize electricity losses. Once the high-voltage power is close to consumers, it will be converted to a lower voltage power at a substation. Finally, low-voltage lines will distribute electricity to consumers.

Some of the types of companies that provide power to consumers include:

- **Municipally Owned Utilities (Muni).** A muni is a publicly owned utility owned by a local government.
- **Co-operatives (Co-ops).** A co-op is a not-for-profit entity commonly found in rural communities where the limited number of consumers limits the profitability of serving them.

- **Investor-owned Utilities.** An investor-owned utility is a for-profit company owned by shareholders.
- **Federally Owned Utilities.** A federally owned utility is a government entity, commonly involving hydroelectric generation, which has authority to buy, sell, and distribute power.

These types of companies can further be described by their customers, operations, or legislatively defined responsibilities:

- **Integrated Utilities.** An integrated power generation utility will own generation, transmission, and distribution assets.
- **Public Utilities.** A public utility or public service company is a company where the legislature has determined that the business affects the public interest and needs to be regulated.
- **Power Marketers.** A marketer is a for-profit company that handles retail sales. Marketing companies typically do not own transmission or generation capability. Power marketers are commonly load-serving entities.
- **Load-Serving Entities (LSE).** An LSE is an entity that provides electric service to consumers. In regulated markets, the LSE is usually a monopoly utility. In deregulated markets, LSEs are typically intermediaries between the power grid operator, the generators, and consumers.
- **Merchant Generators.** A merchant generator sells power to another company (usually a load-serving entity) for resale to consumers.
- **Providers of Last Resort (POLR).** In states providing retail competition, the POLR is the load-serving entity that is obligated to sell power to consumers if they don't choose a supplier or their chosen supplier goes out of business.

Maintaining a transmission and distribution system is extremely expensive. Retail power lines have to be connected to almost every building. These power lines have to be maintained regardless of how much power is used by the consumer. This adds a large fixed component to consumer electrical prices (see Figure 3-3). Approximately half the consumer cost of power is due to the expense of maintaining the transmission and distribution system. As a result, special terminology is used to differentiate the price that generation facilities get paid, called *wholesale power*, and the price that consumers pay for power, called *retail power*.

The amount of power lost in transmission depends on the length of the power lines as well as their voltage. There is a trade-off between efficient generation a long way from consumer regions and less efficient generation located closer to consumers. For a variety of reasons, most power grids have adopted large generation units a long way from consumers. One reason is that a popular technology for generating power, steam turbines, is substantially more efficient

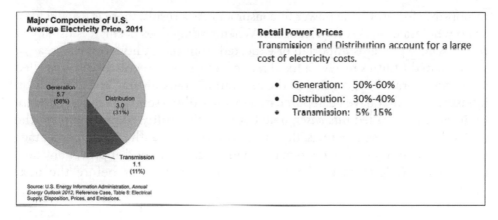

FIGURE 3-3 · Retail Power Prices

when built on a very large scale. Another reason is that these plants often depend on polluting or nuclear fuels. Consumer groups often protest construction of these units "in their backyard." The decision to construct large generation units a long distance from consumers comes at the cost of more power losses during transmission and less reliable power grids.

Key Concept

Wholesale and Retail Prices

Most trading is based on wholesale power prices. This is different from the price that consumers pay for power due to costs associated with the transmission and distribution of power.

- **Wholesale Price.** The price paid to the generator for placing power onto the power grid.
- **Retail Price.** The cost paid by the consumer. The customer pays the wholesale price of power, transmission, and distribution costs.

Regulated Markets & Power Purchase Agreements (PPAs)

In a regulated market, a government commission, usually called a *public utility commission* or a *public service commission*, determines consumer electricity prices by setting the rates that a utility can charge its customers. In these markets, an integrated utility (one that owns both transmission and generation) is typically responsible for supplying power to consumers. As a result, there is usually little or no wholesale market for electricity. When trading does occur, it is usually at points where power is imported or exported from the utility's service area.

Regulated utilities receive a fixed rate of return on a regulatory value called a *rate base*. A rate base consists of the generation, transmission, and distribution infrastructure that have been purchased by the utility (see Table 3-1). Rates are set in meetings, called *rate cases*, held between the utility commission and the utility. During these meetings, the utility commission authorizes a percentage rate that the utility is allowed to make on its investments and approves any new investments (additions to the rate base) that will occur before the next meeting.

Authorized return on rate base = (Rate Base) * (Authorized Percentage Rate of Return)

Rate Base =
Net Plant in Service
    + Plant in service
    - Accumulated depreciation
Additions to rate base
    +   Construction work in progress
    +   Plant held for future use
    +   Fuel inventories
    +   Material and supplies
    +   Inventories and prepayments
    +   Regulatory assets
    +   Cash working capital
Other Adjustments
    - Deferred income taxes
    - Accumulated deferred investment tax credit (ITC)
    - Customer deposits
    - Regulatory liabilities
    - Other reserves

TABLE 3-1 • Rate Base Calculation

There are a couple of ways that utilities can improve their return on equity. One is by taking on infrastructure projects that increase their rate base. The other is by taking on more debt financing. Both of these approaches need to be approved by the public utility commission. For example, if a company has been approved to receive a 10% return on its rate base, it can increase its return on equity (the money paid to shareholders) by borrowing money at a rate lower than its approved return on its rate base. For example, (see Table 3-2), a utility that is financing half of its capital through bond sales (at an 8% rate) can improve its return on equity to 12% even though it still charges 10% on its rate base.

		Annual Rate	Weighted
Debt	50%	8%	4%
Equity	50%	12%	6%
		Weighted Cost of Capital	10%

TABLE 3-2 • Weighted Cost of Capital

Key Concept

Rate Cases

A *rate case* is the formal process that utility commissions follow when setting rates that the utility is allowed to charge consumers.

In regulated markets, the public utility commission has a great deal of responsibility for balancing the need for a solvent utility company, infrastructure improvements, and low consumer prices. The centralized control of the utility commission is both a strength and weakness of regulated markets. Commissioners are often political appointees with limited engineering knowledge serving limited terms. In addition, they often have to balance short-term considerations like cutting consumer prices against long-term considerations like making infrastructure investments needed to ensure a stable power supply in 10 years.

Power transactions will occur even in regulated power grids. Even though most of the generation units will be owned by the utility, some types of generation may require specialty knowledge to build or operate. For example, a utility commission might desire additional renewable energy in its service area and allow private companies to build geothermal, solar, and wind generation facilities. The utility commission would then require the monopoly utility to buy power from the private companies. There are two main ways that the utility can compensate the generation owner. One way is to agree on a fixed price for the generation output called a *Power Purchase Agreement* (or PPA). The other is to compensate the generation owner based on the avoided cost of the utility.

- **Power Purchase Agreement (PPA).** A Power Purchase Agreement (PPA) is a legal contract where the utility agrees to buy power from a generator at a fixed cost. For example, if an integrated utility is under a legislative requirement to build more renewable power, it may sign a long-term contract to purchase power from a renewable generation facility owned by private investors. This agreement will typically fix a price for the power when the generation unit is first built and the price will last for the expected life of the facility. PPAs are typically linked to the physical facility and, if the facility is sold to a new owner, the PPA will transfer along with the physical unit.

Most commonly, PPAs are signed at a price proportional to the cost to construct a facility and provide a sufficient return to the investors who paid for construction. There is no set of standard terms that will apply to every PPA contract. For example, the contracted prices may be flat, escalate over time, or use any other set of mutually agreeable terms. The prices will determine the rate of return for the investors who financed the construction costs. Investors often see a return on equity in the 7.5% to 12% range.

- **Avoided Cost.** In cases where a utility does not sign a PPA with a generator, the public utility commission may require the utility to purchase power from certain generators at the cost that it would have paid to generate the power. Each service area will have its own rules governing who is allowed to sell power at the utility's avoided cost. However, renewable power generation is one of most common types of generation where private investment can fund construction costs. To incentivize private construction of renewable power, the public utility commission commonly allows the developers to sell power to the regulated utility.

Key Concept

Independent Power Generation

Even in regulated markets with an integrated utility, there are cases where independent power generation makes sense. While the exact rules vary between power grids, there are two main ways that independent power producers are compensated. One way is for the power producer to be provided a fixed payment for their generation through a Power Purchase Agreement. The other way is to compensate the independent producer based on the avoided cost of the utility.

Deregulated Market Pricing

Deregulated markets use a market pricing mechanism to set the price of power. In these markets, wholesale power prices are determined by the operating cost of the most expensive generation unit that needs to be online. With this pricing mechanism, power plants are activated in order of their cost to generate electricity (from lowest to highest) until consumer demand for power is completely met.

The last power plant activated sets the wholesale price of power for the power grid. The cost of bringing the last unit of electricity into the market is called the *marginal price of power* and the most recently activated plant is the *marginal producer*.

Key Concept

Marginal Pricing

In deregulated power markets, power prices are determined by the cost of generating power. This ensures that consumers pay the lowest price for their power on the average, even though prices will occasionally spike in the short term. For example, prices may spike due to a shortage of generation capacity, downed power lines, or heavy congestion on power lines.

- **Marginal Producer.** The marginal producer is the most expensive generation unit needed to meet consumer demand in markets where the lowest price generation unit is activated first.
- **Marginal Price of Power.** In a deregulated market, the price of power is the cost of generating the last unit of energy used by the market—typically the cost of the marginal producer.
- **Avoided Cost.** Avoided cost is a way to apply marginal pricing principles in a regulated market. When an independent generator gets paid the avoided cost of the utility, the independent generator gets compensated based on the generation unit that the utility left inactive.

A list of all of the power plants within a region, ordered from cheapest to most expensive operating costs is called a *generation stack* (see Figure 3-4). The amount of consumer demand (the *cumulative operating capacity*) determines how many generation units need to be online. The variable operating cost of operating the last unit sets the price of power in the region.

The demand for energy varies over time. For example, more power is used during the middle of the day than during the middle of the night. Generation facilities are commonly described by how much they operate.

- **Baseload.** A baseload unit operates almost all the time. Baseload plants typically include nuclear generation, hydropower dams, and fossil fuel generation units that are either highly efficient or that have very low fuel cost. Commonly, these units have high fixed costs or they cost a lot of money to build.

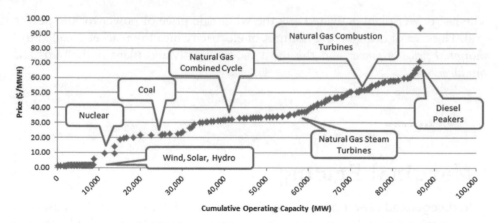

FIGURE 3-4 • Typical Generation Stack

- **Mid-merit.** Mid-merit plants run part of the year. These are typically older, less efficient fossil fuel plants or newer fossil fuel plants designed to minimize fixed operating costs.
- **Peaking Unit.** Peaking units operate only occasionally and often need to start up and shut down quickly. These units are commonly not very fuel efficient. Their lower efficiency is offset by lower fixed costs. These units operate only in high demand periods (like the middle of the afternoon during a heat wave).

Key Concept

Generation Stack

A generation stack is an ordered list of all generation units in a region sorted from the lowest cost units to the highest cost units. The generation stack is commonly split into three main portions:

- **Baseload.** A generation unit that runs constantly. Baseload generation will almost never set the price of power in a region.
- **Mid-merit.** A generation unit that runs part time, usually during the summer and the middle of the day. Commonly mid-merit units are the marginal units which determine the price of power.
- **Peaking Unit.** A generation unit that runs infrequently and whose primary role is to help balance the power grid during periods of peak demand. These units will set the price of power when they operate.

Part of the cost of generating power is the cost of the facility, regular maintenance, and the salaries of the required staff. These are all fixed costs. The variable cost of running a generation facility depends on fuel prices, the efficiency of the generator at converting fuel into electricity, and the cost that the incremental wear and tear from starting up will have on maintenance costs.

The efficiency at which fuel is converted into power is called a *heat rate*. This heat rate is in units of fuel needed to produce one unit of power. Lower heat rates are better—a low heat rate plant uses less fuel per unit of output than a high heat rate plant. Even in highly efficient generation units, about half of the heat energy gets wasted before it is turned into electricity (see Table 3-3).

Heat Rate (MMBTU/MWH)	Comment
3.4	Perfect conversion of heat to electricity
7.0 - 7.5	Most efficient generation units, Modern Combined Cycle Natural Gas units
9-10	Most common marginal unit efficiency, Mid-Merit generation, advanced Natural Gas peaking units, and large scale, modern steam turbines
12+	Peaking units

TABLE 3-3 • Typical Heat Rates

The efficiency of a generation plant is one of its most important characteristics, since it largely determines when the unit can operate profitability. However, efficiency is only one characteristic of a generation unit. Generation units with the same heat rate may be very different units. For example, some units can start up very quickly (within 5 minutes) and others require 24-hour notice to start up. Fast-starting units are far more useful for the purpose of balancing the power grid and often can obtain secondary payments (called *ancillary service* payments) for their role.

To estimate the profitability of a generation unit, power prices can be compared to the operating costs of the unit. These operating costs can be estimated by adding the fuel used by the unit to the variable operating and maintenance costs. For natural gas generation, this calculation is called a spark spread (see Figure 3-4).

Other terms are used for other spreads:

- **Spark Spread.** Profitability of a natural gas generation facility.
- **Dark Spread.** Profitability of a coal generation facility.
- **Clean [Dark] Spread.** A spread that incorporates cost of complying with environmental regulations.

Spark Spreads	
Spark Spread = Power Price − Heat Rate * Fuel Price − VOM	
Factor	**Description**
Power Price	The price
Heat Rate	The efficiency at which fuel is turned into electricity. This needs to be in the same units as power and fuel prices.
Fuel Price	The cost of fuel
Variable Operations & Maintenance Cost (VOM)	The variable cost of operating the unit. In most cases, maintenance costs are proportional to the number of starts for the year and this is a pro-rated cost based on the expected operations of the unit.

TABLE 3-4 · Spark Spread Definition

For a variety of reasons, power plants tend to offer power for sale close to their marginal generation costs. Regulatory pressure, competition from other generators, and the risk of not being operational all contribute to this bidding process. As a result, it is possible to estimate the efficiency of the marginal generation unit by looking at the ratio of power and fuel prices observed in the forward market. The ratio between power prices and gas prices is called the *implied heat rate*. In general, units with lower heat rates than the implied market heat rate will be able to profitably operate. Generation units with higher heat rates will be unprofitable to operate.

Key Concept

Heat Rates and Spread

Heat rates describe the efficiency at which a unit can convert fuel into electricity. Spread describes profitability.

- **Heat Rate.** A measure of a generation unit's efficiency measured in units input/units output. Lower numbers represent more efficient generation units.
- **Implied Heat Rate.** The forward price of power divided by the forward price of the marginal fuel (typically natural gas).
- **Spark Spread.** Spark spreads are a way to estimate the profitability of natural gas-fired generation units.
- **Dark Spread.** Dark spreads are a way to estimate the profitability of coal-fired generation units.

Another factor that adds to the complexity of the power grid is that the amount of power used by consumers varies over the course of the day. The largest source of variation in consumer demand for power is due to heating and cooling needs. Typically, prices are highest during periods of peak consumer demand (see Figure 3-5). In the winter, this is typically during early morning and evening hours when heating is required. During the summer, peak demand occurs during mid-afternoon when temperatures are the hottest.

Usually there are two types of auctions coordinated by RTO/ISOs— day-ahead and real-time auctions. A day-ahead auction sets the price of power for the following day. This auction is commonly completed in the early afternoon of the day before delivery. This allows power producers time to arrange fuel and operating schedules based on their expectations of what will happen the next day. A second price auction, the real-time price auction, sets prices during the actual delivery date. These prices are commonly used to true up the electricity that is actually needed to do what was expected.

Key Concept

Day-ahead and Real-time Pricing

In deregulated markets, most power is scheduled the day before it is needed. The prices set at this time are called day-ahead prices. *Day-ahead* prices are based on expectations of what will happen the following day. A smaller amount of power, usually less than 10%, is transacted in the *real-time* market. The real-time market sets the price based on actual conditions.

Generally, real-time prices are slightly more expensive than day-ahead prices because fewer units can activate on short notice. In addition, real-time prices are typically more volatile than day-ahead prices.

Most electricity trading contracts are based on average power prices over blocks of time in a day. For example, electricity is commonly traded in monthly peak and off-peak contracts. For example, a peak contract might specify the average price of power every non-holiday weekday in a month between 7 a.m. and 11 p.m. A corresponding off-peak contract would cover weekday nights between 11 p.m. and 7a.m., and all day on weekends and holidays.

- **Peak.** A 16-hour block of power, five days (Monday to Friday) or six days (Monday to Saturday) a week
- **Off-Peak.** Hours not in the peak contract: nights, weekends, and holidays
- **Around the Clock.** 24 hours a day, 7 days a week

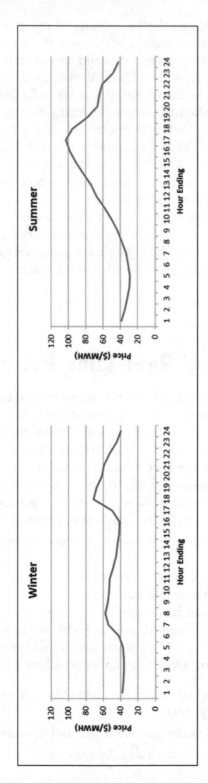

FIGURE 3-5 • Daily Variation in Load

To reduce the confusion about names meaning different things, it is common for the days and hours to be included in naming. For example, 5×16 peak prices will refer to a 16-hour block 5 days a week. 7×8 off-peak will refer to an 8-hour block (11 p.m.–7 a.m.) every day of the week.

- **5×16 Peak.** Daytime prices, Monday–Friday, 7 a.m.–11 p.m., excluding holidays
- **6×16 Peak.** Daytime peak prices, Monday–Saturday, 7 a.m.–11 p.m., excluding holidays
- **7×8 Off-Peak.** Nighttime prices, every day, 11 p.m. –7 a.m.
- **2×16 Off-Peak.** Weekend/holiday daytime prices, 7 a.m.–11 p.m.
- **Off-Peak Wrap.** All non-peak hours (includes both 7×8 and 2×16 prices)
- **7×24 ATC.** Around-the-clock prices

There is no magic to the choice of 16-hour blocks for peak prices, except that it appeals to a wide audience. Contracts can be found on smaller parts of the day too. However, it is harder to find trading partners for uncommon time periods and trading costs might be prohibitively high.

Key Concept

Peak and Off-Peak Prices

Financial contracts typically trade in power based on the average price over a number of hours. A variety of naming conventions are used to indicate which hours are included in the average price. In cases of confusion, the terms can be found spelled out in the trading contract.

In addition to the time of the day and the auction that is setting the price, another complication is the location of the power that is being delivered. Power lines can only transmit a limited amount of power before they will melt. When a power line can't transport any more power, it is said to be *congested* and requires a generation plant on the far side of the congestion to be brought online to meet consumer demand. This will force the prices on either side of the congested point to diverge from one another. Power plants brought online to alleviate congestion will not be the cheapest generation unit on the grid (or they would have already been active). Instead, they will be activated *out of merit order*, and the consumers that required that plant to come online will pay a higher cost for their power than consumers in less congested parts of the power grid.

Historically, power grids were often broken into *zones* that had very few lines that would get congested within the zone. This allowed consumers in the entire zone to pay the same price for their power. Modern technology has taken this a step further by making it possible to calculate a power price at every point within a power grid (see Table 3-5). Points within a power grid are called *nodes*. Nodes are usually physical hardware like generation facilities, transmission substations, or bus-bars that allow power to enter or leave the power grid.

Zonal System	Nodal System
• No significant transmission constraints within the zone • A single price of power for the zone called a *zone price* • Zone systems are being phased out in favor of nodal systems.	• Each node has its own price called a *Locational Marginal Price* (LMP). • *Hub Prices* are average price of a large number of nodes that have limited transmission constraints between them. • For financial contracts, hub prices serve the role of zone prices.

TABLE 3-5 • Zonal *versus* Nodal Systems

Key Concept

Nodal and Zonal Systems

Zonal power grids are being replaced by nodal systems. There are substantial engineering hurdles involved in making a switch. However, from a financial standpoint, it is primarily a terminology change as hub prices replace zone prices.

- **Zone System.** In a zone system, the power grid is divided into geographic areas (called zones) where the price of power is the same everywhere in the zone.
- **Nodal System.** A nodal system is a refinement on the zone system, where each node on the power grid has its own price assigned to it.
- **Node.** A node is any piece of physical hardware that is part of the power grid where a location-specific price can be calculated.
- **Marginal Price.** A marginal price is a power price that is determined by marginal generation costs. Most deregulated markets, whether they are nodal or zone based, set prices in this manner.
- **Locational Marginal Price (LMP).** A locational marginal price is a marginal price used in a nodal system. A LMP describes the price of power at a specific node and is sometimes called a *node price*
- **Physical Transmission Constraint.** A constraint is a limitation on how much power can be transmitted over a power line. Constraints exist in both

nodal and zone systems. A major reason for transitioning from a zone to nodal system is to better manage transmission constraints.

- **Congestion.** Congestion is caused when generation units have to be acti vated out of merit order to allow the system to avoid physical transmission constraints. If there is no congestion on a power grid, everyone pays the same price for power. When congestion occurs, prices will diverge, with the most congested regions paying the highest price for their power.

Types of Generation Plants

Before it can be delivered to consumers, electricity needs to be generated from another form of energy. There are several methods that can be used, but the most common approach is to create electricity by spinning a wire in a magnetic field. In the early 1800s, British scientist Michael Faraday discovered that magnetic fields can be used to generate electrical currents, and vice versa. Later scientists expanded this research into the study of electromagnetism.

When a coiled wire is rotated inside a pair of magnets (or magnets are rotated around a coiled wire), the wire will build up an electromagnetic charge. This potential energy can be discharged by connecting the wire into a circuit. This allows current to flow through the wire. By continuing to spin the coiled wire in a magnetic field, a continuous supply of electricity can be generated. The process of generating electrical current in this manner is called electromagnetic induction (see Figure 3-6).

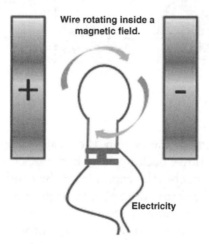

FIGURE 3-6 · Electromagnetic Induction

Generation Technologies

Most power generation uses electromagnetic induction by forcing some type of fluid (steam, liquid, air) through a rotating engine called a *turbine*. A turbine is a rotary engine containing blades that spin the engine when fluid is forced through the turbine enclosure. The design of turbines can vary quite a bit. Nuclear and coal plants might heat water to create pressurized steam that is used to rotate the turbine. Hydroelectric dams will use flowing water to drive a turbine. Wind farms will use the large propellers to rotate the turbine.

Steam turbines

Steam turbines are the most common type of generation technology. About 80% of the electricity in the world is generated using this technology. Steam turbines work by creating superheated water in a boiler (see Figure 3-7). This superheated water is kept under high pressure so that it can be converted into steam as the water moves past a turbine. As water turns into steam, it rapidly expands and causes the turbine to spin. The power produced by the expanding steam is converted into electricity using the Faraday induction process described previously.

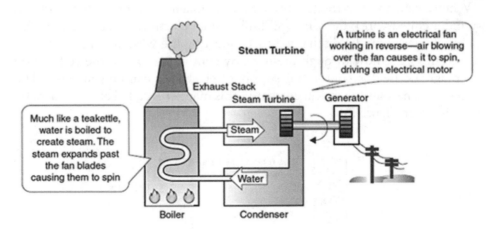

FIGURE 3-7 · A Steam Turbine

To improve efficiency of the system, the steam can be reused by cooling it just enough so that it flows back into the boiler. A condenser is a cool metal chamber. When steam touches the cool sides of the condenser, it turns back into water and is then sent back into the boiler to begin the process again. The most fuel-consuming part of operating a steam turbine is turning it on and heating the system. It takes less energy to boil already hot water than it takes to boil cold water. When the condenser cools the steam, the water is still very hot. It only needs to be cooled to a temperature slightly below its boiling point.

In addition to the extra fuel required, heating up a turbine places substantial stress on the components. Going from cold to hot enough times will eventually cause damage to the generation unit and lead to higher maintenance costs. As a result, steam turbines are most efficient when they operate continuously.

Steam turbines also have a large economy of scale. Larger units are more efficient than smaller units. Technology also has an effect. Large scale, modern units can often operate around at a level of 10–11 MMBtu/MWh, while less efficient units operate at 11–14 MMBtu/MWh.

Combustion turbines

Another major technology for producing electricity is the combustion turbine. Combustion turbines are also called *gas turbines*. A combustion turbine produces a controlled explosion to create superheated gas in the same way that a jet engine operates. Most commonly, superheated gas is created directly through combustion by igniting a mixture of natural gas and air. In the proper proportions, this will create an overpressure in the ignition chamber that forces the superheated gas to move past a turbine on the way out (see Figure 3-8).

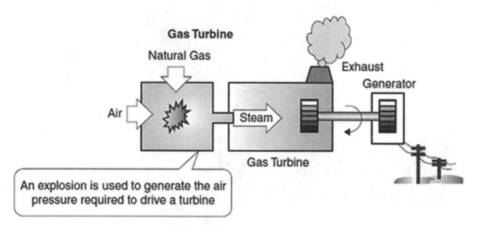

FIGURE 3-8 • A Combustion Turbine

Combustion turbines are generally simpler to build and maintain than steam turbines. Another advantage of combustion turbines is that there is no lengthy process required to heat up the water into steam. As a result, gas turbines can start producing power at peak efficiency very soon after they are turned on. Combustion turbines are commonly used when the power grid needs generation units that can turn on and off quickly. On the downside, combustion turbines are less efficient than steam turbines because the exhaust gas of a combustion turbine can't be reused in the same way that water can be reheated. Combustion turbines also depend on fuel being able to create a consistent explosive exhaust. This eliminates the possibility of using most solid fuels like coal or biomass.

Combined cycle generation

A combined cycle plant uses a combination of combustion-turbine and steam-turbine technology. In a combined cycle plant, the exhaust from the combustion turbine is used to heat water for the steam turbine (see Figure 3-9). The combustion turbine exhaust is no longer expanding, so it can't be used to directly drive a turbine. However, it is still very hot. Instead of exhausting the hot gases (primarily carbon dioxide and water vapor) into the atmosphere, heat from that gas can be used to heat steam for a steam turbine.

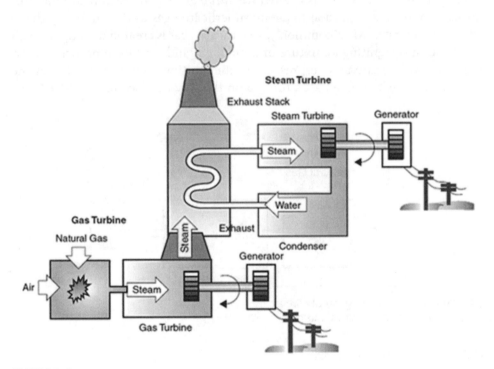

FIGURE 3-9 · Combined Cycle Generation

Combined cycle plants are more complex than either combustion turbines or steam turbines alone. However, they are also much more efficient.

Cogeneration

Some generators can sell superheated hot water and steam as products in addition to the electricity that they produce. While this is not practical for all generators, it can provide a second source of income in cases where it makes economic sense. First, there needs to be a local buyer who wants to purchase superheated water. Second, there needs to be some way to get the superheated water to the buyer. This is easiest if the client is located adjacent to the generation plant.

The downside of cogeneration is that a long-term contract to produce steam limits the operational flexibility of the generation facility. Most generators can shut down when they are not able to operate profitably. If a cogeneration facility has agreed to supply an industrial plant with steam, the facility may not be able to shut down.

Key Concept

Generation Technologies

Electricity can be generated using a variety of technologies.

- **Steam Turbines.** A steam turbine operates by allowing steam heated in a pressurized vessel to drive a turbine that is linked to a generator. On a small scale, a similar effect is caused when water is boiled in a tea kettle and the escaping steam creates a whistling sound.
- **Combustion Turbines.** Combustion creates an explosion that is directed past a turbine, which drives a generator. This is similar to how the exhaust from a jet engine might drive a propeller.
- **Combined Cycle.** A combined cycle generation plant uses both combustion and steam turbines. Excess heat from the exhaust of the combustion turbine will be used to heat steam for the steam turbine.
- **Cogeneration.** A cogeneration plant will sell both steam and electricity. Selling the steam does not make the unit more efficient. However, since the steam provides a secondary income source, it can defray fuel costs.
- **Dual Fuel.** A dual fuel generation unit can operate using two different types of fuel. For example, a dual fuel unit might be able to use wood chips or coal.

Renewable Power (Biomass, Solar, Wind, Hydro)

Renewable power is produced from resources that can be replenished indefinitely. In general, these renewable resources are currently more limited and more expensive than fossil fuels. According to the U.S. Energy Information Administration, renewable energy currently supplies about 10% of the energy needs of the United States (see Figure 3-10). Of this generation, about 50% of renewable power is produced from burning biomass like wood chips or municipal waste.

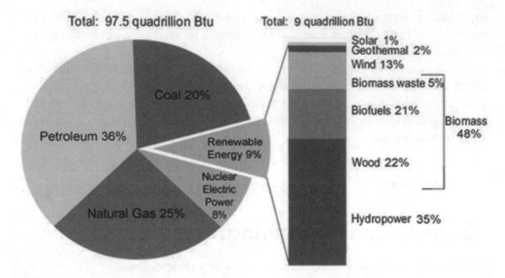

FIGURE 3-10 · Energy Consumption by Source
Source: U.S. Energy Information Administration, *Monthly Energy Review*. Table 10.1 (March 2012), preliminary 2011 data

Approximately, 35% of renewable energy in the United States comes from hydropower (hydroelectric dams).

Many renewable units produce power only when their energy source (like sunlight, flowing water, or wind) is available. They can't be activated on demand (*dispatched*) by the power grid. As a result, their power production is generally a small fraction of what they might produce if they operated full time and they contribute less to the reliability of a power grid than similarly rated fossil fuel generation.

Key Concept

Capacity Factors

Some terms are commonly used to describe generation units. These terms apply to both conventional and renewable generation units.

- **Nameplate Capacity.** A size assigned to a generation unit to describe the maximum power it can produce at any time.
- **Capacity Factor.** The ratio of the actual output of a plant relative to its output if it had operated at full nameplate capacity.
- **Availability Factor.** The percentage of time that a unit operates when it has fuel or another energy source available. When a unit is not available, it is usually down for maintenance.

Biomass

Biomass is organic material composed of plants and animals whose production can be sustained over time. Historically, this has been a popular form of heating fuels. For example, wood and manure can both be used as a fuel for heating and cooking. Other examples of biomass are municipal waste and fuels like ethanol or biodiesel.

- **Wood and Wood Waste.** Wood and wood waste like bark, sawdust, wood chips, wood scrap, paper mill residue, and some agricultural by-products like grape vines can be burned to produce heat and electricity. Depending on the technology and fuel, burning these products can result in a substantial amount of air pollution and carbon dioxide (CO_2) released into the atmosphere. Waste wood generation facilities are often viewed as carbon neutral since an equivalent amount of CO_2 can be captured through growing new biomass to replace what was burned.

- **Municipal Solid Waste (MSW).** Burning solid waste has two purposes. First, it generates electricity and heat. Second, it reduces the amount of waste that has to be buried in landfills. MSW generation units typically need advanced technology to prevent harmful emissions, since a variety of chemicals get thrown away in garbage. When burned, these chemicals may produce dangerous by-products. Typically, waste-to-energy furnaces operate at very high temperatures (2,000°F) to assist in breaking down dangerous compounds.

- **Landfill Gas (Biogas).** Methane is a common by-product of sewage treatment plants, waste landfills, and livestock manure management systems. Methane is the primary component of natural gas, and can be burned to produce both heat and electricity. Since methane is a stronger greenhouse gas than carbon dioxide, burning methane reduces greenhouse gas emissions.

- **Biofuels (Ethanol and Biodiesel).** Ethanol and biodiesel are types of biomass fuels used in vehicular engines. They are rarely used to produce electricity or heat. Biofuels are considered carbon-neutral, since plants used to make biofuels absorb carbon dioxide as they grow.

Key Concept

Biomass

In the context of energy markets, the term *biomass* refers to plant and animal material which can be replaced through a sustainable cycle of cultivation and harvesting. In the energy industry, biomass that isn't being replaced (like coal, petroleum, natural gas) is typically referred to by the term *fossil fuel*. Biomass generation is often capable of using either biomass or fossil fuels. If a unit can run on multiple fuels, it is called a *dual fuel* unit. This gives all the benefit of a renewable generation system, as well as standby capacity in case the power grid needs additional power.

Hydropower

Hydropower is a way of mechanically converting swiftly flowing water into electricity. The flowing water spins a turbine connected to a generator to produce electricity (see Figure 3-11). In a run-of-the-river system, the current of the river produces the pressure needed to drive the turbine. In a storage system, water accumulated behind a dam is released on demand to produce electricity.

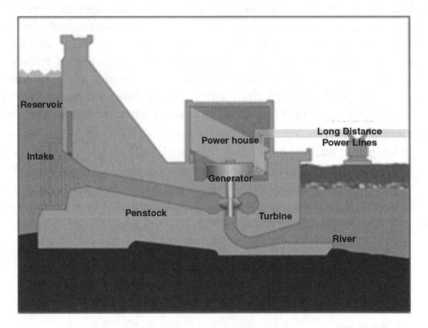

FIGURE 3-11 • A Hydroelectric Dam
Source: Tennessee Valley Authority (Public Domain)

The type of hydroelectric facility has a large impact on the reliability of the power produced by the facility. For example, run-of-the river facilities depend on water flowing in the river to produce power. These facilities tend to produce the most power in the late spring when snow melts, and relatively little power in the summer and fall.

Building a dam over a river will produce a reservoir of water which can be released on demand. This is much more valuable economically since the water can be saved until electricity prices are highest. It also makes dams a more reliable producer of electricity than run-of-the-river hydroelectric units. However, any type of dam can change the water temperature and chemistry of the river on which it is located. This can negatively impact the native plants and animals that rely on the river. Dams can also obstruct the migration of fish in a river from reaching their spawning areas. These environmental issues are not limited to electricity producing dams. Only a small percentage of dams produce electricity. Most dams have been built to supply flood control, irrigation, and water to nearby communities.

Capacity factors of hydropower generation vary widely. Run-of-the-river systems are very sensitive to snow melt, rainfall, and drought conditions. This gives a seasonal shape to their generation. The capacity factor of hydropower units with storage systems is harder to characterize. For example, a dam-based generator might add more turbines for a higher peak output. This will allow the generator to sell more electricity during periods of peak demand. However, this will lower the unit's overall capacity factor since the total output of the unit continues to be limited by the amount of water stored in the reservoir.

Key Concept

Hydropower

Hydropower is historically one of the largest providers of renewable energy. However, most of the best locations for hydropower are already in use and the use of hydropower is not expected to expand significantly in the future.

- **Run-of-the-River.** A hydropower generation facility that depends on flowing water in a river without relying on a dam.
- **Storage System (Dam).** A hydropower generation facility that blocks the river with a dam. This allows more control of the water flowing through the facility but affects the environment of the area more than a run-of-the-river facility.

Solar Power

Photovoltaics

With photovoltaic power, sunlight is used to create electricity using special semi-conductors called *solar panels*. Electromagnetic radiation, like sunlight, causes electrons in various bands of the semiconductor to move to an adjacent band. This creates a current of electrons that can be used to provide electrical energy if the solar panel is connected to a circuit. The amount of energy provided by photovoltaic solar power depends on the amount of sunlight in a given area. In general, dry, arid climates (like a desert) close to the equator will produce the most power. As the distance from the equator increases, sunlight has to pass through additional layers of atmosphere, reducing the amount of energy contained in sunlight.

Solar panels are often installed at a fixed angle facing towards the equator. Fixed panels have the advantage of having very few moving parts and limited maintenance. By adding motorized components, it is possible for panels to track the sun as it moves through the sky. This will increase the effectiveness of the solar panel. Motorized units will be more expensive to install and maintain relative to fixed installations.

A fixed-panel solar array will typically have a 13%–20% capacity factor. For example, out of 8,760 hours in a year, a 1 kW solar panel will typically produce 1150 to 1750 kW-hours of electricity. A solar panel with a fixed tilt that tracks the sun east and west (single-axis tracking) will be 25% to 30% more efficient than a fixed panel and typically have a 17% to 25% capacity factor. A solar panel that tracks the sun on both the east-west axis and tilts up and down will be 30% to 40% more efficient than a fixed panel solar array and have an 18% to 27.5% capacity factor.

The major arguments against solar power are limited efficiency, a high cost to make and distribute solar panels, and the amount of petroleum products needed to manufacture the panels.

Key Concept

Solar Power

Solar power uses the photovoltaic effect to produce an electrical current from sunlight using special semiconductors called solar panels. Power is produced only when the sun is shining and the *solar panel* is clean of obstructions (like condensation, dust, or snow). Power is produced during peak hours.

- **Fixed Tilt Panel.** A solar panel that sits at a fixed tilt and facing (typically) towards the equator at an angle equal to the latitude of the installation. Output is approximately 13%–20% nameplate capacity.
- **Single-Axis Tracking Panel.** A solar panel that is motorized to track the sun as it moves east to west but has a fixed tilt. Output is approximately 17%–25% nameplate capacity.
- **Dual-Axis Tracking Panel.** A solar panel that is motorized to track the sun east to west and change its tilt. Output is approximately 18%–27.5% of nameplate capacity.

Compared to most types of electrical generation, a unique aspect of photovoltaic solar power is that solar cells have limited economy of scale. Solar panels are equally efficient in both large and small installations. They also do not produce harmful emissions during operation. As a result, solar power can often be distributed throughout consumer regions rather than located a long distance away. This simplifies the transmission grid and helps relieve congestion over long-distance transmission lines.

Distributed Generation

Most types of electrical generation units are most efficient when built on a large scale. Solar units are no more or less effective when placed in a large installation. As a result, solar power can relieve congestion on power lines since it can be located close to consumer areas.

Solar thermal power

Solar thermal is a technology designed to collect heat energy from sunlight. The uses of solar thermal power range from low-temperature units used to heat water in swimming pools to high-temperature units used to drive steam turbines. Medium-temperature units are used to provide hot water and air for residential and commercial usage.

Thermal solar is much more efficient than photovoltaic generation since a majority of the energy of sunlight can be kept as heat. However, it can be difficult to concentrate the heat sufficiently to provide electrical generation. As a result, some more common applications of solar thermal are:

- Heating water for swimming pools
- Residential and commercial heating
- Drying wood and agricultural products
- Distillation of drinking water

Wind Power

Wind generation uses the kinetic energy in wind to mechanically drive a turbine connected to a generator. The turbines are typically placed along tops of ridges or shorelines where steady winds are common. These units typically produce much of their electricity at night and during the spring and fall. They produce relatively less power during hot summer afternoons when power demand is at its highest.

Wind generation is often concentrated in remote areas. This can create problems, since all of the units in an area are all likely to be producing (or not producing) power at the same time. When the wind is blowing, transmission lines to get the power from where it is produced (the remote area) to where it will be used (a populated area) can become highly congested. This can limit the ability of wind generators to profitably sell their power. In addition, when the wind stops blowing, all of the wind turbines will stop producing power simultaneously. The irregular power production of wind requires backup generation be able to come on- and off-line very quickly. If the fast start generation is not located near the wind units (and it usually is not), this can prove challenging for the power grid to balance flows throughout its network.

Wind generation involves building large mechanical installations in remote areas. Maintaining these units can be problematic since specialized technicians, vehicles, and tools are often required. For example, changing the oil on a turbine requires vehicles capable of carrying large amounts of oil to the wind turbine. Maintenance may also require a sufficient number of trained mechanics that are physically capable of carrying the necessary tools up a ladder to the top of a twenty-story tower.

The output of wind generation depends on its location. Even locations very close to one another may experience very different wind conditions. For example, there is a big difference in the wind at the top of a hill compared to the wind behind the shelter of the hill. Another problem is that when one wind turbine is downwind of another, the downwind facility will experience chaotic wind flow due to the disruption in wind caused by the upwind facility. This typically necessitates wind farms be spread out in lines or organized to minimize disruption from nearby units. Wind installations typically require several years of study before the best locations to site wind turbines can be determined.

As a rule of thumb, a typical utility scale wind turbine unit with an advantageous site has an annual capacity factor around 35%. For example, since there are approximately 8760 hours in a year (365 days * 24 hours/day), a 100 MW unit with a 35% capacity factor will produce (100 MW) * (.35) * (8760 hours) = 306,600 MW-h of production each year. Wind turbines in very advantageous wind locations (for example, an offshore unit in a windy area) might have capacity factors as high as 40% to 50%. Wind turbines in areas with few advantageous sites (for example, continental Europe) will often have capacity factors around 25%.

Wind Power

The output of a wind turbine can vary substantially year to year but is commonly 25% to 40% of its rated capacity.

- Output is approximately 25% of nameplate capacity in most locations and 35%-40% in advantageous locations
- Power is produced around the clock with slightly more production during dawn and dusk than the middle of the day (prices are approximately equal to the around the clock price of power).
- The capacity factor typically increases with height of the installation due to increased wind speeds high above the ground. Utility scale installations (at 80-100 meters high) produce substantially more power than shorter installations (at 40-60 meters high).

Wind power is commonly paired with natural gas turbines to guarantee reliability.

Renewable Energy Certificates (RECs)

Renewable energy is commonly traded through a type of financial instrument called a *renewable energy certificate* (or REC). The motivation for the creation of REC markets is a government or regulator's desire to encourage the generation of power from renewable or nonpolluting sources in a market-based environment. A market-based system sets prices based on activating the cheapest way to generate electricity. This will rarely be sufficient to build renewable or nonpolluting generation. One way that market regulators address this problem is to create intangible tradable commodities (RECs) that certain market participants are required to purchase. Renewable energy certificates and related products like emissions credits, CO_2 allowances, and SO_x allowances are all examples of intangible assets created by regulators to achieve certain policy goals.

Environmental certificates and emissions allowances typically have no intrinsic value. They have value because regulators require certain market participants to purchase them or be required to pay some type of penalty (sometimes called an *alternative compliance payment*). This creates a great deal of uncertainty in the pricing of RECs and similar regulatory products. When there is too little supply, prices quickly get bid up to either the penalty price or the cost of new construction (whichever is lower). When there is too much supply, prices rapidly fall to zero.

Some features of RECs and similar environmental products are:

- They have no inherent value.
- Demand stems from a need to comply with regulations.
- Prices are very sensitive to supply and demand.
- They are only useful within the geographic area overseen by the regulator.

RECs are a common type of certificate created by regulatory bodies, which are designed to increase the amount of renewable energy used in a service area. The regulatory body overseeing the services area establishes annual renewable targets (called a *Renewable Portfolio Standard* or RPS) that load-serving entities (LSE) must meet. For example, a regulator might require that 20% of all retail electricity sales be from renewable sources by a particular date. The RPS also typically specifies a penalty fee that each LSE will need to pay if they fail to comply with the regulations.

From the perspective of a generator, an RPS will typically define the types of generation facilities that can be considered renewable power. Some common criteria used to define renewable power are geography, technology, and start-up date. For example, Ohio might establish a requirement that 10% of all consumer power must be met from renewable power—at least half of which needs to be from solar photovoltaic generation. It might also require that half of that required generation—for both solar and nonsolar—comes from facilities within the state that have been built in the last five years. This will lead to four traded products: Ohio in-state solar REC, Ohio in-state nonsolar REC, Ohio out-of-state solar REC, and Ohio out-of-state nonsolar REC.

When a renewable generator produces power, it will typically generate one renewable energy certificate for each megawatt of power that it produces. That renewable energy certificate can then be sold to someone who needs to meet their regulatory requirement. The RECs and electricity can be sold together (*bundled*) or separately (*unbundled*) depending on the rules set out in the RPS. In either case, the electricity is placed onto the power grid and the REC created at the same time is placed into a tracking system (often called a *registry*). The REC registry is used to track the owner of the REC as the products are traded to ensure each company is compliant with the appropriate regulations.

In general, REC products are also quoted in terms of the year in which the REC was generated. This date, called a *vintage*, determines the window of time that an REC can be used to meet compliance requirements set out in the RPS. For example, an RPS may specify that RECs have to be used within three years of the date that they were generated.

Key Concept

Renewable Energy Certificates

A renewable energy certificate (REC) is an intangible asset which can be used to meet regulatory requirements related to purchasing a specific amount of power coming from a renewable source.

- **Renewable Portfolio Standard (RPS).** An RPS is a regulatory body's goal for renewable generation within its service area.
- **Vintage.** The vintage of an REC is the year in which the REC was produced. Each RPS will specify the window of time that an REC can be used for compliance purposes.
- **Voluntary RECs.** Voluntary RECs are national programs not tied to a specific regulator that allow anyone to participate in REC markets.

Ancillary Services

In addition to supplying power to consumers, the power grid operator must keep the power grid operating safely and consistently. Supplying power to consumers is the primary service of a power grid. The other responsibilities of a power grid are commonly called *ancillary services*. These responsibilities include:

- Scheduling and dispatching generation units
- Maintaining a constant voltage and current on the power grid
- Ensuring units can be started quickly to recover from outages
- Ensuring sufficient standby units are available to meet consumer demand
- Protecting the hardware of the power grid
- Matching consumer demand with generation

To carry out these responsibilities, the power grid operator will contract with power generators to reserve a variety of services on short notice. For example, the power grid operator might pay a generator for the ability to reduce the generator's output by 100 MW within five minutes notice. There are several common types of ancillary services, although each power grid may have their own terminology and requirements.

- **Regulation Up (Reg-Up).** Reg-Up is an ancillary service used to stabilize the frequency of the AC power by increasing the power it is placing on the power grid within a couple of seconds (for example, three to five seconds).

- **Regulation Down (Reg-Down).** Reg-Down is an ancillary service used to stabilize the frequency of the AC power by reducing the power it is placing on the power grid within a couple of seconds (for example, three to five seconds).

- **Spinning Reserve (Responsive Reserve).** Spinning reserve is online reserve capacity that is operating but not placing power on the power grid. Typically spinning reserve needs to be able to place power onto the power grid within a couple of minutes (for example, within 30 seconds to 1 minute of being notified).

- **Non-Spinning Reserve.** Non-spinning reserve is an ancillary service where a power plant is not operating but can be ramped up and synchronized to the power grid within a couple of minutes (for example, 10 minutes).

- **Replacement Reserve.** An ancillary service that is not operating but can be ramped up and synchronized to the power grid within 30 minutes to an hour.

When a generator agrees to provide ancillary services to the power grid, the generator is obligated to operate their facility in a certain manner. Most generators have the option to turn off when they can't run profitably or to ramp up production during high-price periods. That ability to optimize operations is given up when ancillary services are sold to the power grid. As a result, generators typically have to weigh the advantages against disadvantages when it comes to selling ancillary services to the power grid. This is helpful from a valuation perspective, because the price of ancillary services can be compared to the expected profit of selling wholesale power.

When a generator has the option of providing ancillary services to the grid or to selling power into the market at wholesale prices, the ancillary and wholesale power prices become linked. Whenever the price of ancillary services and the profit from selling wholesale power diverges, generators should choose to sell into the more profitable market and drive that price down. In other words, the price for providing various ancillary services should be equal to the expected profit from selling power directly into the market.

Key Concept

Ancillary Services

Ancillary services is a term used to describe all of the responsibilities of the power grid other than providing power to consumers.

Capacity Markets

Seasonal variation in consumer demand has an important impact on the power grid. The number of generation units required to meet peak demand is much higher than the number of generators needed to meet average consumer demands. Power grid operators usually need to keep a reserve margin of at least 10% generation capability that will never be used. As a result, in a typical year, a number of power plants will operate infrequently and others won't operate at all. This creates a problem for the power grid, because if the units are not operating, their owners are not being paid. No one will pay to construct a new power plant unless they think that they can get a reasonable return on their investment.

Efficient power plants tend to be expensive to construct but have low variable costs. Since wholesale power prices (and therefore generator revenues) are based on variable costs, a power grid with lots of efficient generation will have low-priced power. However, those low prices come at a cost—low prices may force units out of operation or discourage new construction. This can lead to a vicious cycle where units are closed without being replaced by new construction even in periods of rising consumer demand. If this cycle is not stopped, it will ultimately lead to insufficient capacity to meet consumer demands and brownouts or rolling blackouts.

A special type of energy market, called a *capacity market*, has developed to help the power grid resolve some of these issues. Capacity markets are a way for a power grid operator or similar agency to compensate owners of generation assets for ensuring a stable supply of power in future years. In theory, these markets should help fund new construction by providing an secondary source of income for merchant generators. Capacity markets vary widely between regions and no model has proven completely successful in achieving its goals.

Auction-style capacity markets set a capacity payment based on the volume of power that generation operators agree to maintain for some period of time in the future. Bilateral capacity markets will require load-serving entities to acquire sufficient capacity to meet the needs of their customers. Typically, this is done by entering into contracts with generators to guarantee certain levels of power production.

Over the long term, capacity prices are generally expected to reach an equilibrium price that is sufficient to compensate new construction. The reasoning for this is that, at some point, new generation units will be needed to provide energy and no one will build them if there is no possibility of making a return on that investment.

Key Concept

Capacity

Capacity is a term that has a lot of meanings in the energy market. It generally refers to a quantity of power. For example, the quantity of power needed to meet consumer demand or an amount of power that can be delivered under a contract. However, it can have a variety of meanings that vary by context. Some of the more common uses are:

- **Capacity Market.** An auction-based system designed to compensate less-utilized or unutilized generation units for providing a safety margin for the power grid.
- **Capacity Price.** The price paid in a contract for the option to use some physical asset. For example, the amount of money, per MW-hour, giving the buyer the right to rent a power plant's ability to convert fuel into electricity.

QUIZ

1. **In the context of power grids, what is not an ancillary service?**
   A. Balancing the load being served by each power line.
   B. Providing power to consumers.
   C. Ensuring sufficient generation capacity exists to meet consumer demand.
   D. Ensuring sufficient reactive power is available to keep the power grid synchronized.

   Correct Answer: B

   Explanation: Providing power to consumers is the primary service provided by a power grid. All of the other answers describe services provided by the power grid in addition to its primary service. These additional services are called ancillary services.

2. **Which of the following statements is true?**
   A Transmission and distribution commonly account for about 40% of the cost of retail power.
   B. Transmission and distribution commonly account for about 25% of the cost of retail power.
   C. Transmission and distribution commonly account for about 10% of the cost of retail power.
   D. Transmission and distribution are commonly negligible components of retail power prices.

   Correct Answer: A

   Explanation: Transmission and distribution costs account for about 40% to 50% of the cost of consumer (retail) power prices. Some of these costs come from line losses. Other costs come from the cost of maintaining power lines to any building wired for electricity, whether it is economic to do so or not.

3. **What is a drawback of alternating current (AC) power?**
   A. AC power can't be scaled to higher or lower voltage.
   B. AC power needs to be converted to DC power before it can be used to power an electric motor.
   C. AC power requires each generator to produce an AC wave with identical frequency and timing.
   D. AC power is difficult to produce using a mechanical process.

   Correct Answer: C

   Explanation: Answer C is correct, all of the other answers are incorrect.

4. **Which of the following choices is the most efficient way to transmit AC power?**
   A. High-voltage AC power with synchronized generation.
   B. Low-voltage AC power with synchronized generation.
   C. High-voltage AC power with unsynchronized generation.
   D. Low-voltage AC power with unsynchronized generation.

Correct Answer: A

Explanation: High voltage power lines are more efficient at transmitting power than low voltage lines. If generation on a power grid is not synchronized, the AC waves produced by each power plant will cancel and a substantial amount of power will be lost.

5. **Choose the best answer. If financially settled day-ahead 5×16 Peak prices are $50/MWh, Off-Peak prices are $40/MWh, and the legislated price cap for power prices is $5000/MWh, are financially settled day-ahead 5×4 super-peak prices of $271/MWh reasonable?**
   A. No, the super-peak price is too high compared to the 5x16 Peak price.
   B. No, because 5x4 power is not commonly traded.
   C. Yes, any price less than the legislated price cap of $5,000 is reasonable.
   D. Yes, because 5x4 power is illiquid and it may have large transaction costs.

Correct Answer: A

Explanation: It would be very unusual for $271/MWh super-peak prices to be reasonable. It costs $800 to buy power for a 16-hour block ($50/MWh * 16 hours). Even if power prices for every hour except the four most expensive hours in that block is zero, the maximum price for a 4-hour super-peak block is $200 ($800/4 hours). While power prices can go negative, this usually occurs overnight, and off-peak prices are positive.

6. **Which of the following statements is correct about retail and wholesale electricity prices?**
   A. Wholesale prices are usually substantially higher than consumer prices.
   B. Wholesale and consumer prices are about the same.
   C. Wholesale prices are usually substantially lower than consumer prices.
   D. Since every area is different, it is difficult to generalize.

Correct Answer: C

Explanation: Since power is lost in transmission, and transmission and distribution companies need to recover the cost needed to maintain the power grid and repair downed power lines, retail prices (the price paid by consumers) are almost always higher than wholesale prices (the price paid to generators).

7. **If a power grid has to build a new power plant, is a 7.4 MMBtu/MWh heat rate generation plant better than a 10.2 MMBtu/MWh heat rate generation plant?**
   A. Yes, a 7.4 MMBtu/MWh unit is more efficient than a 10.2 MMBtu/MWh unit.
   B. No, a 10.2 MMBtu/MWh unit is more utilized than a 7.4 MMBtu/MWh unit.
   C. Yes, a 7.4 MMBtu/MWh unit is has lower maintenance costs than a 10.2 MMBtu/MWh unit.
   D. There is insufficient information to make the determination.

Correct Answer: D

Explanation: This is a trick question. While a 7.4 MMBtu/MWh is more efficient than a 10.2 MMBtu/MWh unit, efficiency is only one characteristic of a power plant. The speed at which the unit can start up, the amount of pollution that it produces, the desire for diversified fuels on a power grid, and consumer support for a project can all contribute to decisions on which generation unit is deemed the best in a particular instance.

8. **A natural gas-fired power plant requires 6,000 MMBtu of fuel to generate 500 MWh of electricity. Based on this information, what is the heat rate of the power plant?**
    A. 6 MMBtu/MWh
    B. 10 MMBtu/MWh
    C. 12 MMBtu/MWh
    D. 30 MMBtu/MWh

    Correct Answer: C

    Explanation: The heat rate of a power plant can be determined by dividing the quantity of fuel it uses by the quantity of power that is produced. 6,000 MMBtu / 500 MWh = 12 MMBtu/MWh.

9. **In the electricity market, which of the following best describes the term capacity?**
    A. Capacity represents the maximum output of a generation plant.
    B. Capacity refers to the quantity of power that can be transported over a transmission and distribution network.
    C. Capacity refers to the volume of power available to a power grid for the purpose of meeting peak consumer demand.
    D. The term *capacity* can mean all of these things

    Correct Answer: D

    Explanation: The term capacity means different things to different people. Capacity generally refers to a volume or quantity of power. However, there is no single definition for the word capacity that applies to all market participants.

10. **What defines an electrical company as a public utility?**
    A. The company owns transmission and distribution lines needed to supply consumers.
    B. The legislature has designated the company as a utility.
    C. The company owns transmission, distribution, and generation assets.
    D. The company owns generation assets.

    Correct Answer: B

    Explanation: A government entity (usually a legislature) designates a company as a public utility and determines that it should be subject to government regulation. This determination can be done at a national, state, or local level.

Part II

Trading & Investing

Chapter **4**

Trading Essentials

This chapter describes terminology related to trading and forward prices, and introduces the groups involved in trading at an institutional level.

CHAPTER OBJECTIVES

After completing this chapter, the student should have an understanding of

- Trades and trading positions
- Features of commodities
- Different types of prices
- Types of groups involved in trading organizations

Trades and Positions

A *trade* is a transaction. It is a legally binding contract that involves the buying and selling of some type of good. The people who are transacting are called the *parties* to the transaction. From the perspective of either party, the trader on the other side of the transaction is the *counterparty*. Without someone willing to take the other side of the transaction, there can be no transaction. In other words, every trade requires both a buyer and a seller.

Trades

Trades involve both a buyer and a seller.[1]

- **Buyer.** The trader paying cash for something.
- **Seller.** The trader receiving cash for something.
- **Party.** A trader involved in a transaction.
- **Counterparty.** From the perspective of each trader, the other trader involved in the transaction.

It is impossible to make a trade without a trading partner. If you are a buyer, you have to find someone willing to sell. If you are a seller, you have to find someone willing to buy. Investors are often used to thinking about commodities as items for which prices are readily available. However, the price of an asset becomes very subjective whenever neither buyers nor sellers can be found.

Traders use the term *liquidity* to indicate markets when buyers and sellers are easy to find. A *liquid market* allows a trader to easily convert the commodity being traded into cash (or vice versa). An *illiquid market* is one where it is difficult or impossible to find a trading partner. An example of an illiquid market is selling a house. When selling a house, the ultimate sale price won't be known until a transaction occurs. There may also be a significant time between listing the house for sale and the completion of the transaction. Moreover, the sale price may depend on the willingness of both buyers and sellers to wait for a better price.

Liquidity

Liquidity is a term that describes how easily counterparties can be found who are willing to transact at reasonable prices.

- **Liquid Market.** A market where it is easy to find people who are willing to transact.
- **Illiquid Market.** A market where finding a counterparty willing to transact at a reasonable price is difficult or impossible.

There are a variety of ways to find a trading partner. The simplest is to directly contact someone that you know is willing to transact. Alternately, you could enlist a third party to find a trading partner (a broker) or go to a location where people willing to trade congregate (an exchange).

Trades negotiated directly between two traders are private contracts and are referred to by the name *bilateral transactions*. Bilateral trades can be highly customized. Other trades are done on the *exchange*. An exchange is an organized market where traders can transact with one another. These trades are very standardized. Most exchanges allow anonymous trading and act as the counterparty for each trader after the trade price is negotiated (see Figure 4-1).

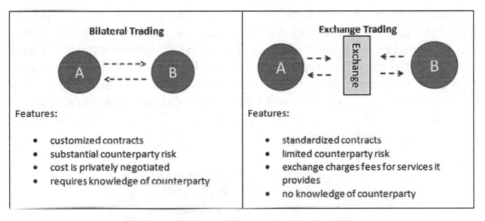

FIGURE 4-1 • Bilateral and Exchange Trades

Key Concept

Types of Trades

There are three primary ways to find a trading partner.

- **Bilateral.** A trader has the option of directly contacting potential trading partners to see if they would like to transact. For example, a trader might telephone or use instant messaging software to reach contacts at other firms. This approach works well for traders that have substantial industry contacts.
- **Broker.** A trader can contact a *broker* to help find him a trading partner. For a fee, the broker will do the legwork of finding trading partners who are interested in transacting. A broker has the advantage of providing some

anonymity for the trader, insight into current markets, and giving traders access to a larger pool of potential trading partners than they might have by themselves. Brokers may also handle much of the paperwork necessary for trading.

- **Exchange.** For benchmark products where there is a lot of trading activity, an exchange can provide a centralized location for finding trading partners. Exchanges can provide anonymity and limit exposure to counterparty risk.

Exchanges allow anonymous trading through the use of *limit orders*. A limit order allows traders to post a price at which they are willing to transact. A limit price for a trader willing to buy is called a *bid price*. A price for a trader willing to sell is called an *ask price* or *offer price*. The difference between the bid and ask prices is called the *bid/ask spread* (see Figure 4-2). Because these prices set a limit on the maximum price that a trader is willing to pay (for buy orders) or minimum price that a trader is willing to receive (for sell orders), bid and ask trades are called *limit orders*. A third type of order, called a *market order*, makes a transaction at the best available price.

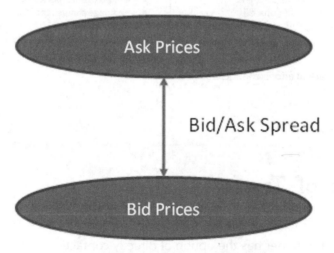

FIGURE 4-2 · Bid/Ask Spread

If an ask price is placed below the best bid price, or a bid placed above the lowest ask price, a trade will immediately take place. This is called trade *execution*. Trading will continue until either the buy or sell orders are exhausted. Then a bid/ask spread will be re-established. The combination of the best bid and ask is called the *inside quote*.

Exchange Trades

Some trading is done on an exchange. On an exchange, traders anonymously negotiate prices. When there is agreement to trade, the exchange will become the counterparty for each trader.

- **Bid Price.** A bid price is the highest price that a buyer will pay.
- **Ask Price.** An ask price (sometimes called an offer price) is the lowest price that a seller is willing to accept.
- **Limit Order.** A limit order is an order that limits the price that the trader is willing to accept. Bid and ask prices come from limit orders—bid prices come from buy limit orders, and ask prices come sell limit orders.
- **Market Order.** A buy or sell order for immediate execution (no limit on the price to be paid).

Regardless of where a transaction occurs, most trades have the following features:

- **Buyer.** The person who is paying cash.
- **Seller.** The person who is receiving cash.
- **Trade Date.** The date at which agreement to trade occurs.
- **Expiration Date.** The date the transaction will take place. For some transactions that occur on the spot (*spot transactions*), the trade and expiration dates are the same.
- **Settlement Date.** The date the money will be transferred. This will affect timing of cash flows and is typically a day or two after the expiration date.
- **Commodity Transacted.** Details about what has been transacted
- **Price.** The price per unit that the buyer will pay the seller.
- **Quantity.** The amount that has been traded.

For trades that have unusual or unique features, those features will be specified in a legal contract. All trades are a form of binding legal agreement. As a result, there is always paperwork that documents the transaction. An example of paperwork for a bilateral transaction is shown in Figure 4-3.

The Terms of the particular transaction to which this confirmation relates are as follows:

Transaction	Swap
Trade Date	28 September 2012
Commodity	Natural Gas
Quantity	Total 3,600,000 MMBTU
	Period: See below
Term	01 January 2013 to 31 Dec 2013
We pay you:	Fixed price of 5.7000 USD per MMBTU
You pay us:	NYMEX Henry Hub Natural Gas
	contract settling price of last three trading days each month (see Schedule A)
Payment	Exactly 5 business days after the end of the relevant determination period.

Schedule A

Pricing Month	Quantity (MMBTU)
January 2013	310,000
February 2013	280,000
March 2013	310,000
April 2013	300,000
May 2013	310,000
June 2013	300,000
July 2013	310,000
August 2013	310,000
September 2013	300,000
October 2013	310,000
November 2013	300,000
December 2013	310,000

FIGURE 4-3 · Bilateral Trade Example

Because a trade is a contract between two parties, it is necessary for both sides to honor their obligations. The risk that your trading partner won't honor the agreement is called *counterparty credit risk*. Counterparty credit risk tends to be different than other types of risk, since a trader is at risk when they have entered into a profitable trade and their trading partner owes them money. There is relatively little uncertainty involved with owing someone money—it's generally assumed that sooner or later they will try to collect.

Spot transactions typically have limited credit risk due to the short time between transaction and settlement. For these trades, cash flows are commonly finalized two days after trading. However, in commodity markets, there may be an extended period between trading and delivery. For example, it is relatively common to line up fuel deliveries 6 to 12 months in advance. In the months between when the transaction was entered and the delivery date, the price of the commodity might have changed substantially.

The markets have developed a variety of ways to help minimize credit risks. One way to reduce this risk is to transact on an exchange. Exchanges are extremely creditworthy counterparties and set up rules that allow them to minimize credit risk. As a result, exchanges are generally considered to represent zero credit risk. Another way to reduce counterparty credit risk is to write additional terms into trading contracts. Some of the more common terms include:

- **Margining.** An amount of collateral that needs to be deposited to offset potential credit exposure. Margining is a standard feature of any contract traded on an exchange (like a future) but can also apply to bilateral agreements (like forwards).
- **Master Netting Agreements.** A standard clause in many commodity contracts that consolidates all transactions between two parties and allows net settlement of cash flows. This can reduce the gross exposure between two parties into a net exposure.

Key Concept

Counterparty Credit Risk

When traders transact with one another, they are at risk of the other party defaulting on their obligations. This risk is called *counterparty credit risk*. This risk can be mitigated through a variety of ways including margining, master netting agreements, and knowing your trading partner.

Where a trade is a transaction, a *position* is the net exposure that results from one or more trades. For example, if a trader makes two trades that each purchase 500 shares of IBM stock, the result is a 1,000 share position in IBM stock. Positions use different terminology than trades. In the same way that buy and sell might describe trades, the terms *long* and *short* describe positions.

- A *long position* profits when the price of the underlying asset increases and loses money when prices drop.
- A *short position* profits when the price of the asset drops and loses money when prices rise.
- A *flat position* does not either gain or lose money when prices change.

Because the terms long, short, and flat describe exposures, it is necessary to define what exposure is being analyzed. For example, a *put option* allows the owner of the option the right to sell stock at a fixed price. This option gets more valuable when the stock goes down in price. As a result, the trader's position is "long the option" (she benefits when the option becomes more valuable) and "short stock prices" (she benefits when stock prices decline). In most cases, it is necessary to infer from the context which exposure is being discussed. For example, if a trader says that she is "long a crude oil put" or "long crude oil futures," the context is that the trader is referring to a specific contract rather than the trader's exposure to crude oil prices.

This terminology also applies to spreads. A long spread benefits when the spread gets larger, and loses money when the spread gets smaller. It also applies to factors that might affect the value of positions like volatility. For example, options get more valuable when volatility rises. As a result, a trader that owns options will be described as "long volatility."

Key Concept

Positions

A position is an exposure that results from various transactions or commitments that a trade is obligated to meet. The terms *long* and *short* describe the economic effect of prices on those exposures.

- **Long Exposure.** Benefit when price rises or, in the case of a spread between two prices, the spread gets larger.
- **Short Exposure.** Benefit when price declines or, in the case of a spread between two prices, the spread gets smaller.
- **Flat Exposure.** There is no exposure.

Features of Commodities

The energy market deals with commodities. A commodity is a physical item that is interchangeable with other items of the same type. There are several differences between commodities and financial contracts like stocks and bonds. First, commodities come in different levels of quality or grade. Second, commodities typically exist in a physical location. There is often a substantial cost associated with storing and transporting commodities. Third, many commodities are consumed (destroyed) when used and their value comes from being in the right place at the right time.

The necessity of dealing with physical issues makes commodities much more complicated than financial contracts. It also raises the possibility of severe problems related to scheduling delivery of the commodity. For example, if a trader needs to deliver crude oil to a port, transposing two numbers when reserving space at the dock may be very difficult to correct. In a financial contract, both parties can agree there was an error and fix it. However, commodities transfers may involve other people, for example, the dock with the necessary equipment might have been reserved by someone else by the time the error is identified.

Key Concept

Commodities

Commodities are physical items and need to be in the right place at the right time. The physical properties of commodities are important and they tend to have high operational risks.

- High operational risks.
- Location is important.
- Quality and grade of product are important.

Different Types of Prices

There are many types of prices involved in the energy markets.

- **Spot Prices.** A spot price is a price at which an asset has recently been bought or sold for immediate delivery.
- **Forward Prices.** A forward price is a price at which traders have agreed to transact at some point in the future. This type of price involves two dates: the valuation date (the date when the price was quoted) and the delivery date (when the product needs to be delivered).
- **Quotes.** A price where someone is willing to buy or sell some quantity of an asset for either spot or forward delivery (but no transaction has taken place). Bid and ask prices are examples of quotes.
- **Historical Prices.** These are prices of transactions that have occurred at some point in the past. There are historical spot prices, forward prices, and quotes.

In general, the price of an asset is defined as the price that other people are willing to pay for it. Changing supply and demand conditions cause assets to change in value over time. As a result, most valuations of trading assets are based on what the asset is worth right now (this is called the *market price*) rather than what was originally paid for the asset. In the example below, an asset goes up and down in value from the inception of the trade to its termination. (See Figure 4-4.)

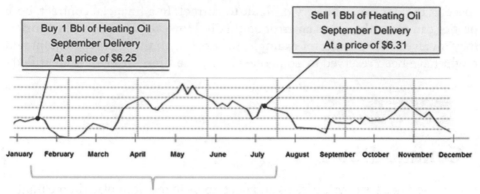

Price of an asset changes after it is traded.

FIGURE 4-4 • Asset Prices

In many financial markets, like the stock market, the most commonly quoted price is the spot price—the price for immediate delivery of an asset. In energy markets, spot prices are still commonly quoted, but often less important than prices for future delivery. The reason is that commodities like energy, need to be transported and stored. This is easier to arrange with some lead time. For example, while a trader often has little trouble arranging delivery with a month of advance notice, arranging delivery may not be feasible on short notice. As a result, many energy and commodity products are traded for future delivery.

Spot prices also tend to be less predictable than forward prices. Forward prices are based on expectations of the future. In contracts, spot prices are based on what is happening at that time. A tree falling on an electrical transmission line, a delay in off-loading crude oil onto a dock, or a sudden winter storm that creates an unexpected demand for fuel can all cause short term changes in prices that will disappear upon a return to normal conditions.

Because forward prices are based on expectations, they often show a predictable cyclical pattern (see Figure 4-5). The first price on the curve is commonly the spot price, and the future delivery dates are shown on the x-axis. Difficulty in storing energy products often leads to seasonal cyclical prices. Markets where storage is widely available at low cost generally won't exhibit the same cyclical nature.

The reason that forward prices show cyclicality is due to the way forward prices are developed rather than underlying behavior of spot prices. Forward prices are determined by no-arbitrage concepts.[2]

For example, a common arbitrage relationship is related to the cost of buying an asset and then storing it until it is needed. If the storage is more expensive during some parts of the year than others, a cyclical pattern of prices will show up in the forward curve.

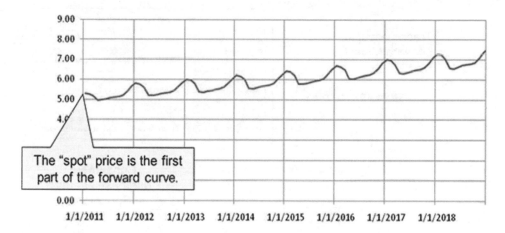

FIGURE 4-5 · Natural Gas Forward Prices

Spot prices typically don't show the same predictable cyclicality as forward prices. These prices are typically determined by the supply and demand based on what's on hand for a given day. As a result, spot prices don't necessarily behave the same way as forward curves. For example, forward curves would seem to indicate that natural gas prices in the winter were consistently higher than prices in the summer. However, that relationship doesn't show up when examining spot prices (see Figure 4-6).

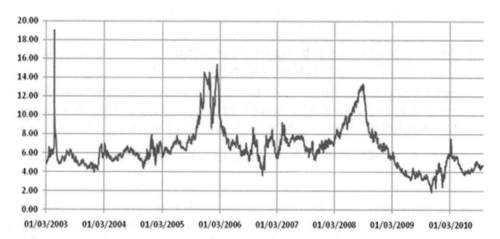

FIGURE 4-6 · Natural Gas Spot Prices

For every date, there is both a spot price and a forward price curve (see Figure 4-7). Most commodities trades occur in the forward market. Traders will line up their expected requirement for a particular delivery date and then use the spot market to balance their expectations of consumer demand with actual consumer demand.

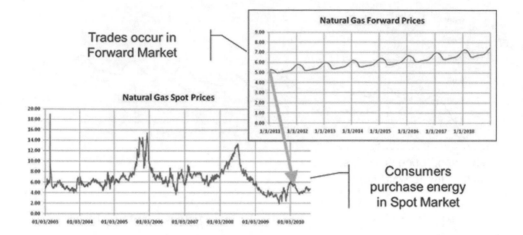

FIGURE 4-7 • Spot and Forward Curves

Spot and Forward Markets

Spot and forward prices have different dynamics and traders will have different reasons for trading in each.

- **Forward Market.** Used by traders to obtain the expected supply of a commodity. These prices are usually relatively predictable.

- **Spot Market.** Used by traders to balance actual consumer demand against expectations. Spot prices tend to be less predictable than forward prices.

A common assumption in most financial markets is that spot and forward prices will exist for a wide variety of commodities. In practice, that isn't always a safe assumption. A reason for limited availability of prices is commonly that markets are illiquid. In the energy industry, where transportation and storage are difficult, there may not be two people interested in trading the exact same product to be delivered at the same location and time. Lack of trading can commonly lead to long periods of flat prices followed by a sudden jump in prices (see Figure 4-8).

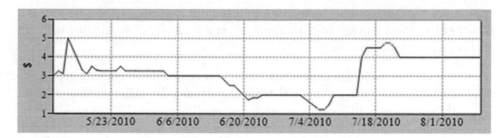

FIGURE 4-8 · Intermittent Trading

Generally, intermittent trading requires that current prices be inferred based on the price of related commodities (like the same product in a nearby location) or through gathering indications of trading interest through brokers or surveys. Some of the common sources of prices in the energy market are exchange-based prices, exchange over-the-counter (OTC) clearing prices, and bilateral prices.

Exchange Based Prices

Exchanges will publish recent transaction prices and the prices that they use to make margin calls on trades executed on the exchange.[3] As a result, exchange-traded prices are the most visible source of pricing in the energy market. However, exchanges only allow trading on a small number of contracts. In addition, most trading occurs in contracts that will be delivered within eighteen months. Exchange-based prices are often used as industry benchmarks but can only be used to price a small portion of physical trades.

Exchange OTC Clearing Prices

Exchanges will often allow traders to clear trades arranged bilaterally on the exchange. To traders, this will offer many of the benefits of trading on the exchange (like eliminating credit risk) while reducing the need for the exchange to build up sufficient trading volume to support exchange-based trading. When an exchange interposes itself between the two traders (*clears the trade*) it will publish daily prices, which it will use to margin the traders.

Bilateral Prices

A substantial portion of the energy trading is done bilaterally. Bilateral trades are private contracts between two companies. There is no requirement for the either trading partner to make the trade prices publically known. If those bilateral prices are revealed, public knowledge of those prices could put the traders at a competitive disadvantage. Instead, these prices are usually disseminated through voluntary surveys or brokers.

- **Broker Prices.** In the energy market, traders commonly employ brokers to help them identify potential trading partners. To assist in this process, these brokers will disseminate indications where they think people will be willing to transact. In some cases, to get access to market quotes, it is often necessary to be willing to transact. This involves a level of trust between both the broker and the traders.
- **Survey-based Prices.** Several companies survey traders to get nonbinding estimates of trading prices. Using one of these sources assumes that other traders have better information and are willing to share it. There is the possibility that everyone is ignorant of prices and exchanging bad information. In these cases, bad information can exist for extended periods. Prices may only get corrected when trading in that location becomes more common.

Key Concept

Pricing Availability

Spot and forward prices have different dynamics and traders will have different reasons for trading in each. Some of the more common sources of prices are:

- **Exchange and OTC Clearing.** Prices used by the exchange to determine daily margining.
- **Brokers.** Nonbinding indications where the broker believes that they will be able to find someone willing to trade.
- **Surveys.** Nonbinding, anonymous surveys of market participants that ask where they believe trading to be possible.

Groups Involved in Trading

In a trading organization, there are a wide variety of people involved in making trades. Commonly these groups are divided into a couple of major categories: Front office, middle office, back office, and various support groups. (See Figure 4-9.)

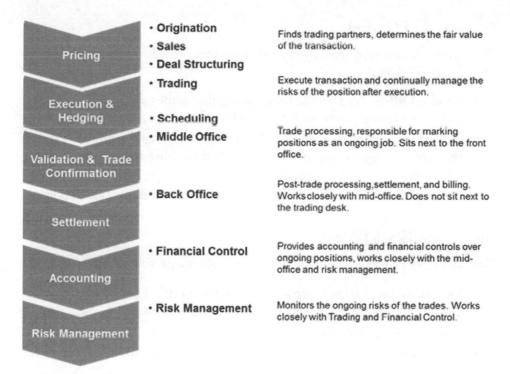

FIGURE 4-9 • Groups Involved With Trading

Commercial Groups (Front Office)

In a trading organization, the *front office* is comprised of the commercial teams whose goal it is to make money for the organization. These teams include:

- **Sales and Origination.** Responsible for identifying potential trading partners and their potential trading needs.

- **Structuring.** Responsible for calculating fair prices and valuing complex (*structured*) transactions. These are typically quantitative, math-heavy groups.

- **Scheduling.** Responsible for managing the physical delivery and scheduling of energy. Scheduling teams need to understand minute details of the markets for which they are responsible.

- **Trading.** Responsible for executing transactions, managing the existing positions, and hedging positions to reduce risk.

- **Proprietary Trading.** Responsible for making transactions on behalf of the company rather than facilitating client orders. This may or may not be separate from the regular trading desk.

Support and Control

The trading desk is supported by several teams that provide operational controls over the trading desk.

- **Middle Office.** Responsible for ensuring that trades are properly entered and that existing positions are marked to market on a daily basis.
- **Risk Management.** Makes sure that traders are not taking on too much risk and keeping management informed of ongoing risks to the existing portfolio.
- **Financial Control.** Responsible for accounting and profit and loss reporting.

Processing (Back Office)

The *back office* provides post-trade processing, settlement, and clearing functions.

- **Reconciliation.** Making sure that the counterparty's back office agrees on the terms of every trade (quantity, price, location, etc.)
- **Margin.** Responsible for posting and receiving margin calls.
- **Documentation.** Responsible for much of the paperwork necessary for trading.

QUIZ

1. In a trading organization, which group is responsible for scheduling and coordinating physical deliveries?
   A. Trading
   B. Scheduling
   C. Risk management
   D. Middle office

   Correct Answer: B

   Explanation: Because of the high operational risk involved in physical delivery, energy companies typically have a team dedicated to coordinating physical deliveries called the schedulers or scheduling team. This team is responsible for knowing minute details related to physical deliveries, physical issues that might delay or prevent delivery, and having the necessary contacts for fixing problems.

2. Brianna, a trader at a refinery, is long a 3-2-1 crack spread. What is Brianna's position relative to crude oil, gasoline, and diesel fuel prices?
   A. Short crude oil, short gasoline, short diesel
   B. Long crude oil, short gasoline, short diesel
   C. Short crude oil, long gasoline, long diesel
   D. Long crude oil, long gasoline, long diesel

   Correct Answer: C

   Explanation: This question requires knowledge of the definition of a 3-2-1 crack spread. A 3-2-1 crack spread is defined as: 2* Gasoline Price + 1* Diesel Price – 3*Crude Oil Price. Since she is long, Brianna benefits when the spread gets larger. As a result, she is long gasoline and diesel prices and short crude oil prices.

3. In a trading organization, which group is responsible for monitoring risk and reporting it to senior management?
   A. Trading
   B. Sales and marketing
   C. Risk management
   D. Middle office

   Correct Answer: C

   Explanation: The risk management group is typically responsible for monitoring risks and reporting these risks to senior management.

4. In a trading organization, which group is responsible for marking the positions every night and calculating whether the trading desk made or lost money?
   A. Trading
   B. Sales and marketing
   C. Risk management
   D. Middle office

   Correct Answer: D

   Explanation: Marking positions and calculating P&L (Profit and Loss) is typically the responsibility of the middle office.

5. **What is the primary difference between physical and financial products?**
    A. Physical products have an associated location.
    B. Physical products have different levels of quality.
    C. Physical products can be very difficult to deliver.
    D. All of the above.

    Correct Answer: D

    Explanation: All of the above describe issues that are important to physical commodities.

6. **In a trading organization, which group is typically responsible for maintaining the trading positions and hedging them to reduce risk?**
    A. Trading
    B. Sales and marketing
    C. Risk management
    D. Middle office

    Correct Answer: A

    Explanation: The trading desk is typically responsible for maintaining the firm's positions. A large part of that job is monitoring the risk associated with those positions and taking corrective steps to stay in line with the firm's trading and investing policies.

7. **If a tree falls over and knocks out a power line due to a surprise storm, which type of power price is most likely to be affected?**
    A. Spot prices
    B. Forward prices
    C. Historical prices
    D. None of these are likely to be affected.

    Correct Answer: A

    Explanation: An outage on a power line could have a dramatic impact on spot prices. Power might have to be brought in from another area or expensive power plants brought online to balance the power grid. This would have little effect on forward prices because the power line is likely to be fixed prior to the delivery date. Historical prices will not change—they are historical records.

8. **Yongyan, a trader with a bank, is long 500 barrels of crude oil. If prices rise by $3/BBL,**
    A. Yongyan will make money.
    B. Yongyan will lose money.
    C. Yongyan will neither make nor lose money.
    D. The results can't be determined from the information provided.

    Correct Answer: A

    Explanation: A trader with a long position benefits from a rise in prices. In this case, Yongyan will make $1,500 (500 BBL x $3/BBL profit).

9. **Spencer owns 10 options on IBM stock. What is Spencer's exposure?**
   A. Spencer is long IBM stock prices and long volatility.
   B. Spencer is short IBM stock prices and long volatility.
   C. There is insufficient information to determine whether Spencer is long or short IBM stock prices but he is definitely long volatility.
   D. Spencer is long IBM stock prices and there is insufficient information to determine whether he is long or short volatility.

Correct Answer: C

Explanation: Without knowing what type of option, it is impossible to determine whether Spencer will benefit from rising or falling prices. However, he will benefit from an increase in volatility whether he owns calls or puts.

10. **Which statement is false?**
    A. It is cheaper to trade on an exchange than bilaterally.
    B. Bilateral trades can be more highly customized than exchange trades.
    C. Exchange trades largely eliminate counterparty risk.
    D. Bilateral trades are private contracts between two parties.

Correct Answer: A

Explanation: Because exchanges charge fees for their services, they are not usually the lowest cost option. The cost of exchanges has to be weighed against the cost of having lawyers draw up bilateral contracts and counterparty credit monitoring. For the other answers, exchanges typically trade a limited number of contracts. To get a specific item anywhere except the location used for exchange settlement usually requires a bilateral contract. Exchanges largely eliminate counterparty credit exposure. This is a major reason that exchanges are utilized.

Chapter **5**

Forward Prices

Obtaining a fair price is important to the success of any energy trading or investing strategy. *Fair prices* are prices that allow neither buyer nor seller a risk-free profit at the expense of the other trader. This is a mathematical constraint on prices that defines a fair price in relation to other prices. Defining fair prices in this way allows investors to move away from opinions and benefit from a concrete way to measure fairness.

In cases where there are active trading markets, the market can usually be relied upon to give a fair price. However, a large number of energy markets don't experience active trading. As a result, these markets can't be relied upon to provide fair prices to investors. In these cases, investors need to develop an estimate of a fair price.

CHAPTER OBJECTIVES

After completing this chapter, the student should have an understanding of

- The difference between forecasts from fair prices
- Time value of money and interest rates
- The term *volatility* as used in the financial markets
- Statistical terminology used to describe forward curves
- How to extend forward price curves
- How to extend forward volatility curves

The Difference between Forecasts and Fair Prices

Investors, whether buying or selling, are interested in transacting at fair prices. Among individual investors, there is often confusion about what constitutes fair prices in the future. However, in finance things are a bit simpler—a *fair price* is a price where neither party to a transaction can make a risk-free profit at the expense of the other party. This is a mathematical concept that, in financial literature, is often called a *no-arbitrage* price. As a result, a fair price is not just an opinion. A fair price is defined by a mathematical linkage between the prices of various commodities.

A wide variety of predictions on the future called *forecasts* can be found from a variety of sources. Forecasts may often be mistaken for fair prices, but they are not the same thing. A forecast is an opinion about where prices will be in the future. Unlike a fair price, forecasts are not necessarily no-arbitrage prices. Some forecasts may be based on economic analysis. Other forecasts may be developed by the government or prestigious think tanks. These forecasts may provide the justification or catalyst for a trade. However, a *forecast* is not a *fair price*.

Arbitrage opportunities often come from the ability to convert, store, and transport commodities. For example, if a trader could buy a ton of coal and enter a binding contract to sell it in one month at a $200 profit, he could make a risk-free profit assuming he had little or no storage costs. Regardless of where prices are forecasted to be in a month, the ability to buy coal today and store it creates a linkage between current prices and the fair price in the future. Any other price would allow traders to make a risk-free profit. The fair price would be the price at which neither party could make a risk-free profit.

In liquid financial markets, prices obtained from recent trades are generally assumed to be fair prices. The logic is that if trading prices provided arbitrage opportunities, traders would start making risk-free profits and continue to do so until prices reached non-arbitrage levels. Ultimately, the market would reach an equilibrium that prevented arbitrage profits from occurring. The term used to describe a market where no arbitrage opportunities exist is called an *efficient market*.[1]

Key Concept

Fair Prices

A fair price is one where neither party can make a risk-free profit. In other terms, a fair deal is one that leaves all parties equally aggrieved.

- **Arbitrage.** An arbitrage is a risk-free opportunity for profit.

- **Fair Price.** A fair price allows neither side of a trade the potential for a risk-free profit. (As a result, a fair price is sometimes called a no-arbitrage price.)
- **Forecast.** A forecast is a prediction of the future prices. A forecast is not necessarily a fair price in the financial sense.

In practice, energy and commodities are characterized by extreme illiquidity,[2] physical constraints, and physical transactions rather than by the trading of cash-settled financial products found in other markets. Efficient markets rely on trading to create fair prices. In markets where trading is impossible or difficult, market prices may or may not be representative of fair prices. For example, it's possible to have a transaction market (I buy a cheeseburger) without the ability to trade cheeseburgers (I can't resell the cheeseburger tomorrow). Even though a trader is willing to sell, there may be no buyer for the product. Most of these limitations can be minimized or eliminated by allowing delivery at some point in the future.

Interest Rates and the Time Value of Money

Interest rates link money today with money in the future. Simply described, it is better to have cash in hand rather than a promise to get paid at some point in the future. As a result, interest rates are a fundamental building block of fair prices and provide a way to mathematically compare cash on hand to the promise of future payments.

Key Concept

Interest Rates

Money, like any other asset, changes in value over time. The value of money at some point in the future is equal to its value today plus any interest that could be obtained by investing it at a risk-free rate. In cases where money cannot be lent without some risk, a higher interest rate needs to be applied to the cash flows. This higher interest rate is called a *risk premium* and can be thought of as the cost of buying insurance to ensure repayment.

An *interest rate* is a payment received for loaning someone else money for a period of time. Interest rates depend on the certainty that the loan will be repaid. The interest rate on a loan that is certain to be repaid is called the *risk-free rate*. A loan to a counterparty that has a chance of not repaying the loan is called a *credit-adjusted rate*. The most commonly accepted standard for risk-free interest rates is the London Inter-Bank Offer Rate (LIBOR). LIBOR is the interest rate at which large, high credit quality (low probability of bankruptcy), banks loan money to one another.[3]

Key Concept

Interest Rates

Some key terms related to interest rates:

- **Interest Rate.** An interest rate is a fee paid for the use of someone else's cash.
- **LIBOR.** The London Inter-Bank Offer Rate (LIBOR) is the primary benchmark for risk-free interest rates.
- **Risk-Free Rate.** The risk-free interest rate is the interest paid by someone with no risk of default.
- **Credit-Adjusted Rate.** A credit-adjusted interest rate is higher than the risk-free rate and paid by someone who has a chance of not repaying the cash that was borrowed. The credit quality of the borrower will determine how much higher the credit adjusted rate is than the risk-free rate.

The mathematical formula that links cash prices (the *present value*) to future prices (the *future value*) is called the *continuous compounding formula* (see Equation 5.1). In this formula, a mathematical constant, called *e* (approximately 2.718281828), is raised to a power that depends on interest rates and time.

Continuous Compounding

$$FV = PV * e^{rt}$$
or   (5.1)
$$PV = FV * e^{-rt}$$

Where

PV	**Present Value.** The value of cash today
FV	**Future value.** The value that cash will be worth in the future
r	**Interest rate.** This needs to be in the same units as t (Time). The standard convention is that this is an annual interest rate.
t	**Time.** The standard convention is that a date 1 year in the future is 1.0, six months in the future is 0.5, and so on.
e	**Standard exponent.** An important constant (approximately 2.718281828) associated with continuous compounding.

The choice of interest rate will depend on whether there is any counter-party risk involved in the valuation. If there is no counterparty risk, the risk-free rate will be used. In the energy market, many trades are considered to have no *counterparty risk*. For example, exchange-based trades (like futures) typically have no counterparty risk because the exchange is heavily collateral-ized. Physical positions (like physically owning oil) will also have no counter-party risk.

In the context of fair pricing, interest rates link the fair prices of commodities in the future to today's prices. These interest rates have two components: a risk-free component and costs associated with holding the commodity. Even when items are riskless and free to store, prices will rise in the future due to the alternative (holding cash). This is due to the fact that money in the future is worth less than money today. It might take $1.50 eighteen years in the future to equal $1.00 today (see Figure 5-1).

Fair price of $1

FIGURE 5-1 • Time Value of Money

Economic studies, like the type funded for government agencies, commonly exclude the time value of money effect and represent their results in *real* or *constant* dollars. In a real (constant) dollar study, $1 in the future is equal to $1 today. This is useful to understand how supply and demand evolve. However, contracts and trading are never in real dollars. Contracts are written in *nominal* dollars—the price named in the contract is what gets paid regardless of what has happened to inflation or interest rates. [1]

Key Concept

Time Value of Money

Money is similar to other commodities in the way that it changes value over time.

- **Time Value of Money.** The concept that money today is worth more than money in the future because money today can be used to earn interest on risk-free loans.
- **Real (Constant) Dollars.** Reports in constant dollars exclude time value of money. In other words, in these reports, the value of a dollar is constant over time ($1 today is equal to the promise of $1 tomorrow). This is typically calibrated to a *base year*.
- **Nominal Dollars.** The value of a dollar depends on time (typically $1 today is worth more than a promise of a $1 tomorrow). Contracts and trading are always in nominal dollars.

There are a variety of sources where interest rates can be obtained. Interest rate curves from different sources may not be identical. Interest rates can trade 24 hours a day. A London-based investor might choose rates as of the close of the London markets, while a U.S. based investor might take rates as of the close of the U.S. markets. An example of an interest rate report, the H.15 Report, is published by the U.S. Federal Reserve every week (see Figure 5-2).

Data from these reports can be used to construct a risk-free curve (see Table 5-1). In this example, the U.S. federal funds rate was chosen as the overnight risk-free rate, Eurodollar deposits for maturity dates between one day and one year, and LIBOR swaps for maturities one year and longer. *Maturity date* refers to the date when the loan must be repaid.

To get interest rates at intermediate points, it is necessary to interpolate between nearby points. For example, to make interest rates easier to use, it is common to fit a smooth line to the observed points (see Figure 5-3). This makes interest rates easier to use with spreadsheet and computer programs, since formulas are easier to use than lookup tables. The actual method of interpolation, whether it is using a spline (curved lines) or a straight line, usually has minimal effect on commodity valuations. As a result, in the energy industry, the methodology used to create a smooth interest rate curve is usually chosen for ease of use.

In this example, the interpolation is a based on a Nelson–Siegel–Svensson (NSS) approach shown in Equation (5.2). The NSS approach assumes that interest rates can be described by a predefined functional form. It then uses an optimizer to pick the parameters that best fit the observed points. The reason

FEDERAL RESERVE statistical release

H.15 (519) SELECTED INTEREST RATES
Yields in percent per annum

For use at 2:30 p.m. Eastern Time
April 8, 2013

Instruments	2013 Apr 1	2013 Apr 2	2013 Apr 3	2013 Apr 4	2013 Apr 5	Week Ending Apr 5	Week Ending Mar 29	2013 Mar
Federal funds (effective)[1][2][3]	0.16	0.15	0.14	0.14	0.15	0.12	0.15	0.14
Commercial Paper[3][4][5][6]								
Nonfinancial								
1-month	0.12	0.10	0.08	0.08	0.09	0.09	0.07	0.10
2-month	0.12	0.11	0.11	0.10	0.11	0.11	0.10	0.13
3-month	0.12	0.13	0.13	0.13	0.12	0.13	0.13	0.15
Financial								
1-month	0.07	0.11	0.11	0.09	0.10	0.10	0.11	0.11
2-month	0.09	0.14	0.16	0.16	0.16	0.14	0.11	0.13
3-month	0.19	0.19	0.21	0.17	0.17	0.19	0.12	0.15
CDs (secondary market)[3][7]								
1-month	0.18	0.18	0.18	0.18	0.18	0.18	0.17	0.17
3-month	0.21	0.21	0.22	0.21	0.21	0.21	0.21	0.21
6-month	0.27	0.27	0.28	0.27	0.27	0.27	0.27	0.27
Eurodollar deposits (London)[3][8]								
1-month	0.23	0.23	0.23	0.23	0.23	0.23	0.23	0.23
3-month	0.28	0.28	0.28	0.28	0.28	0.28	0.28	0.28
6-month	0.44	0.44	0.44	0.44	0.44	0.44	0.44	0.44
Bank prime loan[2][3][9]	3.25	3.25	3.25	3.25	3.25	3.25	3.25	3.25
Discount window primary credit[2][10]	0.75	0.75	0.75	0.75	0.75	0.75	0.75	0.75
U.S. government securities								
Treasury bills (secondary market)[3][4]								
4-week	0.06	0.06	0.06	0.07	0.05	0.06	0.06	0.08
3-month	0.08	0.07	0.06	0.07	0.07	0.07	0.08	0.09
6-month	0.11	0.11	0.10	0.10	0.10	0.10	0.11	0.11
1-year	0.13	0.14	0.13	0.13	0.13	0.13	0.13	0.14
Treasury constant maturities								
Nominal[11]								
1-month	0.06	0.06	0.06	0.07	0.05	0.06	0.06	0.08
3-month	0.08	0.07	0.06	0.07	0.07	0.07	0.08	0.09
6-month	0.11	0.11	0.10	0.10	0.10	0.10	0.11	0.11
1-year	0.14	0.14	0.13	0.13	0.13	0.13	0.14	0.15
2-year	0.23	0.25	0.24	0.22	0.24	0.24	0.25	0.26
3-year	0.36	0.36	0.34	0.33	0.33	0.34	0.37	0.39
5-year	0.76	0.78	0.73	0.69	0.68	0.73	0.78	0.82
7-year	1.23	1.26	1.20	1.15	1.12	1.19	1.25	1.32
10-year	1.86	1.88	1.83	1.78	1.72	1.81	1.90	1.96
20-year	2.70	2.72	2.66	2.60	2.50	2.64	2.73	2.78
30-year	3.08	3.10	3.05	2.99	2.87	3.02	3.12	3.16
Inflation indexed[12]								
5-year	-1.47	-1.44	-1.45	-1.44	-1.42	-1.44	-1.45	-1.43
7-year	-1.03	-0.99	-1.02	-1.01	-1.02	-1.01	-1.00	-0.97
10-year	-0.65	-0.63	-0.65	-0.70	-0.74	-0.67	-0.62	-0.59
20-year	0.14	0.16	0.13	0.06	-0.03	0.09	0.17	0.19
30-year	0.58	0.60	0.56	0.48	0.38	0.52	0.61	0.62
Inflation-indexed long-term average[13]	0.08	0.10	0.06	-0.01	-0.10	0.03	0.11	0.13
Interest rate swaps[14]								
1-year	0.35	0.34	0.33	0.33	0.32	0.33	0.36	0.33
2-year	0.41	0.41	0.40	0.39	0.37	0.39	0.42	0.40
3-year	0.52	0.52	0.51	0.50	0.48	0.51	0.54	0.53
4-year	0.70	0.71	0.69	0.67	0.65	0.69	0.73	0.73
5-year	0.94	0.95	0.93	0.90	0.87	0.92	0.97	0.98
7-year	1.42	1.45	1.42	1.38	1.33	1.40	1.46	1.48
10-year	1.99	2.01	1.98	1.94	1.87	1.96	2.03	2.05
30-year	2.97	2.99	2.96	2.91	2.78	2.92	3.00	3.03
Corporate bonds								
Moody's seasoned								
Aaa[15]	3.89	3.90	3.86	3.79	3.68	3.82	3.90	3.93
Baa	4.77	4.79	4.74	4.66	4.54	4.70	4.83	4.85
State & local bonds[16]				3.96		3.96	3.99	3.96
Conventional mortgages[17]				3.54		3.54	3.57	3.57

See next page for footnotes.

FIGURE 5-2 • U.S. Federal Reserve H.15 Report. *Source:* U.S. Federal Reserve

1. The daily effective federal funds rate is a weighted average of rates on brokered trades.

2. Weekly figures are averages of 7 calendar days ending on Wednesday of the current week; monthly figures include each calendar day in the month.

3. Annualized using a 360-day year or bank interest.

4. On a discount basis.

5. Interest rates interpolated from data on certain commercial paper trades settled by The Depository Trust Company. The trades represent sales of commercial paper by dealers or direct issuers to investors (that is, the offer side). The 1-, 2-, and 3-month rates are equivalent to the 30-, 60-, and 90-day dates reported on the Board's Commercial Paper Web page (www.federalreserve.gov/releases/cp/).

6. Financial paper that is insured by the FDIC's Temporary Liquidity Guarantee Program is not excluded from relevant indexes, nor is any financial or nonfinancial commercial paper that may be directly or indirectly affected by one or more of the Federal Reserve's liquidity facilities. Thus the rates published after September 19, 2008, likely reflect the direct or indirect effects of the new temporary programs and, accordingly, likely are not comparable for some purposes to rates published prior to that period.

7. An average of dealer bid rates on nationally traded certificates of deposit.

8. Source: Bloomberg and CTRB ICAP Fixed Income & Money Market Products.

9. Rate posted by a majority of top 25 (by assets in domestic offices) insured U.S.-chartered commercial banks. Prime is one of several base rates used by banks to price short-term business loans.

10. The rate charged for discounts made and advances extended under the Federal Reserve's primary credit discount window program, which became effective January 9, 2003. This rate replaces that for adjustment credit, which was discontinued after January 8, 2003. For further information, see www.federalreserve.gov/boarddocs/press/bcreg/2002/200210312/default.htm. The rate reported is that for the Federal Reserve Bank of New York. Historical series for the rate on adjustment credit as well as the rate on primary credit are available at www.federalreserve.gov/releases/h15/data.htm.

11. Yields on actively traded non-inflation-indexed issues adjusted to constant maturities. The 30-year Treasury constant maturity series was discontinued on February 18, 2002, and reintroduced on February 9, 2006. From February 18, 2002, to February 9, 2006, the U.S. Treasury published a factor for adjusting the daily nominal 20-year constant maturity in order to estimate a 30-year nominal rate. The historical adjustment factor can be found at www.treasury.gov/resource-center/data-chart-center/interest-rates/. Source: U.S. Treasury.

12. Yields on Treasury inflation protected securities (TIPS) adjusted to constant maturities. Source: U.S. Treasury. Additional information on both nominal and inflation-indexed yields may be found at www.treasury.gov/resource-center/data-chart-center/interest-rates/.

13. Based on the unweighted average bid yields for all TIPS with remaining terms to maturity of more than 10 years.

14. International Swaps and Derivatives Association (ISDA®) mid-market par swap rates. Rates are for a Fixed Rate Payer in return for receiving three month LIBOR, and are based on rates collected at 11:00 a.m. Eastern time by Garban Intercapital plc and published on Reuters Page ISDAFIX®1. ISDAFIX is a registered service mark of ISDA. Source: Reuters Limited.

15. Moody's Aaa rates through December 6, 2001, are averages of Aaa utility and Aaa industrial bond rates. As of December 7, 2001, these rates are averages of Aaa industrial bonds only.

16. Bond Buyer Index, general obligation, 20 years to maturity, mixed quality; Thursday quotations.

17. Contract interest rates on commitments for fixed-rate first mortgages. Source: Primary Mortgage Market Survey® data provided by Freddie Mac.

T	Rate	NSS Model	Source
0.0028	0.17%	0.17%	Fed Funds
0.0833	0.30%	0.29%	Eurodollar Deposit
0.25	0.43%	0.46%	Eurodollar Deposit
0.50	0.63%	0.58%	Eurodollar Deposit
1	0.55%	0.60%	Libor (Interest Rate Swap)
2	0.56%	0.54%	Libor (Interest Rate Swap)
3	0.63%	0.62%	Libor (Interest Rate Swap)
4	0.78%	0.78%	Libor (Interest Rate Swap)
5	0.97%	0.98%	Libor (Interest Rate Swap)
7	1.34%	1.35%	Libor (Interest Rate Swap)
10	1.77%	1.75%	Libor (Interest Rate Swap)
30	2.49%	2.49%	Libor (Interest Rate Swap)

TABLE 5-1 • Selected Interest Rates

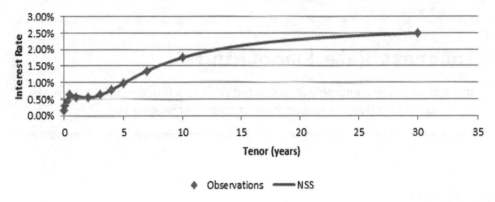

FIGURE 5-3 · Interest Rate Interpolation

that this fitting formula is fairly complex is because six-month interest rates are commonly higher than one-year rates. In this approach, interest rates are assumed to follow a trend where rates rise between overnight and six months and hit a local high value at six months. After the six-month mark, rates fall slightly before steadily rising again.

The Nelson–Siegel–Svensson Model:

$$NSS\,(T, B_0, B_1, B_2, t_1, t_2) = B_0 + B_1 \left(\frac{[1 - \exp(-\frac{T}{t_1})]}{T/t_1} - \exp(-\frac{T}{t_1}) \right) + B_2 \left(\frac{[1 - \exp(-\frac{T}{t_2})]}{T/t_2} - \exp(-\frac{T}{t_2}) \right) \quad (5.2)$$

where

- T is the time to maturity in years
- B_0, B_1, B_2, B_3, t_1, and t_2 are regression coefficients computed by minimizing the sum of squared errors with a non-linear solver.

The NSS function described above defines a line that is compared to the interest rate observations. The difference between the observation and the NSS defined line is the *error* of each point. A non-linear optimizer can be used to find the parameters (B_0, B_1, B_2, B_3, t_1, and t_2) that best match the observed interest rates.

While widely used, this type of interpolation is not foolproof. Most types of smoothing algorithms make assumptions about the shape of forward interest rates. These algorithms may fail to properly fit observed data, if the observed data doesn't match assumptions about how interest rate curves operate. For example, the NSS algorithm might fail to fit an interest rate curve where the 6-month interest rate was higher than the 30-year rate. When a fitting technique fails, it is necessary to develop a new equation to describe the observed data.

Key Concept

Interest Rate Smoothing

Interest rates are commonly interpolated or fit to a functional form to make them easier to utilize in a spreadsheet or computer program.

Forward Curves

A forward curve is a set of prices, all for the same commodity, that indicate the price at which the commodity can be purchased at various dates in the future. These prices come from trades where a buyer and a seller agree on a price that will be paid in the future when the seller actually delivers the commodity to the buyer. No money changes hands up front. Forward curves derived from trading are always in nominal dollars—the price named in the contract is the actual dollars that need to be delivered (see Figure 5-4).

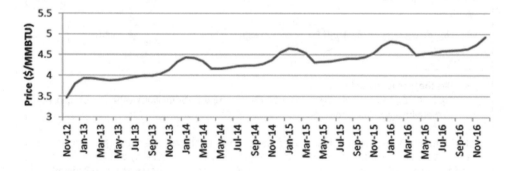

FIGURE 5-4 · Natural Gas Forward Prices

Unique to energy market forward curves is the concept of *seasonality*—a cyclical rise and fall in prices. This is commonly due to seasonal variations in supply and demand and difficulty storing products. For some products, like natural gas and electricity, storage is expensive or impossible. With other products, like gasoline and diesel fuel, seasonality in prices comes from refining practices. When a barrel of crude oil is refined, it produces both gasoline and diesel fuel. Gasoline is heavily used in the summer, which tends to glut the market with excess diesel fuel. In the winter, just the opposite happens. Diesel is used for heating, so when more crude oil is refined to meet the demand for diesel, the excess gasoline gluts the market.

Another way to describe the forward price curve is by the direction that the forward curve slopes. The two most common terms, *contango* and *backwardated*, describe whether prices in the future are higher or lower than spot prices. In a *contango* market, forward prices are higher than spot prices. In a *backwardated* market, forward prices are lower than spot prices. Due to storage costs and time value of money, the normal state of the market is contango (see Figure 5-5).

- **Contango.** A normal market with an upward sloping forward curve
- **Backwardated.** A downward sloping forward curve

Forward curves are also described by how they change over time. When looking at forward curves, there are three major types of changes that can occur in forward curves (see Figure 5-6).

- **Parallel Shift.** With a parallel shift in prices, the entire curve moves up or down.
- **Slope.** When the slope changes, the steepness of the forward curve changes.
- **Seasonality.** For commodities that are consumed, spoil, or are difficult or impossible to store, a change in the seasonality will change how prices oscillate around the annual average price.

Another aspect of energy market forward curves is how spot and forward prices work together. In most financial markets, where storage and transportation are not an issue, current spot prices are a meaningful prediction of the future. The views of every market participant about the future are incorporated into the spot market. For example, if the market consensus is that prices will rise, people will start to buy in the spot market. This will align spot and forward markets in those markets. However, commodity markets have physical constraints and work differently. Spot commodity markets are full of special cases and unusual events.

Commodity spot prices are heavily impacted by events that have no bearing on the future. For example, a trader may have erroneously chosen to take physical delivery of 1,000,000 barrels of oil rather than settling the exposure financially. If he doesn't have a storage facility lined up, he may have to sell the inventory at a fraction of the regular price. Alternately, perhaps a chemical company might need to deliver 50,000 gallons of MTBE, a gasoline additive. If a heavy rain knocked out power at the refinery producing the MTBE, spot prices could skyrocket and the chemical company would have to scramble to find an alternate supplier. In these cases, current spot prices are not an unbiased estimate of future prices.

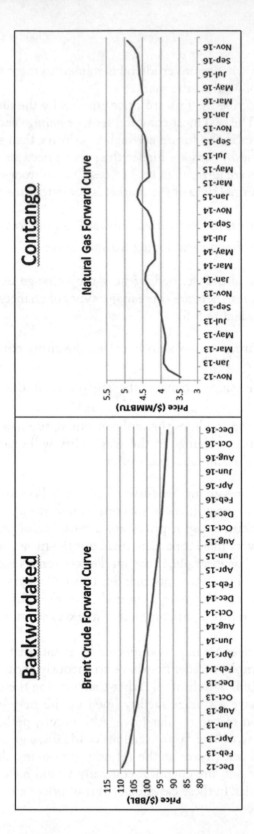

FIGURE 5-5 • Types of Slope

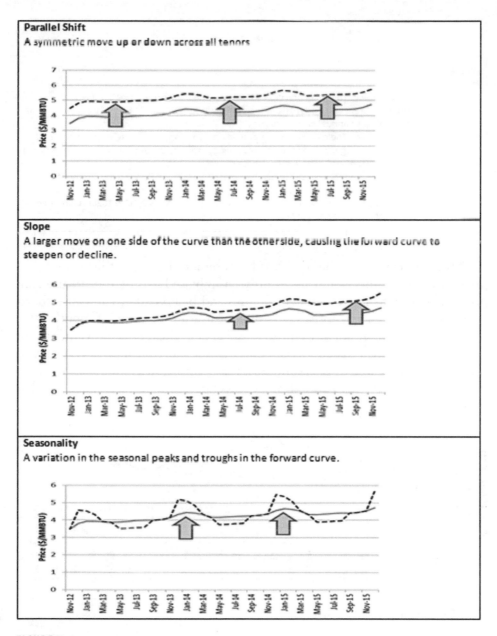

FIGURE 5-6 • Types of Curve Shifts

Extending Forward Price Curves

For financial instruments like stocks and bonds, calculating forward prices is strictly a function of time value of money. In these cases, calculating a forward price is mostly a factor of determining the cost of holding the position (carrying costs). Equation (5.3) shows the forward price formula for non-commodities.

$$FV = PV *e^{(r-q)t} \hspace{4cm} (5.3)$$

Where

PV	**Present Value.** The value of cash today
FV	**Future value.** The value that cash will be worth in the future
r	**Interest rate.** This needs to be in the same units as t (Time). The standard convention is that this is an annual interest rate.
q	**Cost of Carry.** The cost of carrying or holding a position. In the case of commodities, this might be storage, insurance costs, technology reducing production costs, or depletion of reserves leading to more expensive fuels.
t	**Time.** The standard convention is that a date 1 year in the future is 1.0, six months in the future is 0.5, and so on.
e	**Standard exponent.** An important constant (approximately 2.718281828) associated with continuous compounding.

This formula needs to be modified for commodities. First, the current spot price of a commodity is not necessarily an unbiased estimate of future spot prices. Disruptions like equipment failures and bad weather can cause short-term movements in spot prices that disappear after a couple of months. It is also necessary to filter out any type of seasonal or cyclical price movements. For commodities where a traded forward curve exists, short-term price effects typically have disappeared after six months. For example, in Figure 5-7 the prices in the curve after six months follow a cyclical pattern not observed in the first six months.

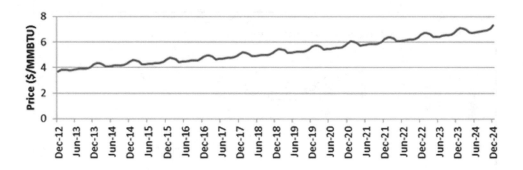

FIGURE 5-7 · Natural Gas Forward Curve

Another complication is estimating the *carrying cost* factor. For commodities, carrying cost can be related to storage and insurance. However, this term also incorporates other factors like technology improvements (which will lower costs) and depletion of easily accessible reserves (which will raise costs). Ways to estimate the cost of carry factor include the use of economic studies or examination of forward markets to determine the market-implied carrying cost.

The market-implied carrying cost can be calculated by examining the year-over-year continuously compounded returns. This calculation can also be performed on a monthly basis, if a seasonality adjustment is made to forward prices. The (r-q) term is defined in the forward price formula [Equation (5.4)]. This formula can be rearranged to solve for the carrying cost term.

Year over Year Continuously Compounded Returns	
Starting From: $Price_1 = Price_0 * e^{(r-q)T}$	(5.4)
Simplifies to: $q = r - [\ln(Price_1/Price_0)]/T$	

Calculating the log return of the prices, the interest rate term (r-q) that is currently being implied by forward prices can be calculated. The year-over-year continuously compounded returns are shown graphically in Figure 5-8.

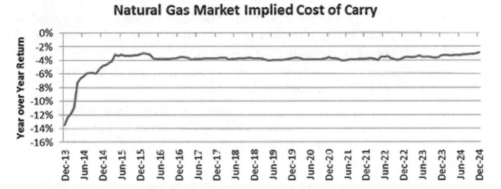

Natural Gas Market Implied Cost of Carry

FIGURE 5-8 • Year-over-Year Returns

The choice of whether to use the longest tenor implied cost of carry, the median cost over the last five years of forward contracts, or an economic study (as long as it is consistent with market observed estimates) is a judgment call. The lack of a prescribed method is due to the fact that distant parts of the forward curves are illiquid—the quality of information that the forward curve provides may not be the same at all times.

Key Concept

Extending Forward Curves

Forward curves can be extended using time value of money concepts. For many commodities, existing forward prices rather than spot prices are used for this analysis. The reason for this is that spot prices are often affected by short-term disruptions that can be expected to disappear after a period of time.

Parent/Child Curves

In many cases, when forward curves don't exist for a commodity, they might be available for similar or related commodities. In these cases, forward curves can be extended by utilizing conversion (arbitrage) relationships with similar products.

Most energy markets have a couple of industry benchmark products with liquid forward markets. These benchmarks are commonly used as "parent" curves that can be modified by expected conversion relationships to produce "child" curves representing less liquid products. For example, Brent crude has a multi-year set of crude oil forward contracts and is an international benchmark for the petroleum industry. Similar crude oils that don't have liquid forward contracts would typically be priced as a spread (or *basis*) to the Brent contract with the same expiration date.

Some common relationships used to extend forward curves are:

- Conversion Relationships: It is often possible to convert one commodity (like Fuel) into another product (like Electricity) through some type of physical process (combusting the fuel to power a generator).

- Transportation Relationships: It is often possible to physically transport a commodity at one location to another location.

- Different delivery dates (Storage): It is often possible to buy and hold (store) a commodity or to arrange future delivery (for example, buying a natural gas and renting a storage facility to store gas for 6 months) to link current and future prices.

For example, if a trader wished to develop a forward curve for Escravos Crude (a light, sweet crude oil from Nigeria) he might examine the historical relationship between Escravos crude oil and Brent crude oil (see Figure 5-9). Brent and Escravos have a similar density and sulfur content and have been priced similarly historically.

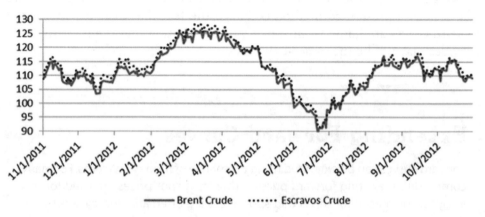

FIGURE 5-9 • Crude Prices

Over the period of one year, Escravos crude traded at a $1–$2 premium over Brent crude (see Figure 5-10). If this relationship is expected to continue into the future, this provides a way to develop a forward curve for Escravos.

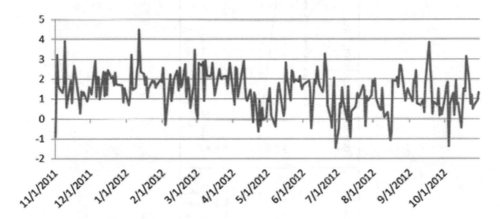

FIGURE 5-10 · Escravos–Brent Spread

There is no single way to model relationships between products. For example, it would be possible to construct a model as Escravos = Brent + spread or to calculate the market implied cost of carry as in the previous section. However, the general intuition is that related products should have similar forward curves (see Figure 5-11).

Key Concept

Parent/Child Relationships

Commodities without forward curves can be extended based on their relationship to similar products where forward curves are available.

It is important to note that when two items are closely related, changes in their prices tend to be correlated. It would be unusual to create a parent/child or even a hedging relationship between two assets where this wasn't the case. In other words, in any period where a parent curve price is rising, the child curve price should also rise. A common situation where problems occur is the transition between an existing curve and a modeled curve.

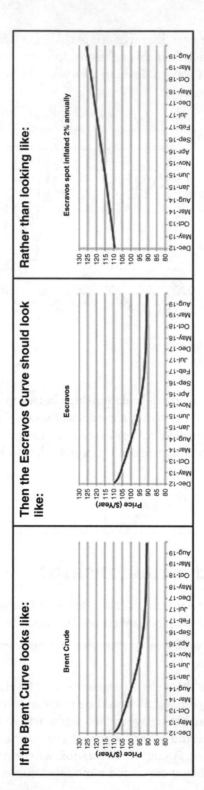

FIGURE 5-11 • Forward Curves

For example, assuming that butane and WTI crude prices are closely related, changes to butane prices should be similar to changes in WTI crude prices. However, problems commonly occur when transitioning between observed market forward curves and modeled curves (see Figure 5-12). In this example, after the forward butane curve ends, it is extended by a modeled curve (arbitrarily chosen to be two-thirds of the WTI price). In this case, a modeled price that shows butane prices falling dramatically while closely related prices (WTI prices) are constant should be viewed skeptically.

WTI/Butane Forward Curves

FIGURE 5-12 · Extending an Existing Forward Curve

Key Concept

Changes in Price

Closely related commodities typically show correlated changes in prices.

- A distinct step up or down in prices is not commonly observed in a forward curve.
- When step changes occur, it is often due to a physical constraint on the market—like a refinery explosion that causes a temporary rise in prices that is expected to disappear at some point.

Statistical Distributions

Forward prices are often thought of as the expectation of where spot prices will end up in the future. Another way to think about a forward price is as the center of a distribution of possible spot prices. The forward price is the most likely end point, but there is also a range of nearby prices where the spot price could end up with slightly lower probability. In the energy markets, the likely distribution of prices is often described using statistical terminology.

The most important description of a distribution is its *central tendency*—the values that are most likely to occur in the future. There are three common measures of central tendency: mean, median, and mode.

- **Mean.** The average value of a distribution. For a finite distribution, the mean value can be found by summing all of the values in a series and dividing by the number of observations. The mean of a series is commonly abbreviated by the lower case Greek letter mu (μ) or by the name of the series with a bar over it. This is the most commonly used measure of central tendency.
- **Median.** The middle value of a distribution. Calculating the median requires sorting the series. This is generally more complicated to calculate than an average.
- **Mode.** The most common value observed in a series. Calculating the mode requires calculating the relative frequency of each value in a series. This is also more complicated to calculate than an average.

There are also several ways to describe the uncertainty within a distribution. Uncertainty describes how much variation exists around the mean of a series. Some statistical distributions have little uncertainty and their elements are closely clustered around the mean of the series. Other distributions may have a lot of uncertainty with elements that are widely spread out (see Figure 5-13).

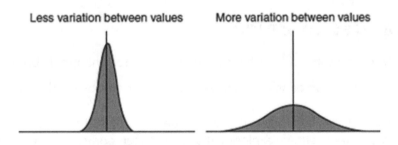

FIGURE 5-13 • Variation

The two most common measures of uncertainty are *variance* and *standard deviation*. Both of these calculations are based on calculating the square of the difference between each value and the average value as shown in Equation (5.5). The choice of using squared numbers is chosen because it is mathematically easy to calculate and results in a positive number. The downside of this approach is that values far away from the average have a disproportionate effect on the standard deviation. Standard deviation is abbreviated by the lower case Greek letter sigma, σ.

$$\text{Variance} = \sigma^2 = \frac{\sum(x_i - \bar{x})^2}{n}$$

(5.5)

$$\text{Standard Deviation} = \sigma = \sqrt{\frac{\sum(x_i - \bar{x})^2}{n}}$$

Other common descriptions of statistical distributions are skew and kurtosis. The *skew* describes the asymmetry of a distribution. If a series has zero skew, it will be symmetric around its central point. If it is skewed right (a positive skew), the right tail will be longer than the left. Similarly, if a distribution is skewed left (a negative skew), the left tail will be longer than the right. *Kurtosis* is a measure of whether the data set is peaked or flat. A data set with a high kurtosis will have a distinct peak near the mean, decline rapidly, and have wide tails. A data set with a low kurtosis will have a flattened peak (see Figure 5-14).

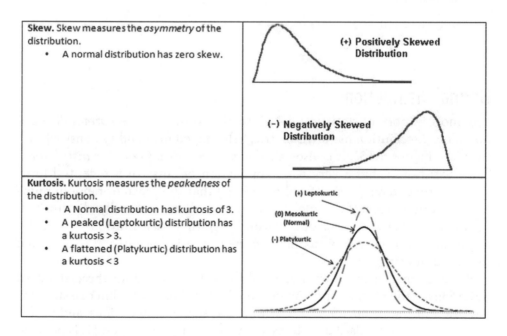

FIGURE 5-14 · Skew and Kurtosis

Key Concept

Statistical Terminology

The following terms are commonly used and need to be memorized.

- **Mean.** The average of a distribution. This is the most commonly used measure of central tendency.
- **Standard Deviation.** Standard deviation is a measure of the variation or uncertainty within a series. It is closely related to the concepts of volatility (of prices) or risk (exposure to large price moves).
- **Skew.** A measure of asymmetry in a distribution. A distribution skewed to the right is positively skewed. For example, a positively skewed distribution is commonly used to model prices, since prices can go infinitely high but can't go negative.
- **Kurtosis.** A measure of peakedness. A sharply peaked series (looks like a witch's hat) will have a kurtosis > 3.
- **Excess Kurtosis.** Excess Kurtosis = Kurtosis −3. Since normal distributions are the most common distribution, kurtosis is often reported as *excess kurtosis*, the amount of kurtosis in excess of a comparable normal distribution.

Normal Distribution

The most important statistical distribution is known as the *normal distribution*. This distribution has a symmetric, bell-shaped probability density function (see Figure 5-15). It is also called a *bell curve* or a *Gaussian distribution*. This distribution has a very wide application because of the central limit theorem that states (with a few limitations) that the mean of random numbers sampled from the same distribution will be normally distributed. To financial markets, a second feature of normal distributions is equally important—it is very easy to calculate the derivative or integral of a normal distribution using Calculus.

For a normal distribution, nearly all the values lie within three standard deviations of the mean. Approximately 68.3% of values are within one standard deviation of the mean, 95.5% are within two standard deviations, and 99.7% are within three standard deviations. Using these approximations, it is possible to estimate standard deviations from sampling. For example, if 95% of the samples fall within the range +10 to −10, and the distribution is known to be normal, the standard deviation is approximately 5.

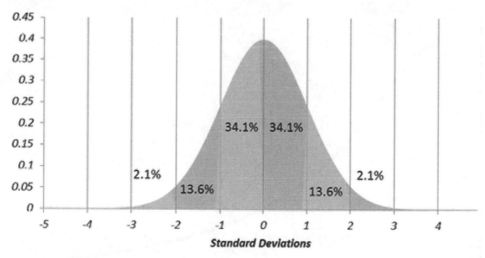

FIGURE 5-15 • Normal Distribution

Normal Distribution

The normal distribution is commonly used to model complex distributions due to its broad applicability and ease of use. In the financial markets, percent changes in price are often modeled as normally distributed. Assuming that a distribution is approximately normal simplifies calculation but runs the danger of not accurately describing the distribution.

- **One sigma.** Approximately 68.3% of values are within one standard deviation of the mean.
- **Two sigma.** Approximately 95.5% of values are within two standard deviations of the mean.
- **Three sigma.** Approximately 99.7% of values are within three standard deviations of the mean.
- **Standard Normal.** A standard normal distribution has a mean equal to 0 and a standard deviation of 1.

Lognormal Distribution

Another distribution that is commonly encountered in financial markets is the lognormal distribution. A lognormal distribution is a continuous probability function of a random variable whose logarithm is normally distributed. Lognormal distributions are important to investors because in the financial markets, lognormal distributions are commonly used as simple models of prices (see Figure 5-16).

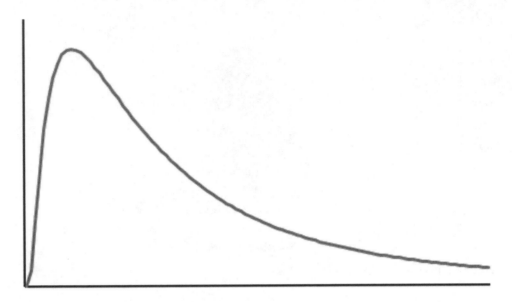

FIGURE 5-16 · Lognormal Distribution

A common assumption is that commodity prices can go to zero, can't go negative, and that they can increase arbitrarily high. For example, oil prices might be at $100/BBL and rise to $400/BBL, but there is no chance of a downward move that takes prices to –$200/BBL. In other words, the distribution of possible prices is skewed to the right and is not symmetrical around the current price. This isn't always the case (electricity prices *can* go negative every so often), but is still a fairly good approximation.

One simple model that incorporates this intuition about price movements is to assume that percentage changes in prices are normally distributed. That way, when prices start to fall, the change in price gets smaller and smaller. When prices start to rise, the movements get larger. When continuously compounded returns are normally distributed, prices are lognormally distributed. This happens because continuously compounded returns are calculated by returns = $\ln(\text{price}_1/\text{price}_0)$.

Key Concept

Lognormal Distribution

In the financial markets, prices are commonly modeled using lognormal distributions. This is the result of the assumption that percent changes in value are assumed to follow a normal distribution.

• Lognormal distributions are skewed to the right.

- The assumption that prices are lognormal is approximately correct for many financial products and widely used.
- Modeling prices as lognormally distributed is a simplification of real life and does not capture every possible price movement. It is only an approximation.

Volatility

As discussed above, variance (σ^2) is how uncertainty is measured in statistics. Applied to a time series, variance is cumulative—it always increases over time. In other words, the further you get from the starting point, the less certainty you will have of being in a specific location. This gives rise to another financial concept, *volatility*. In a mathematical sense, volatility (σ) is the rate at which uncertainty accumulates over time. Because they are closely related, the same symbol (the lower-case Greek letter sigma, σ) is used to represent both volatility and variance.

Since volatility is a rate of change, it depends on the time horizon over which it is measured. Most commonly, volatility is modeled as a specific type of diffusion process, called a Weiner Process or Brownian Motion. In this types of process, which will be most commonly referred to as a *random walk* in this book, volatility will scale with the square root of time. In the simplest type of this process, prices have a 50/50 probability of going up or down one unit. After one period, prices will either rise or fall. However, after two periods, there is a 25% chance that prices will have gone up twice, a 50% chance that prices will be back at zero, and a 25% chance that prices will have gone down twice (see Figure 5-17).

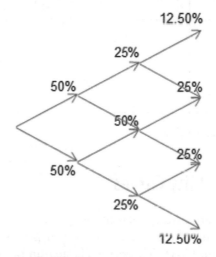

FIGURE 5-17 • A Random Walk

In the financial markets, volatility is typically represented as an annualized number that can then be scaled to other time horizons as needed. The continuously compounded return (also known as the *logarithmic returns* or *log return*) can be found by the formula shown in Equation (5.6):

$$Daily\ Return\ (for\ Day\ T) = \ln\left(\frac{Price_T}{Price_{T-1}}\right) \qquad (5.6)$$

Taking the daily change in the log of daily prices will produce a series of daily returns. The daily volatility is defined as the standard deviation of the daily returns. Assuming that returns are normally distributed, the annual return can be calculated by multiplying the daily return by the square root of time. Some thought needs to be given to how many days are involved. For example, there are typically 252 trading days (non-holiday weekdays) in a year. For commodities that trade five days a week, scaling will be based on non-holiday weekdays rather than calendar days, as shown in Equation (5.7).

$$Annual\ Return = \sqrt{252} * StdDev\ (Daily\ Returns)$$

or more generally (in mathematical notation)

$$\sigma_T = \sigma\sqrt{T} \qquad (5.7)$$

where T = the time horizon difference between original and final units.

Some examples of volatility scaling are shown in Table 5-2.

Conversion	Formula	Assumption
Trading Days to Monthly	$\sigma_{Monthly} = \sigma_{Daily}\sqrt{21}$	21 trading days a month
Monthly to Annual	$\sigma_{Annual} = \sigma_{Monthly}\sqrt{12}$	12 months a year
Annual to Monthly	$\sigma_{Monthly} = \frac{\sigma_{Annual}}{\sqrt{12}}$	12 months a year

TABLE 5-2 · Volatility Scaling Examples

Extending Forward Volatility Curves

In the context of forward prices, volatility is typically used as an input to models that need to describe the likely dispersion of prices at some point in the future as shown in Figure 5-18. There are a large number of models that can be

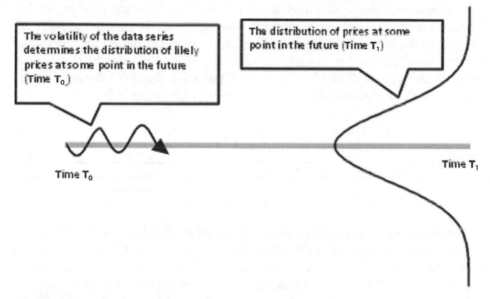

FIGURE 5-18 • Volatility Creates a Dispersion of Future Prices

used to do this task. Each volatility value is specific to the model for which it is designed. The volatility used for one model (perhaps a Markov random-walk process) will be different than the volatility parameter used by any other model (like an Ornstein–Uhlenbeck mean-reverting process).

In the energy market, a variety of volatility models are commonly used. Models tend to be chosen for convenience. The reason for this is that energy options (the type of financial contracts where volatility is important) are almost exclusively based on futures rather than the underlying commodity. Futures can't be exercised early. As a result, accurately describing the possible path that energy prices take to their final destination is generally less important than describing the final distribution of prices at the expiration date.

Key Concept

Volatility

For forward prices, volatility is a parameter used to describe the dispersion of prices in the future.

- Volatility is model dependent.
- There are different types of volatility.
- A variety of volatility models are used, although models assuming that returns are normally distributed (follow a random walk) are the most common.

As mentioned above, volatility is model specific. There are a variety of different ways to calculate volatility. Each way will result in a value for volatility that is specific to a certain type of model. The values calculated for one model can't be used for another model. For example, when analyzing historical spot prices, volatility is typically defined as the standard deviation of the logarithmic (continuously compounded) returns as shown in Equation (5.8).

$$\sigma = StdDev\left(\left[\ln\left(\frac{P_1}{P_0}\right)\right]\right) \tag{5.8}$$

Where

σ	Volatility (abbreviated as the Greek letter "sigma")
P_n	Price at Time n
$\ln()$	Natural Logarithm function

Historical volatility can't be used in a forward model that assumes that price returns are a random walk unless historical prices actually followed a random walk. The amount of error caused by using the wrong volatility measure will depend on how different the historical prices were from a random walk.

By convention, *implied volatility* or *forward volatility* typically refers to the volatility that could be used to solve a Black–Scholes genre option model. Volatility meant for other models will commonly specify that it is intended for another model, as in an *Ornstein–Uhlenbeck volatility*. Black–Scholes style models assume that price returns are normally distributed and follow a random-walk process. This is a convenient approximation for a number of reasons. First, it is relatively easy to scale volatility over different periods for a random walk. For a random walk, volatility scales with the square root of time. Second, it gives a standard convention for valuing many different assets with one set of calculations.

Constant Volatility Implies Dispersion Grows Over Time

If forward implied volatility for an asset is constant over all time frames, this implies that the expected dispersion of the asset is increasing with the square root of time. This is a characteristic of a Wiener (random walk) process. In other words, it is possible to calculate the dispersion of the expected distribution at any future point as shown in Equation (5.9). The most common measure of dispersion is standard devision (σ).

Volatility Scaling

$$\sigma_T = \sigma_{annual}\sqrt{T} \tag{5.9}$$

Where
T = time (in the same units of volatility, typically an annualized number)

For example, the standard deviation of the expected distribution of prices at time T − 2 is the square root of two (1.414214) times the volatility at time T = 1. In other words, with a random walk, the uncertainty of prices grows over time and its accumulation is defined by the volatility (see Figure 5-19).

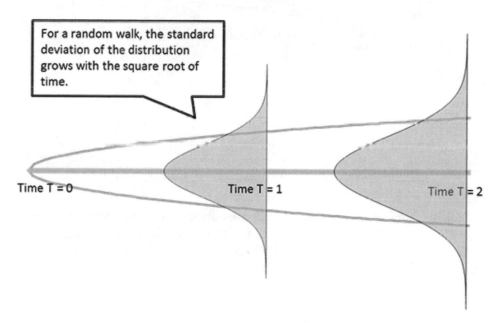

For a random walk, the standard deviation of the distribution grows with the square root of time.

Time T = 0   Time T = 1   Time T = 2

FIGURE 5-19 • Constant Implied Volatility

Constant Dispersion Implies that Volatility Falls Over Time

If the asset doesn't actually follow a random walk, the assumption about dispersion increasing with the square root of time isn't valid. The disconnection between reality and model choice can be corrected by using a forward implied volatility curve rather than a constant volatility term. A common way to reconcile reality with option pricing model assumptions can be done by forcing the implied volatility (using random walk assumptions) to decline over time.

For example, if the amount of dispersion is constant for all time periods (perhaps dispersion is a random spread around a fixed cost of production), the implied volatility (under random walk assumptions) will have to decline over time (see Figure 5-20).

Calibrating a Model Based on Forward Data

When a model has sufficient forward implied volatility estimates that can be observed from options trading, it is possible to observe how the market is correcting for the differences between reality and option model assumptions. It is then

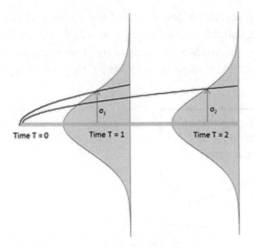

FIGURE 5-20 · Constant Dispersion Implies Volatility Falls Over Time

possible to characterize how quickly the volatility is observed to fall off over time. Instead of falling off with the square root of time, the fall off can be estimated as some other term (see Figure 5-21). This term is commonly called a *Lévy stability exponent*, and is abbreviated by the small Greek letter alpha, α.

$$\sigma_T = \sigma_{annual} T^{(1/\alpha)}$$

FIGURE 5-21 · Lévy Stability Exponent

A common way to calculate a Lévy stability exponent is to use an optimizer to match a smooth curve to the observed forward volatility curve (see Figure 5.22).

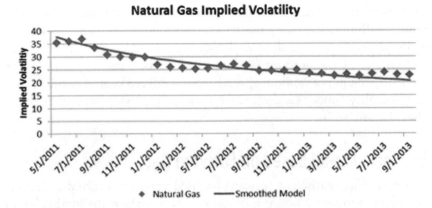

FIGURE 5-22 · An Optimizer Fits a Lévy Stability Exponent to Observed Data

As with any model that is fit through optimization, it is useful to examine the residual errors to improve the explanatory power of the model. In the case of this example, the asset, natural gas, is difficult to store and is used most heavily during the winter for heating. As a result, there is a seasonal effect on implied volatility. In this case, an analysis of the residual errors is used to create a correction factor on top of the Lévy alpha modeling (see Figure 5-23).

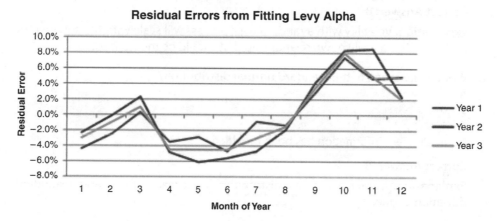

FIGURE 5-23 · Residual errors need to be analyzed after fitting Lévy alpha.

It should be noted that not all commodities will have cyclical residual errors. There is no general approach to determining the cause of the errors except understanding the nuances of the commodity being traded.

QUIZ

1. **If price returns follow a random walk, volatility will scale with:**
   A. The cube root of time
   B. The square root of time
   C. Time
   D. The square of time

   Correct Answer: B

   Explanation: Volatility with a random walk process will scale with the square root of time. This is a well-known relationship that should be memorized.

2. **What is the mean of the standard normal distribution?**
   A. −1
   B. 0
   C. 1
   D. Insufficient information has been provided

   Correct Answer: B

   Explanation: A standard normal distribution has a mean of zero and a standard deviation of one.

3. **In a financial model that assumes that prices are lognormally distributed, what kind of skew is exhibited by the lognormal distribution?**
   A. Positive
   B. Negative
   C. Zero
   D. Insufficient information to answer the question

   Correct Answer: A

   Explanation: The distribution will be skewed to the right (a positive skew). Prices can rise perpetually, but cannot go below zero in these models.

4. **Calculate the present value of $100 payable in 5 years at a 2% interest rate.**
   A. $110.41
   B. $90.48
   C. $105.12
   D. $95.14

   Correct Answer: B

   Explanation: The formula for present valuing is $PV = FV \times \exp(-r \times T)$. In this case, the Future value (FV) is $100. The interest rate (r) is 0.02, and the time (T) is 5. Placing numbers into the formula $PV = 100 \times \exp(-.02 \times 5)$. If you don't have a calculator with a standard exponent function, looking at the answers can help eliminate some answers. Present values are usually less than future values, which eliminates answers A and C.

5. Angela, a trader at an oil company, is looking to develop a forward price for a non-traded commodity. She would like to use observed market prices in related products. What kind of product relationships should she consider?
   A. Products that can be converted into the non-traded commodity
   B. Forward curves for the non-traded commodity at other locations
   C. Prices for the non-traded commodity at different time periods
   D. All of the above

Correct Answer: D

Explanation: A variety of different physical relationships can be used to model prices for non-traded commodities based on traded forward curves.

6. When extending forward curves using time value of money concepts, what factors should be considered in the estimate of the cost of carry term?
   A. Storage and insurance costs
   B. The effect of technology changes
   C. Depletion of low-cost sources
   D. All of the above

Correct Answer: D

Explanation: The cost of carry term is a catch-all that incorporates all of these factors. It is also possible to break these factors into individual components as this can make an analysis clearer.

7. How much excess kurtosis does a distribution exhibit if it has a kurtosis = 5?
   A. 0
   B. 2
   C. 3
   D. 5

Correct Answer: B

Explanation: Excess kurtosis is kurtosis in excess of the kurtosis in a normal distribution. A normal distribution has a kurtosis of 3, so the excess kurtosis is $5 - 3 - 2$.

8. If an economic report does not consider risk-free inflation in an economic analysis of supply and demand fundamentals, what kind of units are the prices?
   A. Present value dollars
   B. Future value dollars
   C. Nominal dollars
   D. Constant dollars

Correct Answer: D

Explanation: When future prices do not incorporate time value of money concepts like risk-free inflation, they are said to be in constant (or real) dollars. This may also be reported as dollars as of a specific year ("2012 dollars") or as *real dollars*.

9. Kai, an analyst working on a trading desk, has been asked by the head of risk management to calculate an implied volatility curve for a random walk process. Can he use a Black–Scholes implied volatility calculator to perform this calculation?
   A. Yes
   B. No

Correct Answer: A

Explanation: This question requires knowledge that an assumption in the Black–Scholes option model is that price returns follow a random walk. As a result, the volatility calculation and its intended model usage will be the same.

10. As defined in economic literature, an efficient market with fair prices has which of the following features:
   A. A large number of buyers and sellers
   B. Prices legislatively determined by a regulatory body
   C. Buyers and sellers who are happy
   D. Extremely limited or no opportunity for risk-free profits

Correct Answer: D

Explanation: Fair, in an economic sense, means that no one can make a riskless profit at the expense of other market participants.

Chapter 6

Swaps, Forwards, and Futures

Energy investors can directly speculate on the price of commodities going up or down by purchasing commodity futures, forwards, or commodity swaps.

- **Futures.** A commodity contract traded on an exchange that will involve physical delivery of a commodity if the contract is held until the expiration date. These are highly standardized contracts.

- **Forward.** A forward is similar to a futures contract except that it is negotiated directly between two traders. Because they are individually negotiated, forwards can be more customized than futures. In most cases, forwards are traded for contracts where there is insufficient liquidity (not enough buyers and sellers) for an exchange-based contract.

- **Commodity Swap.** A futures or forward contract where the payment is settled in cash rather than physical delivery.

CHAPTER OBJECTIVES

After completing this chapter, the student should have an understanding of

- Futures, forwards, and swap contracts
- Margining
- Types of exchange orders

Direct Investments in Commodities

Future contracts (*futures*), forward contracts (*forwards*), and commodity swaps (*swaps*) are a financial contract between two parties to buy or sell a specific amount of a commodity for a fixed price (the *strike price*) for delivery at a specific point in the future (the *delivery date*). These are direct investments that will make or lose money based on movement in commodities prices. Futures are negotiated on a futures exchange which acts as a central gathering place and intermediary between buyer and seller. Forwards are contracts that are negotiated directly between buyers and sellers. Swaps are similar to futures and forwards, but instead of delivering the commodity, the contract is settled in cash. Other than a refundable security deposit (called margin) to ensure creditworthiness and ability to deliver on a contract, these contracts don't cost any money up front.[1]

Key Concept

Strike Prices

The value in a future, forward, or commodity swap contract comes from a difference between the transaction price (the strike price) and the market price at the time of delivery.

Some contracts don't specify a fixed strike price and instead state that the transaction will occur at the market price on the expiration date of the contract. These contracts don't have value—they will always be an exchange of one item (the commodity) for another item (cash) of equal value. As a result, there is zero financial value to this contract.

The value of these futures, forwards, and commodity swaps is determined by some other asset (the *underlying* asset). These investments are also contracts. The term *contract* is used because owning a contract to buy a commodity (like crude oil or cattle) is different than actually owning the commodity. For one thing, unlike buying a physical commodity, entering into a contract generally doesn't require cash up front. In addition, a contract will expire at some point in time. Third, compared to trading a physical commodity, it is relatively easy to buy and sell a contract since physical delivery is not involved.

The party obligated to take possession of the physical commodity is the buyer of the contract. At delivery, the buyer will pay the seller the agreed-upon price for the commodity. The party obligated to deliver the asset in the future is called the seller of the contract. Typically, the buyer is long the underlying commodity (the buyer benefits if the price rises) and the seller is short (the seller benefits if the price declines).

> **Example:** On October 25th, 2014, Alphonse and Betty agree to sign a contract obligating Alphonse to buy 100 barrels of crude oil at $100 per barrel from Betty on July 1st, 2016. Alphonse, the buyer, will benefit if crude oil prices rise. He could pay $100/barrel to Betty and then immediately resell the crude oil at market prices for a profit. In contrast, Betty would benefit from a decline in prices.

To a large degree, futures, forwards, and commodity swaps are all highly standardized. Each contract is required to deliver a standard quantity and quality of a specific product at a specific location. For example, each NYMEX crude oil futures contract requires the seller to deliver 1,000 barrels of light, sweet crude oil to Cushing, Oklahoma. Everyone trading that contract has the same quantity, quality, and location restrictions. This standardization makes it possible to buy a futures contract, resell it, and have all of the contractual terms perfectly offset. The only change in the contract is the price at which it gets bought or sold.

Some of the terms and key features commonly specified in contracts include:

- **Quantity.** Quantity describes the amount of the underlying commodity that needs to be delivered upon expiration of the contract.
- **Currency.** The contract will specify which currency must be used by the buyer to pay the seller.
- **Grade (Quality).** The quality of the commodity will be specified. For example, a crude oil contract will specify an acceptable sulfur content and API gravity.
- **Location.** The delivery location and the acceptable manner of delivery will be specified in the futures contract.
- **Delivery Date.** The date that the commodity must be delivered to the buyer is called the delivery date. In many cases, there will be a month-long window or a period of time specified for delivery.

- **Expiration Date.** Futures will cease to trade before delivery. At that point, anyone who still owns a contract will be obligated to make or accept physical delivery. The majority of futures contracts are liquidated prior to this date.

When these contracts are traded, there is always a buyer and a seller. This is true even for exchange-traded products (futures). The exchange does not trade on its own behalf—it is acting as an intermediary between buyer and seller. As a result, when futures expire there are always equal numbers of buyers and sellers. Each type of contract will specify how buyers and sellers are matched up for delivery.

For private investors, futures are the most commonly traded type of contract. This is because individual investors typically don't want to take physical delivery and futures are the easiest trade to liquidate. Most futures are liquidated through trading rather than through physical delivery. When a future is liquidated through trading, an offsetting contract is purchased or sold to cancel out the original contract. For example, a trader may have bought a futures contract at $110. The trader can sell another contract (which is identical to the contract that was purchased) to liquidate the position. The exchange will keep track of each trader's net position and only match up buyers and sellers with open positions.

Bilateral trades, like forwards, are much harder to liquidate through trading. These are contracts that are negotiated directly between a buyer and a seller. As a result, an offsetting transaction has to be done with the original counterparty. On the other hand, forwards can be more easily customized than futures, so this makes arranging delivery substantially easier.

In other cases, some contracts (*commodity swaps*) might specify a financial settlement rather than physical delivery. With a swap contract, there is no physical transfer of a commodity. The price of the underlying commodity will be compared to the strike price of the contract at the expiration date, and the difference will be settled up in cash. For example, if a Henry Hub natural gas contract with a strike of $5 were financially settled against a commodity price of $6, the seller would end up paying the buyer $1 ($6 − $5 = $1). If a Henry Hub natural gas contract with a strike price of $5 were financially settled against a commodity price of $2, the buyer would pay the seller $3 ($2 − $5 = −$3). In the energy market, contracts with financial settlement are typically called *swaps*.[2]

With commodity contracts, it is important to determine whether the contract will require an actual physical transfer of a commodity or whether the net obligation will be settled in cash.

- **Physical Delivery.** With physical delivery, the seller of the futures contract will need to deliver a physical commodity to the buyer. The buyer will need to pay the seller at this point. For example, a seller needs to deliver 1,000 barrels of WTI crude oil to the buyer for $100/barrel. The seller needs to deliver the oil and the buyer needs to pay $1,000,000 to the seller.

- **Financial Delivery (Cash Settlement).** With a financial delivery, the buyer and seller settle their obligations in cash. For example, if a seller has to deliver 1,000 barrels of oil worth $98/BBL compared to a reference price of $100/BBL, the buyer will need to pay the seller $2/BBL ($2,000). From a credit perspective, financial settlement has a much lower risk than physical delivery, since the actual cash changing hands is much smaller. This is typically called a *commodity swap*, because the buyer and seller are exchanging cash flows—the seller pays the buyer $98 (the floating price), and the buyer pays the seller $100 (the fixed price), for a net of a $2 payment per barrel.

Key Concept

Futures, Forwards, and Swaps

Futures, forwards, and commodity swaps allow buyers and sellers to arrange transactions on commodities at a specific time and place in the future. These contracts allow market participants to directly speculate on commodity prices.

- **Futures.** Futures are traded on an exchange. Most futures are liquidated through trading rather than physical delivery and are commonly used by private investors to speculate on commodity prices.
- **Forwards.** Forwards are contracts directly between a buyer and a seller. They involve increased credit risk but can be more customized than futures. Forwards are commonly used when physical delivery is desired by both parties.
- **Commodity Swaps.** Swaps will settle in cash rather than in delivery of a physical commodity.

Forward Contracts

Forward contracts are private agreements directly between a buyer and a seller. Like futures and commodity swaps, forwards allow traders to arrange a transaction at a specific time and place in the future for a contractually identified price. Negotiating a contract directly has both advantages and disadvantages.

Some of the advantages of forwards are the ability to create contracts for products and locations where futures are not actively traded. As privately negotiated contracts, forwards can also be customized to meet specific requirements that each trading partner wants in the contract. There are also disadvantages to negotiating directly with a counterparty—each trader is exposed to the credit risk of their counterparty.

In practice, most forwards are highly standardized with terms and conditions similar to futures contracts. They are traded under standard contractual terms like the ones specified in the International Swap Dealers Associations (ISDA) Master Agreement. This makes the contracts much easier to transact, since a team of lawyers isn't needed to review every contract.

- **Private Contracts.** In order to cancel the contract, an offsetting transaction must be made with the original counterparty.
- **Credit Risk.** Each trader depends on the other trader to meet their obligations.
- **Settlement at delivery.** Forwards typically have zero value on the trade date since they are commonly an agreement to transfer a commodity for its equivalent in cash. Forwards acquire value when the value of the commodity changes and the cash price stays fixed. As a result, there is very little up-front cost involved in trading forwards.
- **Delivery will commonly take place.** Forwards are commonly physically delivered.

Forward contract example

On June 1, 2012, Andrew a trader at Widgets4You, Inc., agreed to purchase 50,000 gallons of widget fuel from Barry, a trader at WidgetFuel Co., at a price of $100/gallon for delivery in a barge in New York Harbor on December 1, 2012. Andrew identified that Barry wanted to trade using a broker who introduced Andrew to Barry. For providing this service, Andrew paid the broker a small fee for introducing him to Barry. Andrew and Barry negotiated a deal and signed a trade contract, the key details of which are summarized in Table 6-1.

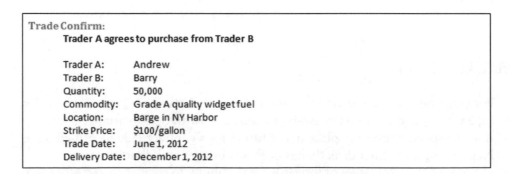

Trade Confirm:
Trader A agrees to purchase from Trader B

Trader A:	Andrew
Trader B:	Barry
Quantity:	50,000
Commodity:	Grade A quality widget fuel
Location:	Barge in NY Harbor
Strike Price:	$100/gallon
Trade Date:	June 1, 2012
Delivery Date:	December 1, 2012

TABLE 6-1 • Trade Confirm

The prevailing forward price for Grade A widget fuel on July 1 for December delivery was $100, so the contract was signed at fair value. As a result, there was no payment made between Andrew and Barry on the trade date.

On December 1, the spot price for widget fuel had fallen to $90. As a result, the contract represents an above-market sale from Barry to Andrew. To Andrew, the contract is worth −$10/gallon (a loss of $500,000) since he is paying $10 more per gallon for the spot price of fuel. To Barry, the contract is worth +$10/gallon (a gain of $500,000) since he is receiving $10 more per gallon than he would be able to receive on the spot market.

On expiration,

- Andrew pays Barry $5,000,000 (50,000 gallons × $100/gallon).
- Barry delivers 50,000 gallons of Grade A widget fuel to Andrew.

Note that the actual value of the contract ($500,000) created by the difference between the spot price on delivery ($90) and the strike price of the contract ($100) doesn't affect the agreed-upon transaction. Unless Andrew or Barry had an offsetting transaction to buy or sell on the spot market, the fair value of the contract doesn't affect cash flows or delivery. In most cases, Andrew probably needed the fuel (perhaps he needed fuel for the widgets he was selling) and Barry already had the fuel on hand (Barry might be in the refining business).

The forward contract allowed Andrew and Barry to lock in the price of the fuel prior to delivery. This may have been helpful for both parties. Andrew may have agreed to sell a large order of widgets and the fuel needed to operate them to one of his customers. By locking in a fuel price, he may have been able to pass that cost directly to the client. If he had waited to buy fuel on the spot market, he might have made additional profit, but also risked losing money if prices had risen. As a refiner, Barry also may have benefited from being able to arrange a sale of a known quantity of fuel ahead of time.

Key Concept

Forwards

Forwards are nontransferable contracts directly between a buyer and a seller that allow traders interested in physical delivery the ability to lock in prices and volumes at some point in the future.

Forward trades and credit risk

One of the major drawbacks to forward trades is the counterparty credit risk that comes from a direct agreement between a buyer and a seller. In the previous example, each trader relies on the other party to meet their obligations. The buyer, Andrew, might need a large quantity of relatively rare fuel to meet his other obligations. If he doesn't have the fuel needed, he might miss delivery to his client (who is purchasing both widgets and widget fuel). The seller, Barry, might also need this sale. Not only has he locked in a good price, he might not be able to sell a large quantity of fuel into the spot market without collapsing the market.

To minimize credit risk, traders that are involved in forward trading may require margin or other guarantees (like evidence of a guaranteed line of credit from a bank) from the other trader in order to make a transaction. Another way to limit credit risk with forwards is to use an exchange-based OTC clearing service. With this type of service, the trading partners arrange the trade themselves and then record the trade with the exchange. The exchange becomes the counterparty to each trader, essentially converting the forward into a future (see Figure 6-1).

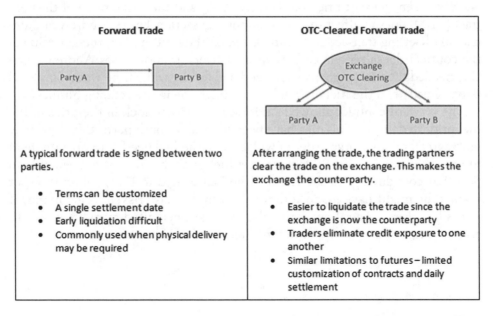

FIGURE 6-1 • OTC Clearing

Another way for forward traders to reduce credit risk is to transact under *a master netting agreement*. With a master netting agreement, trading partners will sign a single agreement that will govern all the transactions between the two companies (this is the *master agreement*). This agreement won't initially have any trades, but each subsequent transaction will become a portion of this larger agreement. This allows traders to net cash flows payable on the same day and in the same currency. It allows traders who do a lot of business with one another to reduce their gross exposure to one another.

Key Concept

Master Netting Agreement

Master netting agreements allow trading partners to net payments made on the same day and in the same currency. This is vital to trading, since risk reserves only need to be taken against the net exposure payable rather than the gross cash flows.

Futures and Margining

When traders transact on an exchange, they can submit orders to the exchange indicating their willingness to buy and sell anonymously. The exchange will consolidate all of these orders into a trading book, and whenever there is an overlap between where someone is willing to buy and someone else is willing to sell, a transaction will occur. The buyer and seller won't actually know the identity of the other party—the exchange will serve as the counterparty for each trader (see Figure 6-2).

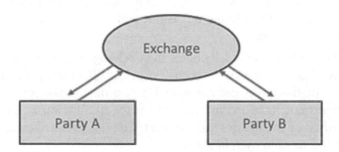

FIGURE 6-2 • An Exchange

By acting as an intermediary, the exchange takes on credit risk that each trader will be able to meet its obligations. Exchanges have developed a variety of methods to minimize these risks. First, the exchange will require that every trader posts a certain amount of collateral, called an *initial margin*, on the trade date. Typically, this will be a percentage of the contract's value (usually between 5% and 15% of the value) corresponding to the size of a very large one-day move in prices. Then, the exchange will feature a cash settlement of the contracts every day prior to expiration. This will result in a daily gain or loss for each investor that will be credited or debited from their accounts, called *daily margin.* Since there are always the same number of buyers and sellers, this involves a reallocation of money. In the event that a trader is required to post additional daily margin and is unable to do so, the exchange will liquidate their trading position on the next trading day. Assuming that prices move less than the initial margin, the exchange will have sufficient collateral to cover the one day of potential losses.

Most individual investors will not trade directly on an exchange. Instead, they will use a broker who will transact on their behalf. The clearing margin charged by the exchange is a financial safeguard to ensure that brokers meet their obligations related to their customers' open futures and options contracts. Typically, brokers will pass those costs along to their clients. As a result, even though clearing margins charged by an exchange are distinct from customer margins that individual buyers and sellers of futures are required to deposit with brokers, they serve much the same purpose.

Margin is not a down payment nor is it representative of the trader's position in the actual commodity. It is insurance for the exchange in case a trader can't meet their obligations. Sometimes margin is described as a *performance bond*, a *good-faith deposit*, or *earnest money*. This money is refunded when a position is closed.

- **Initial Margin.** Initial margin is the minimum amount of equity needed to establish or maintain a futures position. Money in a margin account in excess of the initial margin required for open positions can be withdrawn from the account or used to open new positions. This excess money is called excess equity, although it is not technically an equity (ownership) position in anything.

- **Daily Settlement.** On a daily basis, the exchange will settle all future positions, marking the position to market prices. Essentially, this is similar to closing out the trade and reopening it at a new strike price. As a result, futures do not have a constant strike price like forwards. Every day, the strike price of the futures will be reset. The net proceeds will be credited or debited to each margin account.

- **Settlement Price.** The settlement price is the price chosen by the exchange clearinghouse to value all of the contracts that day. The exchange settlement price may or may not be equal to the closing price (the price of last trade of the day). This discrepancy can occur in cases where a large number of trades gets executed on the market close, or when there is limited trading. In those cases, settlement prices may be chosen by the exchange based on models or other methodology.

- **Maintenance Margin (Daily Margin).** If the daily settlement has resulted in excess money in a margin account, it can be withdrawn. If the amount of money in the margin account has fallen too low, more money will need to be deposited. A *margin call* will alert the trader that additional money needs to be deposited into the account.

In most cases, daily margin is expected to be paid and received on the same day that margin is called. If a margin call is issued and not paid, the exchange has the right to close sufficient positions to meet the margin call. This can present problems for investors trying to manage their cash flows. For example, if an oil well sells crude oil futures and prices move higher, the oil well may have to pay daily on their futures contracts before the crude oil is extracted and ready to sell.

Key Concept

Futures

Futures are standardized, transferable contracts that allow traders to transact for future delivery. They are typically margined and cash settled on a daily basis until the final delivery date.

- Futures are often used for speculation.
- Most futures are liquidated prior to physical delivery.
- Futures are margined.
- Daily settlement can create cash flows throughout the life of the contract.

Types of Futures Orders

For efficiency, exchanges will limit the types of orders that can be executed by the exchange. This is different than bilateral contracts (like forwards) where terms can be individually negotiated. Orders will be combined together to form a limit book.

Market Orders (MKT)

Market orders are executed as soon as possible and should receive the best price available at the time of execution. A market order specifies only the contract (commodity, delivery date) and the action to be taken (either buy or sell). As soon as the order reaches the exchange, it is executed at the best possible price.

- Market orders are the most common type of order.
- Market orders are executed immediately.

Limit Orders (Limit Buy, Limit Sell)

Limit orders will specify the worst price a customer is willing to accept for an execution. For example, a buy limit order will specify the highest price that the trader is willing to accept. A sell limit order will specify the lowest price that a trader is willing to accept.

- Limit orders do not guarantee an execution.
- Limit orders will typically stay around for a while and provide the volume which market orders will be executed against.
- Limit orders have a time priority—the first trader to place a limit order at a specific price receives the first execution.

Stop Orders (Stop Buy, Stop Sell)

Stop orders convert into market orders if the market reaches or goes through a certain price level (the stop price). These are also called *contingency orders*. For example, a trader who is long 10 crude oil contracts may enter a sell stop order at $75 to limit potential losses from prices dropping below that point. Buy stop orders are placed above the current market price and will become market buy orders if the price reaches the stop price. Sell stop orders are placed below the current market price and will become market orders if the price reaches the stop price.

- Stop orders are most commonly used to protect existing investments from ongoing adverse moves.
- Stop orders can also be used to enter positions if the market hits a certain level. For example, a trader following a technical analysis strategy may wish to trigger a buy order if the market rises above some resistance level.

Stop Limit Orders

Stop limit orders combine features of both stop and limit orders. A stop limit order will turn into a limit order when a certain price (the stop price) is reached. Buy stop limit orders are placed with a stop price above current market prices and will convert to buy limit orders. Sell stop limit orders are placed with a stop price below the current market price and will convert into a sell limit order.

- Stop limit orders can protect investors from price moves due to low liquidity (a rising market triggers buy stop orders causing further rises).
- Stop limit orders do not guarantee an execution.

Market-If-Touched (MIT)

Market-If-Touched orders become market orders as soon as the market passes through a specified price—similar to stop orders. They are also called *board orders*. MIT orders are different than stop orders because MIT buy orders are placed below the market, and MIT sell orders are placed above the market. For example, a trader may wish to buy 10 crude oil contracts if prices fall below a certain level.

- MIT/board orders are similar to limit orders. The difference is that a limit order may not get executed if someone else submitted a limit order at the same price at an earlier time.
- The price on an MIT/board order is not guaranteed—the possibility of a bad price is the trade-off for a guaranteed execution.
- MIT/board orders are relatively uncommon.

Another factor in submitting futures transactions is how long the trade will exist on the exchange. Orders can be transacted at a specific time or exist for some period of time before they are triggered. By default, most orders are good only on the day which they were submitted to the exchange and go into effect immediately. However, other instructions are possible.

- **Day Orders.** All day orders are canceled if they are not executed on the day that they were entered. By default, all orders are considered day orders unless otherwise specified.
- **Good-Til-Cancelled (GTC).** GTC orders, also called open orders, remain in effect until they are canceled.
- **Fill-Or-Kill (FOK).** Fill-Or-Kill orders are immediately executed to the extent possible and then canceled. These orders don't have to be fully executed. These are similar to market orders that have a maximum (for buy orders) and minimum (for sell orders) price associated with the order.
- **Market-At-Open, Market-At-Close.** While most orders become active as soon as they are submitted, it is possible to submit orders to transact at the market open or close. Market-At-Close orders are the most common type of order that specify the trading time. As there are occasionally a large number of orders coming in quick succession on the open and close, these orders are not guaranteed to be priced at the official open or close price. These orders are only guaranteed to be executed at a price within the range of prices being traded during the open or close.

Futures Expiration Codes

Futures are often quoted in shorthand. The most common type of shorthand is a four character abbreviation indicating commodity, delivery month, and delivery year. In this type of shorthand, the first two characters of the contract name identify the underlying commodity, the third character identifies the delivery month and the last character is the last digit of the year (see Table 6-2).

Symbol	Month
F	January
G	February
H	March
J	April
K	May
M	June
N	July
Q	August
U	September
V	October
X	November
Z	December

TABLE 6-2 • Futures Codes

For example, as of 2012 and using a four-letter shorthand, CLZ6 is a NYMEX WTI crude oil contract (CL is the symbol for WTI Crude) and the expiration date is December (Z = December) 2016 (6 = 2016). This isn't necessarily a unique name, since the name would be shared with the December 2006 and December 2026 contracts.

Another common naming convention used by trading systems is to use both the exchange name and the abbreviation. For example, NYMEX might be added to the shorthand explained previous and the resulting code would be NYMEX.CLZ6 to help identify the contract. This is helpful if two exchanges both use the same symbol or if a large number of commodities on different exchanges are being traded. In this case, there is no industry-wide convention on abbreviations for exchanges.

Exchange for Physical

An exchange for physical transaction, commonly called an EFP, is a way to convert an exchange trade into a bilateral trade or vice versa.

When futures expire, buyers and sellers are matched up to arrange delivery. If traders do not wish to be randomly matched, they can negotiate an exchange for physical transaction to swap their futures for an equivalent amount of a physical commodity owned by another trader. This can allow delivery of a futures contract away from the typical exchange settlement location. EFP trades are typically negotiated off of an exchange. Once negotiated, they can then be executed on an exchange to cancel a futures position. The location for the physical commodity does not need to be identical to the futures delivery location.

In order to execute an EFP, the two parties involved in the transaction must determine the delivery location and the price differential that the physical commodity at the delivery location should have relative to the futures delivery location.

Key Concept

Exchange for Physical (EFP)

EFPs allow traders to negotiate an exchange of a physical commodity, like natural gas, for a futures contract. This negotiation occurs off of the exchange. Once negotiated, the transaction is registered with the exchange in a process called "clearing." EFP trades are commonly used to facilitate transactions at location other than the futures delivery point.

- **Delivery Location.** The parties to an EFP must determine the delivery location and delivery process.
- **Price Differential.** The parties to an EFP must determine the difference in prices at the futures delivery location and the physical delivery location.

QUIZ

1. **Which piece of information is not needed for a forward trade?**
   A. Strike price
   B. Delivery date
   C. Delivery location
   D. All of these pieces of information are needed.

   Correct Answer: D

   Explanation: All of these pieces of information, and more, are needed to make a forward trade.

2. **What type of trade does not involve physical delivery of a commodity?**
   A. Futures
   B. Forwards
   C. Commodity swaps
   D. All of the financial instruments listed involve physical delivery.

   Correct Answer: C

   Explanation: Commodity swaps are cash settled—futures and forwards are physically settled.

3. **What are ways that a forward trader can reduce counterparty risk?**
   A. Clear the forward on an exchange
   B. Require collateral or letter of credit from counterparty
   C. Execute the trade under a master netting agreement like an ISDA contract
   D. All of these approaches can help reduce counterparty credit risk.

   Correct Answer: D

   Explanation: All of these are ways that a forward trader can reduce counterparty credit risk.

4. **Which piece of information is not needed for a futures trade?**
   A. Strike price
   B. Commodity
   C. Delivery month
   D. A margin account

   Correct Answer: A

   Explanation: Information about the margin account, the commodity to trade, and the delivery date are all needed for a futures trade. The strike price will be determined by the execution price. The strike price is not part of a futures trade, since the contract is cash settled on a daily basis until expiration (when it is physically settled).

5. **What type of futures order guarantees an execution?**
   A. Market
   B. Limit
   C. Stop limit
   D. Market-If-Touched (MIT)

Correct Answer: A

Explanation: A market order will be immediately executed. The other orders have specific conditions that need to be met before they can be executed.

6. **What definition best describes initial margin for a futures contract?**
   A. It is a down payment against future delivery.
   B. It is a good-faith deposit.
   C. It is the difference between the bid and ask price on the exchange.
   D. It is the net profit expected by the trader.

Correct Answer: B

Explanation: Margin is a good-faith deposit. Traders don't have to pay for a commodity up front when they trade futures. However, they must submit some collateral, like cash or securities, as a good-faith deposit against adverse moves resulting from trading.

7. **What is the futures delivery month code abbreviation for December?**
   A. H
   B. J
   C. N
   D. Z

Correct Answer: D

Explanation: The abbreviation for December is Z.

8. **What does the term *grade* refer to when describing a commodity?**
   A. The physical location of the commodity
   B. The quality and specifications of the commodity
   C. The difference in price of the commodity at its particular location relative to the futures delivery location
   D. A rating assigned to the delivery agent indicating the likelihood of the agent being able to deliver the commodity

Correct Answer: B

Explanation: The term *grade* describes the quality and physical specifications of a commodity. Answer A refers to a delivery location, and answer C refers to a basis price.

9. **In the futures market, what does the abbreviation EFP short for?**
    A. Exchange for Principal
    B. Exchange for Physical
    C. Expiration from Proration
    D. Exchange Free Pricing

Correct Answer: B

Explanation: EFP is an abbreviation for Exchange for Physical. An EFP is a way to get delivery of a physical product, using a futures contract, away from the exchange settlement location.

10. **Unless otherwise specified, what is the default timing for futures orders submitted to an exchange?**
    A. Market
    B. Day
    C. On-Close
    D. Open (Good-Til-Cancelled)

Correct Answer: B

Explanation: Unless otherwise specified, orders will be canceled at the end of the trading day on which they were submitted.

Chapter 7

Options

For direct investors looking to limit their exposure to market moves or to investors looking to replicate physical investments like refineries, pipelines, or storage, options are an invaluable tool. Options are a special type of financial instrument known as a derivative. A derivative is any financial instrument whose value depends on the price of some other asset. While futures, forwards, and swaps are all examples of derivatives, another common type of derivative is an option. Options are different from futures, forwards, and commodity swap contracts because they only obligate one party (the seller). Options give the option buyer the right, but not the obligation, to take some action.

- **Derivative.** A financial contract whose value is based on the price of another asset.

- **Option.** A contract which gives the option owner the right, but not the obligation, to do something. Most commonly, options give the option owner the right to buy or sell something at a fixed price.

- **Underlying.** The asset on which the value of a derivative is based. For example, an option to buy 100 barrels of crude oil is a contract whose value depends on crude oil prices. In this case, crude oil is the underlying commodity.

In return for taking on all the risk in the transaction, the option seller is paid an up-front fee, called a *premium*. The math needed to calculate an option premium is discussed in the Chapter 8. However, this premium is often fairly significant in size—options can be very expensive to purchase.

CHAPTER OBJECTIVES

After completing this chapter, the student should have an understanding of

- Call and put options
- Option payoffs
- The difference between American, European, and Asian options
- Put/call parity
- Greeks

Financial Options

Options are contracts between two parties which give the buyer of the option the right to make a decision. In most cases, options give the owner the right to buy or sell an underlying asset at a specific price on or before a certain date. The terms of the contract will specify the rights of each party and any restrictions around this decision. In a general sense, options are also useful when modeling energy markets, since they provide a way to place a value on the ability to make a decision.

- **Buying an Option (Long an Option).** The option buyer pays for the right to make a decision and benefits when that decision gets more valuable. An option buyer (also called an option owner or holder) is long the option.
- **Selling an Option (Short an Option).** The option seller is paid money to become obligated to deliver some commodity at the contracted price if the option is exercised. The option seller (also called an option writer) is short the option.

To enter into an option contract, the buyer of the option will pay the seller an up-front fee, called an *option premium*, for the right to take some action in the future. The right is usually to buy or sell some asset, called the *underlying*, at a fixed price (called the *strike* price). The decision to take action is called *exercise*. The last date that an option can be exercised is the *expiration date*.

From a valuation perspective, options are assumed to be exercised in a manner that maximizes the expected profit to the buyer. For example, if an option buyer purchases the right to buy gasoline in the future for $4.00/gallon, he would only exercise that right when prices were above $4.00/gallon. Otherwise, he would be wasting his money, since gasoline could be purchased from other providers for less money. In this example, the value of the option depends on the probability that prices are above $4.00/gallon.

Option Terminology

Some common terms are used to describe option trading.

- **Option Buyer (Long Position).** The party who has the right to make a decision (usually the ability to buy or sell at a fixed price).
- **Option Seller (Short Position).** The party who is obligated to deliver a commodity at a fixed price (if the buyer exercises the option).
- **Option Premium.** The payment from the option buyer to the option seller in exchange for certain rights (usually to buy or sell at a fixed price).
- **Strike Price.** The fixed price at which the option owner can decide to buy or sell.
- **Exercise.** A decision by the owner to use the rights granted to him by the option contract.
- **Expiration Date.** The last date that the owner of the option can decide to exercise his rights.

The rights of the option buyer, and the obligation of the option seller, depend on the type of option contract. There are two basic types of options—the right to buy at a fixed price (a *call* option) and the right to sell at a fixed price (a *put* option).

- **Calls.** A call option gives the owner the right to buy the underlying asset at the contracted strike price from the seller. The owner of a call option benefits if the price of the underlying appreciates in value. For example, the right to buy gasoline at $2/gallon is more valuable if gasoline prices are $8/gallon than when prices are $4/gallon. The right to buy gasoline at $2/gallon is worthless if gasoline can be purchased for $1/gallon. In other words, the owner of a call option is long the price of the underlying.

- **Puts.** A put option gives the owner the right to sell the underlying asset at the contracted strike price. The owner of a put option benefits if the price of the underlying falls in value. For example, the right to sell gasoline to a trucking company at $6/gallon is more valuable if prevailing prices are $2/gallon rather than $4/gallon. The right to sell at $6/gallon is worthless if gasoline can be sold for more than that amount. In other words, the owner of a put option (the person who is long the put option) is short the price of the underlying.

An option contract is described by the name of the underlying, the date the option will expire, the strike price, and the type of the option (see Table 7-1). In this example, the option buyer has the right to buy (since the option is a call) a May 2014 Henry Hub natural gas futures contract (the underlying asset) for $4/MMBtu.

Underlying	Expiration	Strike Price	Put/Call Type
May 2014 Henry Hub Natural Gas Future	May 2014	4	Call

TABLE 7-1 · Simple Option Contract

When they are traded, options have a price associated with them called the *premium*. This is the amount of money that is paid by the option buyer to the option seller when the option contract is traded. The premium typically has two components, *intrinsic value* and *extrinsic (time) value*. Intrinsic value is the value of the option if it is exercised immediately. Extrinsic value is the amount of value of the option in excess of its intrinsic value.

- **Intrinsic Value.** Intrinsic value is the payoff of the option if it is exercised immediately.

- **Extrinsic (Time) Value.** Extrinsic value is the portion of the option premium in excess of the intrinsic value.

For example, the intrinsic value of a call option with a strike price of $5/gallon and underlying asset priced at $6/gallon is $1/gallon. If executed, the option would allow a purchase of the underlying at $5/gallon, which could then immediately be sold at the market price of $6/gallon for a $1/gallon profit. In general, the price of the option (the premium) will always be greater than the intrinsic value. In many cases, the premium will be substantially higher than the intrinsic value. For example, if the option is trading at $4/gallon, in this example, the portion of the premium in excess of the intrinsic value is $3/gallon (a $4/gallon premium – $1/gallon intrinsic value).

Traders commonly use terminology to describe whether an option can be exercised profitably or not. These terms are *in-the-money*, *at-the-money*, and *out-of-the-money*. Most commonly, options are traded when they are at-the-money. As time passes, and the price of the underlying changes, the option will become more or less valuable.

- **In-the-money.** An option that has a positive intrinsic value is said to be *in-the-money*. These options can be profitably exercised.

- **At-the-money.** An option that has zero intrinsic value is *at-the-money*. These options cannot be profitably exercised.

- **Out-of-the-money.** An option that has a negative intrinsic value is said to be *out-of-the-money*. These options cannot be profitably exercised.

Options contracts have a limited lifespan. An option with a lot of time prior to expiration will typically have a higher extrinsic value than a similar option close to expiration. Intrinsic value isn't as predictable—it fluctuates over time.

Intrinsic and Extrinsic Value

- **Intrinsic Value.** The value of the option if exercised immediately
- **Extrinsic Value.** The value of the option due to the asymmetry of the payoff and the potential for the underlying price to change over time

Option Payoffs

From a transaction standpoint, option trading requires both a buyer and a seller. When the option is purchased, the option buyer will pay the option seller. This is the only payment that must be made by the buyer. At that point, the buyer has the right to determine if future payments will need to made and will exercise that right when it is profitable to do so. The potential value obtained from executing those rights is called the option's *payoff*.

There are several things that can happen after an investor buys an option. First, the option could be resold. In that case, another buyer would purchase the option from the investor. Alternately, the investor could decide to exercise the option. This is less common than the option being sold, because exercising gives up the extrinsic value of the option. Alternately, options are investments with a fixed lifespan. At some point the investor's position will be closed when the option expires.

- **Liquidation (Trading).** If an option owner is long an option contract, one way to close the position is to sell the position. The investor's profit or loss would depend on the difference in the sale price and the purchase price of the option.

- **Exercise.** An option owner can decide to exercise their right to make a decision. In this case, the investors would get paid based on the intrinsic value of the option. This is less common than selling the option because the extrinsic value is lost.

- **Expiration.** If an option hits its expiration date, it will automatically be exercised if it is in-the-money and expire worthless if it is out-of-the-money.

The net benefit that the buyers obtains when the option is exercised is called the *option payoff*. On the expiration date, the payoff of the option will equal the intrinsic value. The payoff primarily depends on the price of the underlying since every option has an exercise or strike price defined as part of the option.

Call Payoff = Asset Price − Strike Price *if the Asset Price > Strike Price at expiration, otherwise zero.*

A put option works similarly. It gives the owner of the option the right to sell an asset at a fixed price. If the market price is greater than the fixed price, a put option is worthless. No one will willingly sell at a lower price than necessary. However, if the fixed price is higher than the market price, the put buyer makes a profit by selling at a higher price.

Put Payoff = Strike Price − Asset Price *if the Strike Price > Asset Price at expiration, otherwise zero.*

Key Concept

Call and Put Payoff

By convention, the option buyer is the one who decides whether the option is exercised and the payoff is described in terms of the buyer's economics. Since the buyer has the option to exercise or not, options with negative payoffs will expire worthless. To calculate the impact on the seller, change the sign of the payoff.

- **Call Payoff** = Max(0, Asset Price − Strike Price)
- **Put Payoff** = Max(0, Strike Price − Asset Price)

Because they have a limited lifespan, financial option contracts, unlike many financial investments, can be all-or-nothing investments. They also tend to be most valuable when first purchased and then tend to lose money over time. In many cases, the purchaser will pay a premium and have the contract expire worthless. Occasionally, the contract will pay off big when an unusual event occurs. Even though the size of the downside is small (losing the premium) compared to the potential upside (a huge profit), the odds of making a profit are stacked against the buyer. As a result, the most common use of options is to guard against a large financial loss—a process called *hedging*. In general, *hedging* means to protect oneself. In the financial markets, hedging means protecting against the risk of financial losses caused by adverse price moves.

American, European, and Asian Options

With some options, it is only possible to exercise the option on its expiration date (these are called *European options*). With other options, it is possible to exercise the option before expiration (these are called *American options*). Historically, the name was a result of the types of options traded on European and U.S. exchanges. However, both types of options are now traded throughout the world. A third type of option, an *Asian option*, uses the average price of the underlying asset over some period of time to determine the payoff.

Exercising early will lock in some of the profits (the intrinsic value) but give up any possibility of any additional profits (the extrinsic value). It is usually more profitable to sell the option than to exercise it early. As a result, options are rarely exercised early. If the option buyer wants out of the position, the option will be sold rather than liquidated.

- **European Option.** The option can be exercised only at expiration.
- **American Option.** An American option can be exercised at any time. In the energy market, when the underlying commodity is usually a futures contract, there is little benefit to early exercise.
- **Asian Option.** An Asian option is an average price option whose payoff is determined by the average price of the underlying over a specified set of dates. Asian options typically cannot be exercised early. In most respects, Asian options are similar to European options with a slightly lower volatility (caused by averaging the underlying price). Differences between Asian and European options are discussed in the Option Valuation section of Chapter 8.

While there are exceptions to this general rule about selling rather than exercising, the exceptions are fairly rare. Sometimes, owning the underlying gives a benefit that isn't accrued to the option owner. For example, a stock might pay a dividend that will reduce the value of the stock and make a call option less valuable. The owner of the stock will receive the dividend to offset the loss in stock price, but the option owner will not. If the dividend is larger than the extrinsic value of the option, it may be worthwhile to exercise the option.

American and European options will have the same value if it is never profitable to exercise the option early. Otherwise, American options will be slightly more expensive. This distinction is not very important in the energy industry. In energy trading, options are typically written on futures or forward contracts rather than directly on the underlying commodity. This is because an actual transfer of a commodity takes time to set up ahead of time. For example, an option to buy electricity will almost always be an option to buy electricity at a specific time (a futures/forward contract), rather than physical electricity at a time chosen by the option buyer.

Having an option written on a future eliminates the complication of the seller being forced to deliver a commodity on short notice. For example, a call option on October off-peak power (relatively cheap power) cannot be exercised early to get daytime power in August (expensive power). If the call option is exercised early, the buyer would get an off-peak futures or forward contract. The buyer would still have to wait until October to acquire power. This tends to eliminate the value of exercising energy options prior to their expiration date.

As a result, most commodity options should be valued using a European option formula rather than an American option formula. The reason for this is that even though commodity spot prices are often very volatile, commodity options are not based on the spot commodity price. Commodity options are based on a future or forward with the same expiration date as the option.

Key Concept

Early Exercise

The option contract will specify when the owner of the option can make a decision to exercise the option. It is extremely rare for a commodity option to be worth exercising early. For most options, it is usually worthwhile to sell the option rather than exercise it. This allows the buyer to keep the extrinsic value. Another reason is that most commodity options are based on futures rather than the spot commodity price. As a result, if the option is exercised early, the owner of the option still doesn't get the commodity until the future expires.

- **American Options.** An American option allows the owner to exercise at any point.
- **European Options.** A European option can only be exercised on the expiration date.
- **Asian Options.** An Asian option is similar to a European option, but the floating price is calculated as an average over a period of time rather than on a single day.

Payoff Diagrams

The profit or loss from holding an option is often explained through the use of payoff diagrams. These diagrams demonstrate the potential payoff of the option as a function of the underlying asset price. For example, the owner of a long future position will benefit when prices at expiration are higher than the strike price, and lose money when prices are lower than the strike price (see Figure 7-1). On these diagrams, the payoff from holding a future is shown on the y-axis and the price of the underlying is shown on the x-axis.

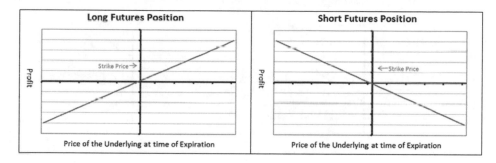

FIGURE 7-1 • Futures Payoff Diagrams

The formula for the payoff of a futures position is:

$$P\&L = V * (F - X) \quad \text{(payoff from a futures contract)}$$

Where:

P&L = Profit or Loss
  V = Volume (negative volume indicates a short position)
  F = Futures prices (as of the valuation date)
  X = Strike price

Graphically, this payoff is depicted on the diagrams. For example, when the futures price expires exactly at the strike price (mathematically, F = X), the payoff is zero. As a result, the payoff line crosses the x-axis at that point. Similar diagrams can be used to demonstrate the payoff of options and combinations of options.

The formula for the payoff of a call option is similar to the payoff of a futures contract with two differences (see Figure 7-2). First, unlike futures that can be entered with no up-front payment, it costs money to buy an option contract. This adds another term to the equation, the option premium (abbreviated P in the formulas that follow). In some cases, since the option premium is an up-front cost it will be excluded from the payoff diagram. Second, the owner of the option has the ability not to exercise. As a result, the option will only be exercised when futures prices are greater than the strike price.

$$P\&L = V * [\text{Max}(0, F - X) - P] \quad \text{(payoff from a call contract)}$$

Where:

P&L = Profit or Loss
  V = Volume
  F = Futures prices (as of the valuation date)
  X = Strike price
  P = Option premium (the cost to purchase the option)

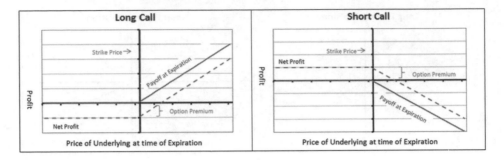

FIGURE 7-2 • Call Payoff Diagrams

 **Key Concept**

Call Option Payoff Diagram

A call option gives the owner the option to buy the underlying asset at the strike price. Call options are valuable when prices rise above the strike price because the asset can be bought at a discount. A good way to remember the payoff graphs is that the combined payoff lines look like a C (the curved part of a C faces to the right).

The owner of a put option has the ability (but not the obligation) to sell an asset at the strike price (see Figure 7-3).

$$P\&L = V * [Max(0, X - F) - P] \qquad \text{(payoff from a put contract)}$$

Where:

P&L = Profit or Loss

V = Volume

F = Futures prices (as of the valuation date)

X = Strike price

P = Option premium (the cost to purchase the option)

For both calls and puts, the buyer of the option pays the option writer a payment (called an *option premium*) when the option contract is signed (on the *trade date*). The option seller gets to keep that payment regardless of whether the buyer decides to exercise his ability to buy or sell.

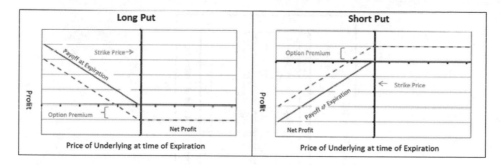

FIGURE 7-3 • Put Payoff Diagram

Put Option Payoff Diagram

A put option gives the owner the option to sell the underlying asset at the strike price. Put options are valuable when prices fall below the strike price because the asset can be sold at a premium.

Put/Call Parity

Since puts and calls each have half the payoff of a future, they can be combined together. For example, it's possible to replicate a future by buying a call and selling a put with the same strike price (see Figure 7-4). The graphs are additive.

Similarly, it is also possible to replicate a call by buying a put and a future. It is also possible to replicate the payoff of a put by buying a call and selling a future. The payoff relationship between calls and puts (with a futures contract as the underlying) and futures is[1]:

Call – Put = Futures   (put/call relationship)

The relationship between puts, calls, and futures means that the prices of each are linked. In other words, it is possible to synthetically create a combination of positions that replicates the payoff of a put or call. For example, the formula can be rearranged to calculate the price of a put, if the price of the future and a call option are known.

Call = Put + Futures   (solve for call payoff)
Put = Call – Futures   (solve for put payoff)

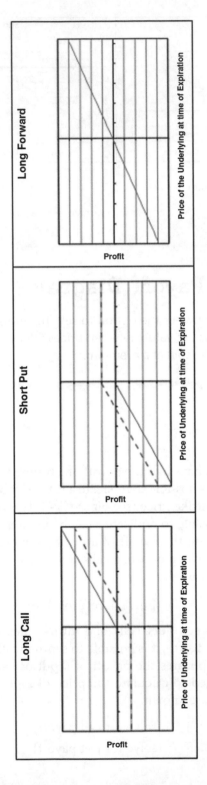

FIGURE 7-4 • Replicating a Future with Calls and Puts

Key Concept

Put/Call Parity

It is possible to replicate the payoff of one type of option with different types of options and futures. This links the value of a call and a put. To replicate a long option position, it is necessary to buy an option of some type. To replicate a short option position, it is necessary to sell an option of some type.

- **Synthetic Call:** Long future, long put
- **Synthetic Put:** Short future, long call

Option Greeks

Finally, because option prices depend on a number of factors, traders often want to know what happens to option prices when those factors change. For example, a trader might want to know what would happen to the value of her crude oil options if the price of the crude oil falls substantially. Some of the most common factors have acquired specific names. These factors are typically represented by Greek letters. Collectively, these factors are called Greeks. The most common Greeks are listed here and summarized in Table 7-2.

- **Delta (Commodity Prices).** Delta is the change in option value for a $1 change in the value of the underlying. Delta is also called the *hedge ratio*, since this is the amount of the underlying needed to duplicate the option payout. Mathematically, this is the first derivative of the option value relative to commodity prices. Delta is the best indicator of how much money the option will make or lose during an average trading day.

- **Gamma (Acceleration).** Gamma is change in Delta for a $1 change in the underlying. Mathematically, this is the second derivative of value of the option relative to commodity prices. Gamma is important because it indicates whether the portfolio will make or lose money during extreme market conditions (like a market crash). An option buyer is always long Gamma. An option seller is short Gamma.

- **Vega (Volatility).** Vega is change in the option value given a 1% change in volatility. Mathematically, this is the first derivative of the option price relative to volatility. Vega is important because it indicates the sensitivity of the option price to a quantity that can't be directly observed. If an option has a high Vega, correctly estimating the volatility becomes extremely important. Rising volatility will benefit the buyer and falling volatility benefit the seller.

- **Theta (Time).** Theta is the decrease in option value over a one-day period. Options are worth less money close to expiration than when they are far from expiration. This is because a long dated option (an option with a long time to expiration) still has time to become valuable. Since the downside of owning an option is limited, volatility and time benefit the option buyer. As time passes, the option will become less valuable. In other words, the extrinsic value of a long option will slowly *bleed* away and this will hurt the option buyer and benefit the option seller.

- **Rho (Interest Rates).** Rho is the change in option price given a 1% change in interest rates. Rho is much more important for interest rate sensitive instruments (like bonds) than physical commodities (like natural gas options).

Greek	Factor	Buyer	Seller
Delta	Price	Call = Long Put = Short	Call = Short Put = Long
Gamma	Change in Price (Delta)	Long	Short
Vega	Volatility	Long	Short
Theta	Passage of Time	Short	Long
Rho	Interest Rates	Call = Long Put = Short	Call = Short Put = Long

TABLE 7-2 · Greeks

QUIZ

1. **A call option with a strike price of zero looks a lot like a:**
   A. Long future
   B. Short future
   C. Synthetic short put
   D. Short Call + Long Future

   Correct Answer: A

   Explanation: Unless prices can go negative, a call option with a strike price of zero acts like a future.

2. **When is an American option worth more than a European option?**
   A. When price of the underlying is worth more in Europe than America
   B. When either option could expire worthless
   C. When exercising early might be preferable to selling the option
   D. When volatility in Europe is lower than volatility in America

   Correct Answer: C

   Explanation: The terms American and European describe the rules on when an option can be exercised. An American option can be exercised at any time. As a result, an American option will be worth more than a European option only if exercising early could be preferable to selling the option.

3. **Excluding time value of money, what instruments can be combined to create a synthetic long put?**
   A. Long Future + Short Call
   B. Short Future + Long Call
   C. Long Future + Long Call
   D. Short Future + Short Call

   Correct Answer: B

   Explanation: A short future plus a long call can be combined to form a synthetic long put. One way to help remember this relationship is that both calls and puts benefit from volatility (they are long volatility). If you want a synthetic long option, you need to buy an option of some type to get a long volatility position.

4. **What is the payoff when a $10/gal strike call option is exercised when the underlying price is $12/gal?**
   A. −$2.00/gal
   B. $0.00/gal
   C. +$2.00/gal
   D. +$8.00/gal

   Correct Answer: C

   Explanation: When a call option is exercised, the payoff Is Max(0, underlying price − strike price). In this case, $12 − $10 = $2. This payoff is the same as the intrinsic value.

5. If widgets are currently trading at $98/ton, what is the extrinsic value of a put option with a strike of $98/ton whose premium is $1.50/ton?
   A. $1.50/ton
   B. $3.50/ton
   C. $5.50/ton
   D. $7.00/ton

Correct Answer: A

Explanation: The put option is at-the-money, so its intrinsic value is zero. The extrinsic value of at-the-money options is equal to their premium.

6. What is the definition of an option's Delta?
   A. The amount the option premium changes due to a 1-day passage of time
   B. The amount the option premium changes due to a 1% change in interest rates
   C. The amount the option premium changes with a $1 change in the price of the underlying
   D. The amount the option premium changes with a 1% change in volatility

Correct Answer: C

Explanation: Answer C is the correct definition. Answer A describes Theta, Answer B describes Rho, and Answer D describes Vega.

7. What is the payoff of a $10 strike put option when the underlying price is $12 at expiration?
   A. −$2.00
   B. $0.00
   C. +$2.00
   D. +$8.00

Correct Answer: B

Explanation: Even though the put option is out-of-the money, the put buyer doesn't have to exercise the option—he can let it expire. As a result, option buyers should never have a negative payoff from an option.

8. What is *not* a way that an option investor might close a long call option position?
   A. Exercising the option
   B. Letting the option expire
   C. Selling the call option to another investor
   D. Buying a put option

Correct Answer: D

Explanation: All of the methods will close out a long option position except for buying a put. If someone is long an option, they need to sell an option of some type to close out the risk. While there are ways to convert a put into a call (discussed in the put/call parity section) cancelling a long position will require selling an option of some type.

9. **If widget fuel is currently trading at $20/gallon, which of the following options is *not* in-the-money?**
   A. Call at $15/gal
   B. Call at $20/gal
   C. Put at $25/gal
   D. Put at $30/gal

   Correct Answer: B

   Explanation: A call written at $20/gal on an underlying whose price is $20/gal is at-the-money. All of the other options would be in-the-money.

10. **What is the correct definition of a European option?**
    A. An option that is traded in Europe
    B. An option that has positive intrinsic value
    C. An option that can only be exercised on the expiration date
    D. An option that is denominated in a foreign currency

    Correct Answer: C

    Explanation: The terms American and European describe the rules on when an option can be exercised. A European option can only be exercised on the expiration date.

Chapter **8**

Option Valuation

A substantial amount of mathematics has been developed over the past century to accurately price options. The most influential option pricing formula, the Black–Scholes formula, was developed by Fischer Black and Myron Scholes for European style options in the 1970s. Subsequent additions to the formula have generalized its use for a variety of other financial products, including energy commodities.

A wide variety of formulas already exist to value options. As a result, it is not usually necessary for option traders to develop their own models. However, valuing options does require knowing which formula to use and how to use it properly.

CHAPTER OBJECTIVES

After completing this chapter, the student should have an understanding of

- Generalized Black–Scholes
- Asian options
- Spread options

Generalized Black–Scholes

Black–Scholes genre option models are the most common type of formula used to value options. As a result, options priced with these formulas are commonly called *vanilla* options to distinguish them from options that need more complicated valuation formulas (*exotic options*).The original Black–Scholes model was published in 1973 for non-dividend-paying stocks. Since that time, a wide variety of extensions to the original Black–Scholes model have been created. Collectively, these are referred to as *Black–Scholes genre* option models. Modifications of the formula are used to price other financial instruments like dividend-paying stocks, commodity futures, and foreign exchange (FX) forwards. Mathematically, these formulas are nearly identical. The primary difference between these models is how the asset gets present valued. To illustrate this relationship, a generalized form of the Black–Scholes equation is explained in this section.

The Black–Scholes model is based on number of assumptions about how financial markets operate. Black–Scholes style models assume:

1. **Arbitrage Free Markets.** Black–Scholes formulas assume that traders try to maximize their personal profits and don't allow arbitrage opportunities (riskless opportunities to make a profit) to persist.

2. **Frictionless, Continuous Markets.** The assumption of frictionless markets assumes that it is possible to buy and sell any amount of the underlying at any time without transaction costs.

3. **Risk-Free Rates.** It is possible to borrow and lend money at a risk-free interest rate.

4. **Lognormally Distributed Price Movements.** Prices are lognormally distributed and described by geometric Brownian motion.

5. **Constant Volatility.** The Black–Scholes genre options formulas assume that volatility is constant across the life of the option contract.

In the traditional Black–Scholes model intended to price stock options, the underlying assumption is that the stock is traded at its present value and that prices will follow a random walk, a diffusion style process, over time. Prices are assumed to start at the spot price and, on the average, to drift upwards over time at the risk-free rate. The Merton formula modifies the basic Black–Scholes equation by introducing an additional term to incorporate dividends or holding costs. The Black (1976) formula modifies the assumption so that the underlying starts at some forward price rather than a spot price. The Black-76 model is the most commonly used formula in the energy markets, since commodities are typically trade based on forward prices rather than spot prices. In a Black-76 model, prices start at the present value of the forward price associated with that delivery month. A fourth variation, the Garman–Kohlhagen model, is used to value foreign exchange (FX) options. In the GK model, each currency in the currency pair is discounted based on its own interest rate.

1. **Black–Scholes (Stocks).** In the traditional Black–Scholes model, the option is based on common stock—an instrument that is traded at its present value. The stock price does not get present valued, but rather starts at

its present value (a spot price) and drifts upwards over time at the risk-free rate.

2. **Merton (Stocks with Continuous Dividend Yield).** The Merton model is a variation of the Black–Scholes model for assets that pay dividends to shareholders. Dividends reduce the value of the option because the option owner does not own the right to dividends until the option is exercised.

3. **Black-76 (Commodity Futures).** The Black-76 model is for an option where the underlying commodity is traded based on a future price rather than a spot price. Instead of dealing with a spot price that drifts upwards at the risk-free rate, this model deals with a forward price that needs to be present valued.

4. **Garman–Kohlhagen (FX Futures).** The Garman–Kohlhagen model is used to value foreign exchange (FX) options. In the GK model, each currency in the currency pair is discounted based on its own interest rate.

The generalized Black–Scholes (GBS) formulas for call and put options are shown in Equation (8.1) using the inputs found in Table 8-1. While these formulas may look complicated at first glance, most of the terms can be found as part of an options contract or are prices readily available in the market. The only term that is difficult to calculate is the implied volatility (σ). Implied volatility is typically calculated using prices of other options that have recently been traded. Implied volatility is discussed in greater detail later in the chapter.

Call Option (C)

$$C = Se^{(b-r)T}N(d_1) - Xe^{-rT}N(d_2)$$

Put Option (P)

$$P = Xe^{-rT}N(-d_2) - Se^{(b-r)T}N(-d_1)$$

Where

$$d_1 = \frac{\ln\left(\frac{S}{X}\right) + \left(b + \frac{\sigma^2}{2}\right)T}{\sigma\sqrt{T}} \qquad (8.1)$$

$$d_2 = \frac{\ln\left(\frac{S}{X}\right) + \left(b - \frac{\sigma^2}{2}\right)T}{\sigma\sqrt{T}} = d_1 - \sigma\sqrt{T}$$

The *cost-of-carry* term, b, varies by formula—it differentiates the various Black–Scholes genre formulas from one another (see Table 8-2). The cost of carry refers to the cost of "carrying" or holding a position. For example, holding a bond may result in earnings from interest, stock dividends, or the like. Those payments are made to the owner of the underlying and not the owner of the option. As a result, they reduce the value of the option.

Symbol	Meaning
S or F	**Underlying price.** The price of the underlying asset on the valuation date t_0. This is commonly abbreviated S if it is a stock and F if it is a future. This will change over time.
X	**Strike Price.** The strike, or exercise, price of the option. This is set in the option contract and will not change over time.
T	**Time to expiration.** The time to expiration of the option in years. In spreadsheets, this is typically calculated as a function of the valuation date and the expiration date where: $$T = (t_1 - t_0)/365$$
t_0	**Valuation Date.** The as/of date on which the option is valued. This will change over time.
t_1	**Expiration Date.** The date on which the option must be exercised. This is set in the option contract and will not change over time.
σ	**Volatility.** The volatility of the underlying security. This will change over time and must usually be estimated from other traded options that use the same valuation formula. Typically abbreviated as the Greek symbol sigma σ. In computer programs that don't support Greek characters, this will have a different symbol that should be apparent by context.
q	**Continuous Yield.** Used in the Merton model, this is the continuous yield of the underlying security. This costs the option holder money since he doesn't own the asset until it is exercised.
r_f	**Foreign Risk-Free Rate.** Used in the Garman–Kohlhagen model, this is the risk-free rate of the foreign currency.

TABLE 8-1 • GBS Inputs

Model	Typical Use	Cost of Carry Formula
Black–Scholes	Stocks	b = r
Merton	Stock options (continuous dividends)	b = r − q
Black (1976)	Futures	b = 0
Garman and Kohlhagen	Currency options	b = r - r_f

TABLE 8-2 • GBS Cost of Carry

For energy options, almost all of the parameters can be found in either the option contract or quoted in the market. The primary exception to this rule is the implied volatility term. The primary way to calculate implied volatility is to solve for the implied volatility (σ) by inverting the Black–Scholes function. Numerical solutions based on guessing an implied volatility term, solving the Black–Scholes equation, and comparing the result to traded price are primary means of calculating the implied volatility. A succession of guesses is used to progressively get closer to the actual market implied volatility.

Generalized Black–Scholes

The Black–Scholes model and its later variants are the most common ways to value options. Almost all of the inputs, except implied volatility, can be observed in the market or obtained from the contract (if it's a stand-alone transaction) or the trade confirm (if transacted under a master-netting agreement). Situations where Black–Scholes style formulas are not appropriate models are relatively rare in the energy markets.

Average Price (Asian) Options

An *Asian option* is an exotic option whose payoff is calculated using the average price of the underlying over some period of time, rather than the price on the expiration date. As a result, Asian options are also called average price options. The reason that traders use Asian options is that averaging a settlement price over a period of time reduces the affect on the value of the option of manipulation or unusual price movements on the expiration date. As a result, Asian options are often found on strategically important commodities, like crude oil, or markets with intermittent trading.

The average of a set of random numbers (prices in this case) will have a lower dispersion (a lower volatility) than the dispersion of prices observed on any single day. As a result, the implied volatility used to price Asian options will usually be slightly lower than the implied volatility on a comparable European option. From a mathematical perspective, valuing an Asian option is slightly complicated, since the average of a set of lognormal distributions is not itself lognormally distributed. However, a reasonably good approximation of the correct answer is not too difficult to obtain.

In the case of Asian options on futures, it is possible to use a modified Black-76 formula that replaces the implied volatility term with an adjusted implied volatility of the average price.[1] As long as the first day of the averaging period is in the future, the following formula can be used to value Asian options as shown in Equation (8.2) and using the inputs listed in Table 8 3.

Call Option (C)	$C = Se^{-rT} N(d_1) - Xe^{-rT} N(d_2)$
Put Option (P)	$P = Xe^{-rT} N(-d_2) - Se^{-rT} N(-d_1)$
Where	$$d_1 = \dfrac{\ln\left(\frac{S}{X}\right) + \left(b + \frac{\sigma_A^2}{2}\right)T}{\sigma\sqrt{T}}$$
	$$d_2 = \dfrac{\ln\left(\frac{S}{X}\right) + \left(b - \frac{\sigma_A^2}{2}\right)T}{\sigma\sqrt{T}} = d_1 - \sigma_A^2\sqrt{T} \qquad (8.2)$$
	$$\sigma_A = \sqrt{\dfrac{\ln(M)}{T}}$$
	$$M = \dfrac{2e^{\sigma^2 T} - 2e^{\sigma^2 T}[1 + \sigma^2(T - \tau)]}{\sigma^4(T - \tau)^2}$$

Symbol	Meaning
S or F	**Underlying Price.** The price of the underlying asset on the valuation date t_0. This is commonly abbreviated S if it is a stock and F if it is a future. This will change over time.
X	**Strike Price.** The strike, or exercise, price of the option. This is set in the option contract and will not change over time.
T	**Time to Expiration.** The time to expiration of the option in years. In spreadsheets, this is typically calculated as a function of the valuation date and the expiration date where: $T = (t_1 - t_0)/365$
τ	**Time to Start of Averaging Period.** The time to the start of the averaging period in years. In spreadsheets, this is typically calculated as a function of the valuation date and the start of averaging date where: $\tau = (t_2 - t_0)/365$
t_0	**Valuation Date.** The as/of date on which the option is valued. This will change over time.
t_1	**Expiration Date.** The date on which the option must be exercised. This is set in the option contract and will not change over time.
t_2	**Start of Averaging Date.** The date on which the averaging period begins. This is set in the option contract and will not change over time.
σ_A	**Adjusted Volatility.** The volatility of the price over the averaging period.
σ	**Volatility.** The volatility of the underlying security. This will change over time and must usually be estimated from other traded options that use the same valuation formula. Typically abbreviated as the Greek symbol sigma σ. In computer programs that don't support Greek characters, this will have a different symbol that should be apparent by context.

TABLE 8-3 · Asian Option Inputs

Key Concept

Asian Option Valuation

Asian options are priced similarly to European options except that they have a slightly lower implied volatility. They have a lower volatility because averaging the floating price over a period is less likely to result in an extreme price than might be observed on any single day.

Spread Options

Spread options are an exotic type of option used to model many energy investments. These instruments are not commonly traded. However, they are used to help value assets that convert one commodity into another commodity. The payoff of a spread option will depend on the size of the spread between two commodity prices rather than the single price found in vanilla option models (Generalized Black–Scholes option models that deal with standard simple options). The payoffs from spread options are similar to normal options, except that spread options have two underlying assets. Spread call and spread put payoffs are determined using the formulas shown in Equation (8.3).

$$C = \max[F_1 - F_2 - X, 0] \qquad \textit{Spread Call Payoff}$$

$$P = \max[X - (F_1 - F_2), 0] \qquad \textit{Spread Put Payoff}$$

(8.3)

Symbol	Meaning
C	**Call Payoff.** The payoff of a call option
P	**Put Payoff.** The payoff of a put option
F_1	**Forward price of Asset 1.** This is the price of the "Finished Product"
F_2	**Forward price of Asset 2.** This is the price of the "Raw Material"
X	**Strike Price.** This is the cost of converting the "Raw Material" into the "Finished Product"

A variety of different assets are commonly modeled using spread options. Some of these assets include natural gas pipelines, electrical generation plants, and refineries.

- **Pipelines (Pipeline Transportation Options).** The owner of firm transportation on a pipeline has the option of transporting gas from one end of the pipeline to the other. When it's profitable to transport the fuel, the profit from transporting the gas will be:

$$\text{Transport Payoff} = \text{Price}_{\text{destination}} - \text{Price}_{\text{origin}} - \text{Transport Costs}$$

- **Power Generation (Heat Rate Options).** The owner of a generation unit has the option to convert fuel into electricity. When it is profitable to convert fuel into electricity, the payoff will be:

$$\text{Generation Payoff} = \text{Price}_{\text{Electricity}} - \text{Heat Rate} * \text{Price}_{\text{Fuel}} - \text{VOM}$$

where Heat Rate describes the efficiency of the unit at converting fuel into electricity and VOM stands for *Variable Operating and Maintenance* costs.

- **Refining (Crack Spread Options).** The owner of a refinery has the option of converting raw materials (crude oil) into finished products (like gasoline and diesel fuel).

$$\text{Refining Payoff} = \text{Price}_{\text{Product}} - \text{Conversion Rate} *$$
$$\text{Price}_{\text{Crude}} - \text{Conversion Cost}$$

Valuing spread options is substantially more complicated than valuing options on single assets. Spread options have to deal with the prices of multiple commodities. In most cases, the two commodities in a spread option will have highly correlated prices. The prices of any two assets with a conversion relationship are usually highly correlated. Similar to how vanilla options have a single variable that can't be directly observed (implied volatility), spread options have three variables that can't be directly observed from the market—the volatility of the first asset, the volatility of the second asset, and the correlation between the two assets.

Similar to Black−Scholes options, implied volatility for spread options is abbreviated by the lower case Greek letter sigma. A subscript is typically used to distinguish the volatility of each asset. This can be numerical (σ_1, σ_2) or descriptive ($\sigma_{\text{electricity}}$, $\sigma_{\text{natural\_gas}}$). The lower case Greek letter rho (ρ) is commonly used as an abbreviation for correlation.

Key Concept

Spread Options

A spread option is based on the spread between two commodities relative to a fixed price. These options are commonly used to model energy investments that convert one commodity (like fuel or crude oil) into another commodity (like electricity or gasoline).

- **Heat Rate Options.** A heat rate option is an option to convert natural gas into electricity. This approximates the economics of owning a power plant.
- **Crack Spread Option.** A crack spread option is an option to convert crude oil into a refined product. This approximates the economics of owning a refinery.

- **NatGas Transportation Options.** A natural gas transportation option is an option to convert natural gas at one location into natural gas at another location. This approximates the economics of owning a natural gas pipeline.
- **Electrical Transmission Option.** An electrical transmission option is an option to convert power in one location to power in another location. This approximates the economics of owning an electrical transmission line.

Analytic formulas similar to the Black–Scholes equation are commonly used to value spread options. One such formula is called *Kirk's approximation*. While an exact closed form solution does not exist to value spread options, approximate solutions can give reasonably accurate results. Kirk's approximation uses a Black–Scholes style framework to analyze the joint distribution that results from the ratio of two lognormal distributions.

In a normal Black–Scholes equation, there is a single unknown variable (implied volatility) that acts like a dial to increase and decrease the value of the option. In a spread option, there are three unknown variables (the volatility of the first asset, the volatility of the second asset, and the correlation between the two prices). When two assets are highly volatile, the dispersion of expected results increases. Correlation has the opposite effect. When two assets are highly correlated, they behave almost like the same asset. As a result, the expected spread between their prices is very low (see Figure 8-1).

Dispersion has a direct impact on option profitability. Option buyers benefit from a wide range of possible spreads because an unusual spread will never result in a loss. In contrast, the seller of an option will benefit from a tight dispersion of possible spreads. An option seller will never make more than the

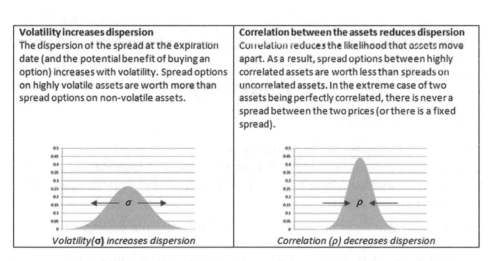

FIGURE 8-1 • Correlation and Volatility

premium, but their losses are unbounded. If either side estimates the correlation between the assets incorrectly, they will consistently lose money to someone that does a better job of estimating correlations.

There is a fundamental difference between spreads and the prices of individual assets. The most common approximation of asset prices (never dropping below zero, but being able to increase much more) doesn't describe a spread very well. Although that assumption of normal returns works for something like a commodity where prices are almost never zero or negative, it doesn't work for a spread between two prices. Spreads between two prices can be zero or negative fairly often. Other standard measures, like the concept of a percent return, don't work either. It is impossible to calculate a percent return on something that starts at a zero price (see Figure 8-2).

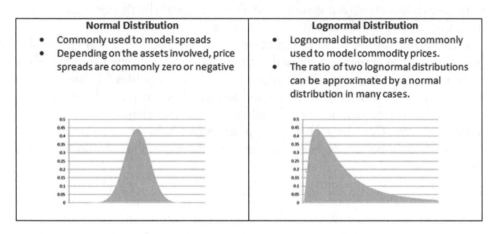

FIGURE 8-2 • Normal and Lognormal Distributions

Key Concept

Spread Option Volatility and Correlation

The spread between the two assets in a spread option model forms a distribution defined by three variables—the volatility of asset 1 (abbreviated σ_1), the volatility of asset 2 (abbreviated σ_2), and the correlation (abbreviated ρ) between the two prices.

- Higher volatility in either asset price will increase the dispersion of the spread between the two prices.
- Higher correlation between the assets will reduce the dispersion in the spread between the two prices.

In a Black–Scholes equation, the distribution of price returns is assumed to be normally distributed on the expiration date. Kirk's approximation builds on the Black–Scholes framework by taking advantage of the fact that the ratio of two lognormal distributions is approximately normally distributed.[2] By modeling a ratio of two prices rather than the spread between the prices, Kirk's approximation can use the same formulas designed for options based on a single underlying. In other words, Kirk's approximation uses an algebraic transformation to fit a spread option into the Black–Scholes framework.

The payoff of a spread option can be algebraically manipulated as shown in Equation (8.4).

$$C = \max[F_1 - F_2 - X, 0] \qquad = \max\left[\frac{F_1}{F_2 + X} - 1{,}0\right](F_2 + X)$$

$$P = \max[X - (F_1 - F_2), 0] \qquad = \max\left[1 - \frac{F_1}{F_2 + X}, 0\right](F_2 + X)$$

$$(8.4)$$

This allows Kirk's approximation to model the distribution of the spread as the ratio of the price of asset 1 to the sum of price of asset 2 and the strike price as shown in Equation (8.5).

$$F = \frac{F_1}{F_2 + X} \tag{8.5}$$

Looking at the valuation formula, the primary difference between the Kirk's approximation formula and the standard Black-76 formula is that the spread option gets multiplied by $(F_2 + X)$ as shown in Equation (8.6), and the F has changed from the distribution of future prices to the distribution of the ratio of F_1 over $F_2 + X$.

Black 76 Model	Kirk's Approximation	
$c = [e^{-rt}\{F N(d_1) - N(d_2)\}]$	$c = (F_2 + X)[e^{-rt}\{F N(d_1) - N(d_2)\}]$	(8.6)

This is a direct result of the transformation formula, where the max() function is valued as an option and then multiplied by the $(F_2 + X)$ term (see Figure 8-3).

That ratio is plugged into the standard Black-76 Formula to create a Black–Scholes genre formula appropriate to value spread options, as shown in Equation (8.7).

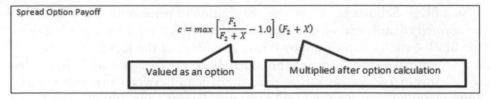

Spread Option Payoff

$$c = max\left[\frac{F_1}{F_2 + X} - 1.0\right](F_2 + X)$$

Valued as an option　　Multiplied after option calculation

FIGURE 8-3 · Payoff of a Spread Call Option

$$c = (F_2 + X)[e^{-rt}\{F N(d_1) - N(d_2)\}]$$

Formula for value of spread call option

(8.7)

$$p = (F_2 + X)[e^{-rt}\{N(-d_2) - F N(d_1)\}]$$

Formula for the value of a spread put option

where

$$d_1 = \frac{\ln(F) + (\frac{\sigma^2}{2})}{\sigma\sqrt{T}}$$

$$d_2 = d1 - \sigma\sqrt{T}$$

The key complexity is determining the appropriate volatility that needs to be used in the equation. The "approximation" which defines Kirk's approximation is the assumption that the ratio of two lognormal distributions is normally distributed. That assumption makes it possible to estimate the volatility needed for the modified Black–Scholes-style equation shown in Equation (8.8).

$$\sigma = \sqrt{\sigma_1^2 + \left[\sigma_2\frac{F_2}{(F_2 + X)}\right]^2 - 2\rho\sigma_1\sigma_2\frac{F_2}{(F_2 + X)}}$$

Kirk's Approximation

(8.8)

Using the following inputs:

Symbol	Meaning
F_1	**Forward price of Asset 1.** This is the price of the "Finished Product"
F_2	**Forward price of Asset 2.** This is the price of the "Raw Material"
X	**Strike Price.** This is the cost of converting the "Raw Material" into the "Finished Product"
σ_1	**Volatility of Asset 1** (typically called "Sigma 1")
σ_2	**Volatility of Asset 2** ("Sigma 2")
P	**Correlation.** Correlation between the prices of Asset 1 and Asset 2 ("Rho")
R	**Risk-Free Rate.** The continuously compounded risk-free rate of return. Because this needs to be in the same units as the time to maturity, by convention this represents an annual return.
T	**Time to Expiration.** The time to expiration of the option in years. In spreadsheets, this is typically calculated as a function of the valuation date and the expiration date where: $T = (t_1 - t_0)/365$
t_0	**Valuation Date.** The as/of date on which the option is valued. This will change over time.
t_1	**Expiration Date.** The date on which the option must be exercised. This is set in the option contract and will not change over time.

Table 8-4 describes several common mathematical functions that are shown in shorthand in the formulas.

N()	The **standard normal density function** is a prebuilt function in most spreadsheet programs and math libraries. It can also be calculated manually. $$N(z) = \frac{1}{\sqrt{2\pi}} e^{-\frac{z^2}{2}}$$
e^x	The e in the **standard exponent function**, "e raised to the power x" is a constant and approximately equal to 2.71828182845904.

TABLE 8-4 · Standard Math Functions

Valuing a spread option depends on properly being able to estimate the implied volatility and correlation needed to define the payoff of the spread on expiration. There is no single way to estimate these parameters. However, it is possible to get reasonable insight into what these parameters need to look like by examining and reversing one of the assumptions used in Black–Scholes genre valuations—the assumption that continuously compounded returns are normally distributed with a constant volatility. To a large extent, this is an approximation chosen to simplify the mathematics needed to solve an option formula. The formula for continuously compounded returns is based on the formula for calculating compound interest as shown in Equation (8.9).

$$P_t = P_0 \left(1 + \frac{r_{nominal}}{n}\right)^{nt}$$
(8.9)

Where

Symbol	Meaning
$r_{nominal}$	**Nominal interest rate.** Interest rate per unit of "t" (usually an annual interest rate)
N	**Compounding periods.** Number of times interest is compounded per year.
T	**Time.** Usually represented in number of years (1.0 = one year, 0.5 = six months, etc.)
P_t	**Price at time "t".** The price at time "t", the ending point for a continually compounded return series that started at P_0.
P_0	**Price at time "0".** The price at time zero – the starting point for a series of continually compounded returns that end at P_t.

When the number of compounding steps (n) approaches infinity, the formula changes to become

$$P_t = P_0 \, e^{rt} \quad \text{when } n \rightarrow \text{infinity}$$

and r changes from a nominal interest rate to a continuously compounded interest rate. Solving for r

$$r_{continuous} = \ln (P_1 / P_0)$$

As a result, this implies that if continuously compounded returns are normally distributed then prices have to be lognormally distributed. Going back to the discussion of Kirk's approximation, the key assumption in Kirk's analytic formula is that the distribution of prices at expiration is approximately normally distributed.[3] This creates a relationship between the starting point, volatility, and the final distribution of the spread.

With two highly correlated assets, spreads tend to be relatively stable over time. The reason for this stability is that one asset can typically be converted into the other asset. If the spread ever gets too large, more conversion units (electrical generation, power lines, pipelines, or refineries) can be built. This dampens the possible variation of future spreads. As a result, it is often possible to estimate the range of possible spreads in the future by looking at how these spreads have behaved in the past and reversing the Black–Scholes equation to calculate the volatility and correlation needed to generate the historically observed relationships (see Figure 8-4).

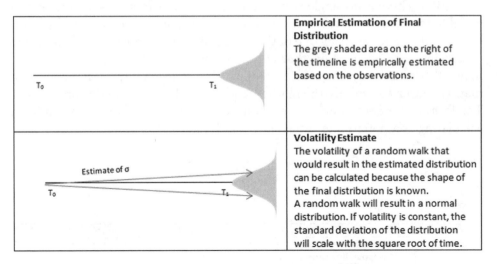

FIGURE 8-4 · Modeling a Spread

Of course, this approach depends on having a pre-ante assumption about the likely distribution of the spread at some point in the future. For both electricity and natural gas markets, the equipment necessary to make the conversion from one commodity to another is expensive and changes little over time. Power plants, long distance transmission wires, and natural gas pipelines all have long lifespans and require substantial capital in construction costs. The factors that might affect spreads like consumer demand, weather, and the state of the economy don't change substantially year-to-year in the forward curve either. For example, our estimate for average high temperatures in August

2035 is much the same as our prediction for average high temperatures in August 2051.

For many energy commodities, there is a strong seasonall component to expected spreads. For example, power prices tend to spike in the summer as consumer demand for air conditioning rises and prices are set by progressively less efficient generation units. However, this is a short-lived phenomenon. By the fall, consumer demand for air conditioning declines and more efficient units are back on the margin. Another example of mean reverting prices come from natural gas. The solid black lines in Figure 8-5 graphically display the price spread between natural gas prices at Florida Gas Pipeline Zone 3 (near Pensacola in the western part of the Florida Panhandle) and Florida City Gates (in central Florida near Orlando). Below those lines are shaded areas showing a normal distribution that best fits the observed historical distribution.

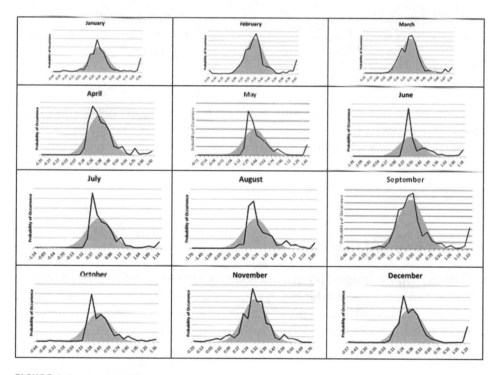

FIGURE 8-5 • Empirical Spreads

When distributions can be empirically measured, it is possible to back into the parameters needed to create the distribution. In a spread option, there are three unknown parameters—two implied volatility terms (σ_1, σ_2) and an implied correlation term (ρ) that can't be directly observed in the market. These terms define the distribution of the spread at some point in the future as shown in Equation (8.10).

$$\sigma_{final} = \sqrt{\sigma_1^2 + \left[\sigma_2 \frac{F_2}{(F_2 + X)}\right]^2 - 2\rho\sigma_1\sigma_2 \frac{F_2}{(F_2 + X)}}$$

Kirk's approximation, repeated   (8.10)

Since the final distribution is already known (having been empirically estimated), the value for the implied parameters will be the values that would make a forward price process based on the Black–Scholes assumptions match the final distribution. Because this problem has too many degrees of freedom, it is possible to fix two parameters (commonly the implied volatilities) and solve for the remaining factor, an "implied correlation," which solves the Kirk's approximation equation, as shown in Equation (8.11).

$$\rho = \frac{\sigma_1^2 + \left[\sigma_2 \frac{F_2}{(F_2 + X)}\right]^2 - \sigma_{final}^2}{2\sigma_1\sigma_2 \frac{F_2}{(F_2 + X)}}$$

Rearranging Kirk's approximation to solve for correlation   (8.11)

It should be noted that because early exercise isn't possible, assumptions about intermediate price movements may or may not bear a strong relationship to actual behavior even if the final distribution is correctly reconstructed.

Key Concept

Spread Options

General purpose spread option models can be extremely difficult to calculate mathematically. However, for highly correlated assets (the type of assets that are typically underlying a spread option), the problem can be simplified enough to allow a closed-form similar to the Black–Scholes equation.

QUIZ

1. **What is an Asian option?**
   A. An option traded in Asia
   B. An option whose settlement price is based on the average price over some period of time
   C. An option which can be exercised at any time
   D. An option that can be exercised only on the expiration date

   Correct Answer: B

   Explanation: An Asian option is an option whose payoff is calculated using the average price of the underlying over some period of time rather than the price on the expiration date. Answer C describes an American option. Answer D describes a European option.

2. **What are advantages of Asian options compared to European options?**
   I. Asian options are less vulnerable to manipulation and price spikes on the expiration day than European options.
   II. Asian options can be exercised at any time.

   A. Neither Statement I nor Statement II is correct.
   B. Only Statement I is correct.
   C. Only Statement II is correct.
   D. Both Statement I and II are correct.

   Correct Answer: B

   Explanation: Asian options can only be exercised on the expiration date. Some other possible answers: For a buyer, the averaging feature makes Asian options less expensive than European options. For a seller, Asian options are less risky than European options.

3. **What is the primary unobservable variable needed to solve a Black–Scholes genre option formula?**
   A. Valuation date
   B. Forward prices
   C. Expiration date
   D. Implied volatility

   Correct Answer: D

   Explanation: Implied volatility is the primary unknown parameter needed to solve a Black–Scholes genre option model. The valuation date is the date when the option is being valued (commonly the current day). The expiration date is specified as part of the contract. Forward prices can usually be obtained from trading markets.

4. **Which of the following is a common closed-form equation used to value commodity spread options?**
   A. Black-76
   B. Garman–Kohlhagen
   C. Kirk's approximation
   D. Merton's formula

   Correct Answer: C

   Explanation: Kirk's approximation is a well-known formula used to value commodity spread options. While it's not the only approach to valuing spread options, and it has many critics, it is one of the more well-known and widely used approaches.

5. **What symbol is commonly used to abbreviate implied volatility?**
   A. alpha (α)
   B. mu (μ)
   C. sigma (σ)
   D. rho (ρ)

   Correct Answer: C

   Explanation: A lower case Greek letter sigma (σ) is a commonly used abbreviation for implied volatility.

6. **What is *not* an assumption made by the Black–Scholes model?**
   A. Arbitrage free markets
   B. Seasonal variations in volatility
   C. Continuous trading
   D. Lognormal price movements

   Correct Answer: B

   Explanation: Black–Scholes models assume constant volatility.

7. **In a spread option model, what parameter is commonly abbreviated by the Greek letter rho (ρ)?**
   A. Implied volatility
   B. Prices
   C. Correlation
   D. Interest rates

   Correct Answer: C

   Explanation: The lower case Greek letter rho is a commonly used abbreviation for correlation.

8. **What are the underlying assets involved in a heat rate option?**
   A. Electricity and a fuel (like natural gas)
   B. Electricity at two different locations
   C. Crude oil and a refined product
   D. Natural gas at two different locations

   Correct Answer: A

   Explanation: A heat rate option gives the owner of the option the ability to convert a fuel, like natural gas, into electricity.

9. **Which Black–Scholes genre option formula is used to value options based on commodity futures?**
    A. Black–Scholes
    B. Merton
    C. Black-76
    D. Garman–Kohlhagen

    Correct Answer: C

    Explanation: The Black–Scholes genre formula used to price options based on commodity futures is the Black-76 formula.

10. **What are the typical underlying instruments for a crack spread option?**
    A. Crude oil and a refined product (like gasoline or diesel)
    B. Electricity and a fuel (like natural gas)
    C. Gasoline and ethanol
    D. Coal and natural gas

    Correct Answer: A

    Explanation: A crack spread is a refining spread—crude oil and one or more refined products (gasoline, diesel, or similar products).

Stocks (Equity Investments)

Stocks, along with bonds, are one of the primary ways that companies raise money to operate and expand their businesses. Stocks provide a partial ownership in a company. This allows stock investors to benefit from growth of the company over time. The biggest driver for company growth is often a growing economy or favorable industry conditions. As a result, stocks typically make a good investment for investors wishing to benefit from a growing economy or improving economic conditions.

CHAPTER OBJECTIVES

After completing this chapter, the student should have an understanding of

- Equity and debt financing
- Corporations
- Ring fencing and structural subordination
- Common and preferred stock
- Dividends
- Voting rights

Financing a Company

Companies need money, called *capital*, to operate. Capital is the cash and physical goods that companies use to generate income. The two primary methods that companies use to raise capital are debt financing (selling bonds) and equity financing (selling stock). When a company issues stock, it is selling a partial ownership interest in the company. When a company issues bonds, it is borrowing money from the investors that buy the bonds. (See Figure 9-1.)

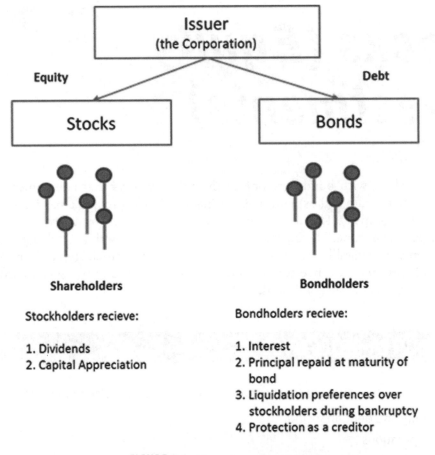

FIGURE 9-1 • Financing a Company

- **Equity Owners (Stockholders).** An equity investor gives money to a company in exchange for partial ownership of that business. As part owners, equity holders help determine the management of the company. Equity holders benefit by cash distributions (dividends) paid by the company and an increase in the value in the company.

- **Debt Owners (Bondholders).** A debt investor loans money to a company which will need to be repaid with interest by some date in the future. Debt holders do not have an ownership interest in a company and have no say in its management. Debt holders benefit by the interest that the company pays them for the use of their money.

The most common type of equity investment is buying *stock* in a corporation. The most common type of debt investment is the purchase of a *bond*.

Key Concept

Equity and Debt

The structure of a company will determine the rights and obligations of owners.

- **Equity.** Equity (commonly in the form of a stock certificate) is an ownership stake in a corporation. A corporation is a limited liability structure where investors can lose their investment (the money they paid for the stock) but are not personally liable for the company's debts.
- **Debt.** Debt is a loan from an investor to a company (commonly in the form of a bond). The investor will receive interest on the money that was lent and be repaid the money at a specified date (the maturity date).

There are advantages to both equity and debt financing. For example, equity financing doesn't have to be repaid. On the downside, giving someone equity in a company makes them a part owner. It is necessary to share profits with them in perpetuity. In the event of a bankruptcy, once the debtors are all paid, the equity owners can divide up the remaining value between themselves.

Debt financing, like a loan, requires that the company make its loan payments in a timely manner. However, none of the profits are shared with the lender and at some point, the loan terminates. This makes loans a useful way to fund projects with a termination date. When the capital is no longer needed, it can be given back to the lender. In the event of a bankruptcy, bondholders get paid before equity holders.

Compared to bondholders, equity holders have a higher potential for both profit and loss. The best a bondholder can do is to make a small return on their investment. In comparison, the equity holder can benefit tremendously if a company grows and becomes successful. However, the equity holders also stand to lose more in the case of a bankruptcy—they are the last people to get paid.

Types of Companies

Stock investments typically relate to corporations. However, there are a variety of ways that energy companies can be organized:

- **Sole Proprietorship.** A sole proprietorship is a company with a single owner who is responsible for making decisions for the company. Sole proprietors have unlimited liability for all of the debts and liabilities that occur while operating the business—they can lose their homes, cars, and other personal assets if the company's assets are insufficient to cover the company's debts.

- **General Partnership.** A partnership is a company where two or more individuals share responsibility for running the company. Like proprietors, partners have unlimited liability for any debts that are incurred when operating the business.

- **Limited Liability Partnership.** Partnerships can be structured so that there is at least one general partner with unlimited liability and one or more limited partners whose liability is limited to their investment. In this kind of corporate structure, the general partner typically operates the company and the limited partners act as investors.

- **Corporation.** A corporation is considered its own entity with assets and liabilities distinct from its investors. As a result, the owners of the company, called shareholders, are not personally liable for any debts or liabilities incurred by the corporation. The ownership of a corporation is divided into portions, called shares. Each share is a claim upon the corporation's assets. For example, if a corporation has issued 10,000 shares of stock, owning 1,000 shares would entitle the shareholder to 10% of the company's assets. Shareholders will typically elect a board of directors that will manage the company for them.

Key Concept

Types of Companies

The most common ownership structure is a *corporation*. A corporation is a legal entity that limits the exposure of shareholders to company losses. Corporations are relatively easy for investors to participate in because investors can buy stock in the company and they are not personally liable for any debts the company might build up.

The Corporation

Many businesses are organized as corporations. Corporations are viewed as a stand-alone legal entity. As a result, corporations may do many of the activities normally restricted to people. For example, a corporation can own property, borrow money, sue other entities, and be sued themselves. Because a corporation is its own entity, the shareholders are not legally responsible for the corporation's debts.

While the size and complexity of corporations can vary substantially, their basic structure is identical. Shareholders elect a board of directors who oversee the company. The board of directors appoints the company's senior managers like the CEO (Chief Executive Officer), who are in turn responsible for running the day-to-day operations of the company (see Figure 9-2).

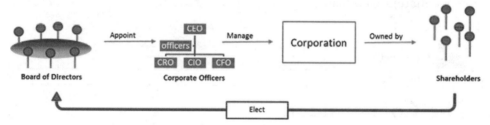

FIGURE 9-2 · The Corporation

When companies have sold stock to the general public, they are called *publically held* corporations. It is generally possible to buy and sell stock for publically held companies. In small companies it is common for a limited group of people to own all the stock and to serve as the corporation's directors and managers. These are called *privately held* companies.

- **Publicly Held Corporation.** A publicly held corporation is owned by stockholders who may or may not be affiliated with the company. It is generally fairly easy to buy and sell shares of publicly held corporations.

- **Privately Held Corporation.** A privately held corporation is owned by a limited group of people. It is common for the owners of privately held corporations to manage the day-to-day operations of the company. It is not generally possible to buy and sell shares of privately held corporations.

Corporations sometimes issue multiple types of stock and bonds. The major difference between the types is the priority that the stock/bondholder gets paid in the event of a bankruptcy.

- **Common/Preferred Stock.** The two main types of stock are common stock and preferred stock. Preferred stock receives preferential payment of dividends and gets paid ahead of common stock in the case of a bankruptcy or liquidation of assets. In the case of a bankruptcy, the creditors (bondholders and trading partners) will get paid before any type of stockholder. Preferred stockholders will be paid next. Finally, if any money is left over, common stockholders will be paid. In exchange for more security of income, preferred stockholders often do not have voting rights.

- **Senior/Subordinated Debt.** When a company issues multiple levels of debt, it may establish a priority order for which bonds will be repaid first in the event of a bankruptcy. The bonds that receive preference are called *senior debt*, and the ones that are repaid second are called *subordinated debt*. Typically, subordinated debt receives a higher interest rate than senior debt. In addition, some debt may be collateralized by specific pieces of property (a mortgage on a house is an example of a collateralized loan).

Key Concept

The Corporation

Buying stocks generally means investing in a corporation. A corporation is a limited liability corporate structure that issues both stock and bonds.

- Corporations can do many activities that people can do (own property, sue other people, get sued, etc.)
- Corporations are limited liability structures—stockholders can lose their investment in the company but are not personally liable to the company's debtors.

In the event of a bankruptcy, the order of repayment is shown in Table 9-1.

Priority	Description
1 (Most Senior)	Wages
2	Taxes
3	Secured Bonds (collateralized bondholders)
4	Unsecured Senior Debt (general creditors, bonds, trading partners, etc.)
5	Subordinated Debt (subordinated bonds)
6	Preferred Stock
7 (Most Junior)	Common Stock

TABLE 9-1 · Liquidation Rights

Priority During Liquidation

During a bankruptcy, there is a priority for people to get their money.

- **Senior Priority.** Someone who is first in line to get paid during liquidation of a company.
- **Junior Priority.** Someone who is behind other people in line to get paid during liquidation of a company.

Ring Fencing and Structural Subordination

Another facet of corporate organizational structure is that energy companies are often conglomerates composed of multiple subsidiaries (see Figure 9-3). In the energy industry, regulatory agencies (public utility commissions) commonly require that companies insulate their regulated operations from the unregulated operations. This has the effect of strengthening one part of the company (the regulated parts) while weakening the rest (the unregulated parts).

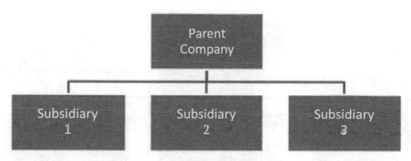

FIGURE 9-3 · A Simple Conglomerate

- **Parent Company.** A parent company is a company that owns a controlling interest in the stock in another company.
- **Holding Company.** A holding company is a special type of parent company whose primary business is holding equity positions in its subsidiaries.
- **Subsidiary.** A subsidiary is a company whose voting stock is controlled (at least 50% owned) by another company.
- **Affiliate.** Companies will have an affiliate relationship when one company owns a substantial, but not majority, interest of the voting stock in the other company or if the companies are both subsidiaries of the same parent.

Corporate structure affects investors because affiliates (subsidiaries of the same parent company) may or may not be liable for obligations made by other subsidiaries of the parent company. In addition, in some cases the assets of the sub-companies (particularly utilities) will not be liable for obligations incurred by the parent company. In these companies, it is important to understand the exact entity with which one is doing business.

Joint Guarantee

In some cases, a holding company and all of its subsidiaries will cross-guarantee the debt and obligations throughout the entities. In these cases, there is no difference created by doing business with and lending to one entity over another.

Ring Fencing

Ring fencing is an economic strategy that legally separates a regulated utility from its unregulated parent or holding company. The effect is to make the parent company a shareholder in the subsidiary. From a regulatory perspective, isolating a utility (or other piece) of a large firm has several effects. First, it tends to improve the credit rating of the utility. This can allow the utility to borrow more cheaply and keep down ratepayer costs. However, it can increase borrowing costs for the rest of the company. Second, it allows the parent company to conduct unregulated activity that could jeopardize the economic health of the utility (see Figure 9-4).

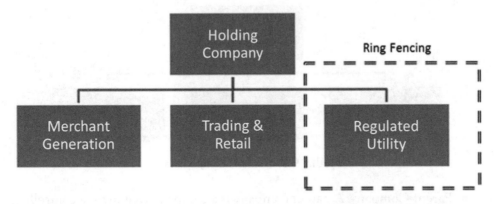

FIGURE 9-4 • Ring Fencing

When a subsidiary is ring fenced, the parent is entitled to dividends from the ring-fenced company and can sell off its ownership stake. However, the parent company often can't set the dividend for the regulated utility (this would usually require approval from the utility's regulator) or liquidate the assets of the subsidiary to pay its own debts. Ring fencing affects both stock- and bondholders.

For stockholders, ring fencing limits the ability of a company to access many of its assets. The utility is likely to own many of the most valuable assets of the holding company. If the trading or retail subsidiaries needed cash, the holding company could not acquire that cash by liquidating some of the assets in the regulated utility. This makes a bankruptcy for the holding company more likely.

For bondholders, there is a big difference between loaning money to the holding company or one of the non-ring-fenced subsidiaries and loaning money to the ring-fenced entity. On one hand, loaning money to the ring-fenced entity is likely to be a very safe investment. On the other hand, lending to the corporate parent might allow the bondholder a cheap way to take over the regulated utility. In the event of a bankruptcy at the holding company level, the bondholders would likely end up owning shares in the regulated utility while the equity holders would be left with nothing.

Structural Subordination

In some cases, a conglomerate will issue bonds or borrow money on several organizational levels (see Figure 9-5). In the event of a bankruptcy, each subsidiary will pay its own creditors first. This will give the lenders at the parent level a subordinate claim on the assets of its subsidiaries. Lenders at the parent level will only get paid after all of the lenders who lent money to the subsidiaries have been paid.

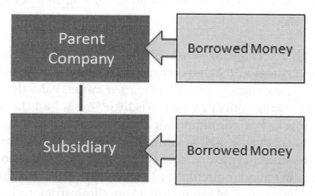

FIGURE 9-5 • Structural Subordination

Structural Subordination and Ring Fencing

Energy companies often have a complicated organizational structure imposed by having to deal with multiple regulators. This corporate structure can have a large impact on how a company's assets are liquidated in the case of a bankruptcy.

Common Stock

Common stock is the basic unit of ownership in a corporation. The holder of common stock is entitled to a portion of the company's earnings proportional to the amount of stock owned. Common stock is the first type of stock that a company issues and represents the most common type of ownership in a company. Owning common stock makes the stockholder the partial owner of a corporation. The price (value) of common stock is typically determined through trading markets. The *market value* of a stock is the price at which the stock trades in the public market.

In most cases, a single share of a stock usually represents only a tiny amount of ownership in a company. As a result, most stocks are traded in batches of 100 shares called a *round lot*. Stock traded in some increment other than a multiple of 100 shares is called an *odd lot* transaction.

- **Round Lot.** A round lot is a batch of 100 shares of stock, or a multiple of 100 shares
- **Odd Lot.** An odd lot is a batch of shares less than 100 shares of stock. For example, 173 shares is one round lot of 100 shares and one odd lot of 73 shares.

There are other accounting values for stocks that are relatively unimportant to most investors but may be confusing for bond investors. For example, common stock is commonly issued with a *par value*. Par value for common stock is an accounting concept which has little impact on the actual market value of the stock. For common stock, par value is an accounting value, unrelated to market value, below which the company guarantees it will not issue any more stock. Typically, this is set to an extremely low value (the lowest unit of currency in circulation) to avoid any chance the company is affected by the par value. Many jurisdictions allow stock to be issued without a par value.

When a corporation is first set up, its charter allows it to issue a certain number of shares of stock. Once a corporation is set up, changing the number of shares that it is authorized to issue requires a majority vote of the shareholders and a revision of the corporate charter.

- **Authorized Shares.** The number of shares that a corporation is authorized to sell is called the *authorized shares*. In many cases, not all of the shares are sold to investors so that the company can issue shares at a later point to raise additional capital.
- **Issued Shares.** The number of shares that has actually been issued to investors is called the *issued shares*.

- **Treasury Stock.** Treasury stock is stock that has been issued to investors and subsequently reacquired by the corporation. Treasury stock does not have voting rights or receive dividends.

- **Outstanding Stock.** Outstanding stock is stock that has been issued and is owned by investors. The amount of outstanding stock is equal to issued shares less any treasury stock. Outstanding stock has voting rights and receives dividends. The amount of outstanding stock determines what percentage of ownership is represented by each share of stock.

Corporations may also decide to distribute some of their earnings to stockholders in the form of a *dividend*. The board of directors for the corporation determines what type of dividend, if any, will be paid to common stockholders. Common stock dividends are not guaranteed and can be changed by the board of directors at any time.

Preferred Stock

Common stock isn't the only type of stock. There are actually two main classes of stock: *common stock* and *preferred stock*. Common stockholders have the right to vote on major company decisions, such as whether or not to merge with another corporation, and receive dividends as determined by the board of directors. Preferred stockholders give up voting rights to receive a minimum dividend and preference in bankruptcy liquidations. Preferred stock is not a better version of common stock—it is a different instrument altogether. Preferred stock is similar to a stock/bond hybrid.

Key Concept

Common and Preferred Stock

Stock gives the stockholder an ownership (equity) position in a company. There are two main types of stock—common stock and preferred stock.

- **Common Stock.** Common stock grants voting rights, but is the most junior security issued by a company.
- **Preferred Stock.** Preferred stock provides greater certainty in dividend payments and priority in case of a bankruptcy when compared to common stock. However, preferred stock generally does not have voting rights. In many cases, preferred stock can be converted into common stock.

Preferred stock is issued by companies that have already issued common stock. Preferred stock has bond-like features that appeal to investors who prefer income to capital appreciation. Like bondholders, preferred stockholders generally do not have voting rights.

Preferred stock is typically issued with a par value of $100 a share and carries a specified dividend. For example, 5% preferred stock will yield an annual dividend of $5/share (5% of the $100 par value). If the company is encountering financial difficulty, the board of directors can decide not to pay the dividend on the preferred stock, but this has repercussions. The repercussions depend on the type of preferred stock.

- **Cumulative Preferred Stock.** Most preferred stock is cumulative. If the board of directors decides not to pay the dividend for preferred stock, the unpaid dividends accumulate and must be paid in full to the preferred stockholders before dividends can be paid to common stockholders. Unpaid dividends are called *dividends in arrears*. For example, if a company did not pay preferred stock dividends on 5% cumulative preferred stock for two years, it has to make a $15/share payment in year 3 before it can pay dividends to common stockholders ($10/share in arrears plus $5/share for the current year).

- **Noncumulative Preferred Stock.** For noncumulative preferred stock, preferred stockholders only have priority over the current dividend. For example, if a company did not pay dividends to noncumulative preferred stock owners for two years, it must pay the preferred stockholders $5/share in the current year before common stockholders can be paid dividends.

In addition, preferred stock may also be callable (the company has the right to buy it back at a specified price) or convertible into common shares. Convertible preferred stock can be converted into common shares at conversion price. For example, $100 par value of convertible preferred stock with a conversion price of $50 can be converted into 2 shares of common stock ($100 par value/$50 conversion price). These features are similar to bonds and discussed in more detail in the bond discussion.

Key Concept

Preferred Stock

Preferred stock is an equity security with bond-like features. It behaves similar to a hybrid between a stock and a bond. It is not inherently better or worse than common stock.

Stock Dividends and Splits

Dividends are always paid on a per-share basis and reduce the value of the shares. For example, if an $85 stock pays a $1 dividend to shareholders, each shareholder will receive $1 per share, and the value of each share will drop $1 to be worth $84. The timeline for dividend payments runs from the announcement of the dividend (*the declaration date*), to the *record date* (owners on that date are entitled to a dividend), to the *payment date* (when the dividends are actually paid to shareholders). A snapshot of owners on the record date is used to determine who is entitled to dividends. The day after the record date is called the *ex-dividend* date.

Dividends represent a transfer of money from the corporation to the investor. As a result, dividends are taxable.

> **Example:** An investor owns 1,000 shares of stock, each with a market value of $50. The company declares a $2.50 cash dividend. On the ex-dividend date, the investor will still own 1000 shares of stock but each share will be worth $47.50 ($50 minus the $2.50 dividend). The stockholder will also receive a check for $2,500, some of which may be held back to pay taxes.

Key Concept

Ex-Dividend Dates

Stock bought prior to the ex-dividend date is entitled to a dividend. Stock purchased on or after the ex-dividend date is not entitled to a dividend. Payment of a dividend will reduce the value of the stock by the amount of the dividend and this change in price occurs on the ex-dividend date.

- **Record Date.** The date on which the snapshot of investors is taken to determine who gets paid dividends.
- **Payment Date.** The date that payments and additional shares are deposited into accounts.
- **Ex-Dividend Date.** The first day of trading after the dividend or stock split.

In all cases, dividends (and splits which will be discussed later) do not usually create trading opportunities for stockholders. They redistribute money between the company and the investors. The value to the investor is the same before and after the dividend (or split).

Stock Dividends

Instead of paying shareholders a cash dividend, the corporation can distribute additional shares to investors rather than cash. On the ex-dividend date, the value of the stock is reduced proportional to the number of new shares distributed to shareholders. As a result, the value of each shareholder's position is unchanged. As a result, stock dividends are not taxable until the shares are sold.

> **Example:** An investor owns 1,000 shares of stock, each with a market value of $50. The company declares a 5% stock dividend. On the ex-dividend date, the investor will own 1,050 shares of stock (1,000 * 1.05) and each share will be worth $47.62 ($50 / 1.05). The fractional difference in prices will be cleaned up when trading begins the next day. If a stock dividend results in a fractional share, the value of the share is usually paid in cash.

Stock Splits

Similar to a stock dividend, sometimes companies decide to split their stock. The company will issue more shares at a fixed ratio to its existing stock. For example, a company might issue a 2-for-1 split and replace each existing share of stock with two new shares. Like a stock dividend, the price of the stock will be proportionally adjusted. For example, after a 2-1 split, each shareholder will own twice as many shares but each share will only be worth half as much.

Many companies try to keep their stock price in the $15 to $100 range. This keeps a round lot (100 shares) in the $1,500 to $10,000, range which is affordable to most investors.

> **Example:** An investor owns 1,000 shares of stock, each with a market value of $150. The company announces a 3-for-1 split. On the ex-dividend date, the investor will own 3,000 shares of stock each worth $50.

Reverse Split

A reverse split is the opposite of a stock split. The company will proportionally reduce the number of shares to raise prices. For example, a 1-for-2 reverse split will double the stock price and give each investor half as many shares.

> **Example:** An investor owns 21,000 shares of stock, each with a market value of $3. The company decides to issue a 1-for-7 reverse split. On the ex-dividend date, the investor will own 3,000 shares (21,000 shares divided by 7) and each share will be worth $21.

For stock dividends, stock splits, and reverse splits, the ex-dividend date is the first business day following the payable day. Between the record date and the payable date, the stock is said to be trading *due bills*. A *due bill* is a tracking mechanism used to make sure that the proper shareholder ends up with the additional shares. To most investors, dividends and stock splits are not major events. The exchange will keep track of everything and make sure everyone gets the correct amount of shares and cash.

Key Concept

Dividends and Splits

Dividends and splits are common types of corporate actions.

- **Dividends.** Dividends redistribute money from the company to the investor. After a dividend is paid, the price of the stock will decrease by the amount of the dividend.
- **Stock Dividends, Splits, and Reverse Splits.** Stock dividends, splits, and reverse splits will change the amount of outstanding shares. The price of each share will change proportionally. For example, after a 2-for-1 split, each stockholder will own twice as many shares. However, each share will only be worth half as much.

Voting Rights

Along with the right to dividends, another important feature of common stock is voting rights. Only common stock grants voting rights, and each share of common stock gives its owner one vote. For example, ownership of 500 shares will give the stockholder 500 votes. Stockholders are primarily responsible for electing the board of directors. However, they also need to vote for corporate events that change the corporate charter. For example, common stockholders vote on stock splits because it is a change in the *authorized shares*. Most corporate decisions are actually made by the board of directors, who are elected by common stockholders. For example, dividends (both cash and stock dividends) are determined by the board of directors.

Electing the board of directors is the most important responsibility of shareholders. Each director is typically elected to serve a fixed term. Director elections tend to be staggered to limit the amount of turnover on the board in any single vote. However, election rules vary substantially from company to company.

- **Director.** A director is anyone who is elected to the company's board of directors.

- **Inside Director.** An inside director is a member of the board of directors who is also employed by the corporation or has a similar meaningful role with the company. For example, if the CEO or company treasurer serves on the board of directors, they would be considered inside directors.
- **Outside Director.** An outside director is one who is not employed by the corporation

When electing directors, there are several common practices. Some companies use statutory voting where each shareholder can vote their shares for each director slot being contested. Other companies use cumulative voting where each shareholder gets a number of votes multiplied by the number of director elections and can use those votes for any director vote.

Example: Statutory Voting. If a shareholder has 100 shares and 3 directors are being elected with statutory voting, the shareholder can cast 100 votes in each election.

Example: Cumulative Voting. If a shareholder has 100 shares and 3 directors are being elected with cumulative voting, the shareholder gets 300 votes to use across all elections. The shareholder could use 100 votes in each election, 150 votes in two of the elections, or cast all 300 votes in one election. This tends to favor minority shareholders since they can focus on electing at least one director who is favorable to their interests.

Shareholders are free to vote themselves or to vote by proxy. When a shareholder votes by proxy, they give someone else the authority to vote on their behalf. For example, a shareholder may grant the authority to have the board of directors vote for them. This helps ensure that a sufficient number of votes are cast during shareholder meetings.

Key Concept

Voting Privileges

Common stock represents an ownership interest in a company. The biggest responsibility of common stockholders is to elect the company's board of directors. The board of directors will hire a CEO and oversee the management of the company.

QUIZ

1. **What is the most common type of equity issued by corporations?**
   A. Common stock
   B. Bonds
   C. Audited financial statements
   D. Preferred stock

   Correct Answer: A

   Explanation: Common stock is the most common type of equity issued by corporations. An equity security gives its owner an equity (ownership) interest in a company.

2. **If a corporation uses cumulative voting rights for board of director elections, during an election for three directors, what is the maximum number of votes a shareholder who owns 100 shares can cast for the first director election?**
   A. 100
   B. 200
   C. 300
   D. Not enough information

   Correct Answer: C

   Explanation: With cumulative voting rights, a shareholder would receive 300 votes (3 elections × 100 votes each) that could be cast across all three elections. The shareholder could use all 300 votes in a single election, 100 votes in each election, or some other combination that added up to 300 votes across all three elections.

3. **A struggling natural gas marketer has issued both 2% cumulative preferred and common stock. The preferred stock dividend was not paid last year. How much money per share must be paid to preferred stockholders prior to dividends being given to common stockholders?**
   A. $2/share
   B. $4/share
   C. $6/share
   D. Insufficient information

   Correct Answer: B

   Explanation: The $2 dividend in arrears and the current dividend of $2 must both be paid to preferred stockholders prior to dividends being paid on common stock.

4. **Who needs to authorize a change in a company's dividend?**
   A. The CEO (Chief Executive Officer)
   B. The board of directors
   C. A simple majority of shareholders
   D. A two-thirds majority of shareholders

   Correct Answer: B

   Explanation: The dividend is determined by the board of directors and does not need to be approved by shareholders.

5. **What is the governing body of a corporation?**
   A. CEO (Chief Executive Officer)
   B. Board of directors
   C. Middle management
   D. Senior bondholders

Correct Answer: B

Explanation: The board of directors is the governing body of a corporation. The board of directors is elected by shareholders and appoints the CEO and senior managers of the firm. In some cases, the CEO and other senior managers of the corporation also serve on the board of directors.

6. **An energy holding company (HoldCo) owns both a regulated utility (UtilCo) and an unregulated energy trading company (TradeCo). The regulated utility (UtilCo) is ring-fenced and has very substantial assets. All of the publicly traded stock and debt is issued by HoldCo and all the assets are held at UtilCo and TradeCo. Large losses in TradeCo exceed the assets held at the TradeCo level. What is likely to happen?**
   A. HoldCo can decide to sell off some of the UtilCo assets to cover the trading losses incurred by TradeCo.
   B. The assets of both TradeCo and UtilCo will be liquidated in bankruptcy proceedings, and the proceeds will first pay the bondholders and then the stockholders of HoldCo.
   C. UtilCo will stay intact and the HoldCo bondholders will end up owning shares in UtilCo (control of the UtilCo shares will pass from the equity holders to the bondholders).
   D. UtilCo will stay intact and will issue new shares in an initial public offering (IPO) that can be used to repay the bondholders of HoldCo.

Correct Answer: C

Explanation: Since UtilCo is ring-fenced, the parent does not have the option of liquidating the HoldCo assets. The owners of HoldCo (the shareholders) may be forced to sell their ownership stake in UtilCo by transferring ownership directly to the bondholders. In some cases, the bondholders may have lent money to HoldCo strictly because they felt a bankruptcy was likely and they wanted to gain control of the UtilCo shares (this is called a "loan to own" strategy).

7. **What type of company gives investors limited liability?**
   A. Partnership
   B. Proprietorship
   C. Corporation
   D. All of the above

Correct Answer: C

Explanation: All stockholders in a corporation structure will typically have limited liability. With limited liability, investors typically cannot lose more money than they invested.

8. **A corporation is:**
   A. A for-profit company
   B. A company that has publicly traded stock
   C. A legal entity that has many of the same abilities as a person
   D. All of the above

   Correct Answer: C

   Explanation: A corporation is a legal entity that has many of the same abilities as a person. While many corporations are for-profit companies and issue publicly traded stock, these do not define a corporation. For example, some corporations are privately held (they have not publicly issued stock) and others are not-for-profit entities.

9. **A reverse stock split creates:**
   A. A larger number of shares
   B. A smaller number of shares
   C. A taxable event for shareholders
   D. A one-time dividend

   Correct Answer: B

   Explanation: A reverse stock split decreases the number of outstanding shares and creates a proportional increase in the price of each share. The value of each stockholder's position is unchanged so there is no tax.

10. **What is preferred stock?**
    A. Common stock with additional voting rights
    B. Common stock with a larger dividend
    C. An equity security that has features similar to both common stock and bonds
    D. A debt security that is junior to subordinated bonds

    Correct Answer: C

    Explanation: Preferred stock is an equity security (it provides an ownership stake in a company). However, it is distinct from common stock, and has both advantages and disadvantages when compared to common stock.

Chapter 10

Bonds (Fixed Income Investments)

Fixed income investments, like bonds, allow investors to loan money to companies and receive interest payments in return. The interest payments are usually reasonably well known when the bond is purchased. As a result, bonds typically make a good investment for investors looking for steady income or a certain amount of money on some date in the future.

Once a company issues bonds, they can be traded to other investors. Bond prices can move substantially during the period after issuance and before they are redeemed. For bonds that are not held to maturity, price movements are a source of both risk and potential profit opportunities. Changing interest rates is one of the major reasons that bond prices change over time.

The value of bonds is heavily affected by the credit of the issuer. Companies at higher risk of defaulting on their payments typically need to pay bondholders higher interest rates than higher credit quality issuers. This can mean higher profits for investors that loan money to poor credit quality companies. However, there is also a greater chance of losing the total investment when lending to poor credit counterparties. Credit situations change over time and heavily impact the value of bonds when traded between investors.

CHAPTER OBJECTIVES

After completing this chapter, the student should have an understanding of

- Bonds
- Interest rates, bond prices, and yields
- Bond ratings
- Convertible, callable, and putable bond provisions

Corporate Bonds

A corporate bond is financial contract similar to a loan. A bond issuer borrows money from an investor and is then obligated to repay the money with interest. The issuer pays the investor interest as a specified amount of money (the *coupon payment*) paid on designated dates (*coupon dates*). The issuer also has to repay the original loan (the *principal*) at a maturity date. Failure to pay either a coupon or the principal when it is due is called a *default* and will generally trigger legal proceedings to enforce the contract. The promises between the bond issuer and the bond buyers, as well as the rights of the bond buyers (the lenders) are set out in a contract called an indenture. This contract is overseen by a trustee who will act in the interest of the bondholders.

- **Par Value (Face Amount, Principal).** The par value of a bond (the face amount or principal) of a bond is the amount of money that the issuer agrees to pay the bondholder at the maturity of the bond. Most bonds are initially sold at their par value—the bondholder pays the issuer an amount of money equal to the principal. After that point, bond prices can diverge from the par value. A bond that is selling for a higher price than the par value is said to be trading at a *premium*. A bond that is selling for less than its par values is said to be trading at a *discount*.

- **Maturity Date.** The issuer is obligated to repay the principal (face amount, par value) to the bondholder on the maturity date. Typically, the bondholder will also receive the last coupon payment at the same time. Maturity dates commonly range from 10 to 30 years.

- **Coupon Rate.** When the bond is issued, the bond issuer agrees to pay the bondholder a stated amount of interest every year (the coupon payment). This is typically expressed as a percentage of the bond's face value—for example, 5% per year. An owner of a $1,000 par value bond paying a 5% coupon would receive $50 per year (5% times $1,000 face value). Typically, this is split into two semiannual payments, so the bondholder in this example would receive $25 twice a year until the maturity date.

Bond Basics

Some common bond terminology:

- **Par Value.** The par value is the amount of money repaid on maturity of the bond. This is the face value and, for many bonds, corresponds to the principal that is loaned to the company.
- **Coupon Payment.** A coupon payment is regular payment made by the issuer to the bondholder in exchange for use of their money. This is also called an interest *payment* or *nominal yield.*
- **Maturity Date.** The issuer of the bond pays the last coupon payment and the par value of the bond to the bondholder on the maturity date.

After they are issued, bonds can be bought and sold between investors. These transactions will commonly not occur at the par value, but fluctuate over time. Bond prices are usually stated as a percentage of the par value. For example, a bond that is trading at 100 is trading at 100% of par value. A bond that is trading at 90 is trading at 90% of par value (it is trading at a discount). A bond trading at 110 is trading at 110% of the par value (it is trading at a premium).

- **Points.** Each 1% increment in price is known as a point.
- **Discount.** A bond price that is below par value.
- **Premium.** A bond price that is above par value.

For example, an investor might buy a $1,000 face value bond, paying a 5% coupon, maturing in 10 years for $1,000. Essentially, the investor is loaning the bond issuer $1,000 for 10 years. If the investor decides to sell the bond a month later, the price of the bond is likely to have changed. If the price of the bond is 98 at the trade date, the original investor will get paid $980 plus any unpaid interest accrued while he was the bondholder. The company who issued the bond is not affected by this change in ownership.

Some bonds don't make regular coupon payments (their coupon rate is zero). As a result, these are called *zero-coupon bonds*. Typically, these are issued and traded at a discount to their par value. For example, a company might issue a zero-coupon $1,000 par-value bond maturing in 10 years for $500. A buyer of these bonds would get $1,000 in ten years for each $500 spent today, if the bonds were held to maturity and the company didn't go into bankruptcy.

Key Concept

Zero-Coupon Bonds

Zero-coupon bonds don't have coupon payments and will always trade at a discount to their par value (assuming positive interest rates).

Bond Yields

Investors will often want to know what return they can get on their investment. In the bond market, this return is commonly expressed as a *yield-to-maturity* or abbreviated as *yield* or basis.[1] There are two components to yield—price appreciation and coupon payments. Price appreciation is the difference between the current price of the bond (where people are willing to buy or sell it) and its value at maturity. Coupon payments are the interest payments that will be paid to the bondholder.

When bonds are first issued, the coupon rate of the bond is set as a percentage of the par value. This rate usually does not change over time and is known as the *nominal yield*. A $1,000 par-value bond with a 10% coupon will pay $100/year in two $50 payments per year for the life of the bond. The 10% yield is known as the nominal yield of the bond [see Equation (10.1)].

$$Nominal\ Yield = \frac{Annual\ Interest\ Payment}{Par\ Value} \tag{10.1}$$

After a bond has been issued, its price can vary substantially. For example, rising interest rates or the threat of bankruptcy can both lead to a decline in bond prices. Bonds issued by those companies may see their bonds trade at a discount to face value. If the $1,000 par value 10% bond is trading at 50, it can be purchased for $500 from another trader. However, the coupon payments are still $100. The coupon yield as a percent of its trading price is called the *current yield* [see Equation (10.2)].

$$Current\ Yield = \frac{Annual\ Interest\ Payment}{Trading\ Price} \tag{10.2}$$

Both of these calculations only measure the effect of the coupon payment on the valuation. There is a second factor that also needs to be considered—the difference in price between the trading price and the amount paid at maturity (the par value). For example, a $1,000 par-value zero-coupon bond trading at 50 will still offer a bondholder a significant profit opportunity because the bond costs $500 to buy and will mature for $1,000. The measure of return (the interest rate) that incorporates both payments and price appreciation is called *yield-to-maturity*.

The definition of yield-to-maturity is the interest rate that makes the present value and all future cash flows equal to one another. As a result, the most common abbreviations for yield-to-maturity are *YTM* or *r* (since it is a type of interest rate). Most spreadsheets and financial calculators will have functions to solve for yield-to-maturity. Manually solving for yield-to-maturity involves creating a present value formula for a bond and solving for the interest rate that satisfies Equation (10.3).

Yield-to-Maturity. Solve for the value of r that satisfies equation

$$P = \frac{F}{(1+r)^n} + \sum_{t=1 \text{ to } n} \frac{C}{(1+r)^t} \qquad (10.3)$$

Where
C = Annual Coupon Payments
F = Face value (par value)
P = Current Price
n = Years to Maturity
r = Yield to Maturity

In most cases, if you have to manually estimate the yield-to-maturity, it is possible to calculate an approximate answer by hand as shown in Equation (10.4).

Approximate Yield-to-Maturity

$$\text{Approximate YTM} = \frac{C + \frac{F - P}{n}}{\frac{F + P}{2}} \qquad (10.4)$$

where

C = annual Coupon Payments
F = Face value (par value)
P = Current Price
n = years to maturity

When yield-to-maturity is quoted by traders, it is commonly just called *yield* or *basis*. Coupon yield and current yield are not commonly referred to as yield.

Yields

Yield describes the percent profit that an investor will make on their investment.

- **Yield-to-Maturity (YTM).** The yield-to-maturity is the expected return on buying a bond. This is commonly quoted in the market along with price and can be calculated using a financial calculator or spreadsheet formula.
- **Yield.** In the bond market, this term typically refers to yield-to-maturity and not coupon yield or current yield.
- **Basis.** In bonds, this term is synonymous with yield-to-maturity. A 6.33 basis and a 6.33% yield-to-maturity are identical descriptions. Note: There are other meanings for the term *basis*. For example, *basis* is used in the natural gas markets to indicate a difference price due to location.
- **Basis Point.** The basis point is equal to 1/100 of 1%. A bond yielding 7.25% is 25 basis points higher than a bond yielding 7.00%.

Interest Rates, Prices, and Yields

A bond investor typically makes money when interest rates fall and loses money when interest rates rise. The reason is that bond investors will buy bonds that will give them the highest yield-to-maturity. If interest rates rise, new bonds will be issued at higher coupons. An existing bond with a lower coupon will need its price to drop to get the same yield-to-maturity as the newly issued bonds. If the bond investor wishes to sell the bond he bought previously, it will need to match the yield-to-maturity of currently issued bonds. In other words, the term *interest rates* and the *yield-to-maturity* rate observed from recent bond trades are mostly synonymous.

Bond investors run the risk that interest rates will change unfavorably while they hold the bond (see Figure 10-1).

The opposite is also true—falling interest rates will make previously issued bonds more valuable (see Figure 10-2).

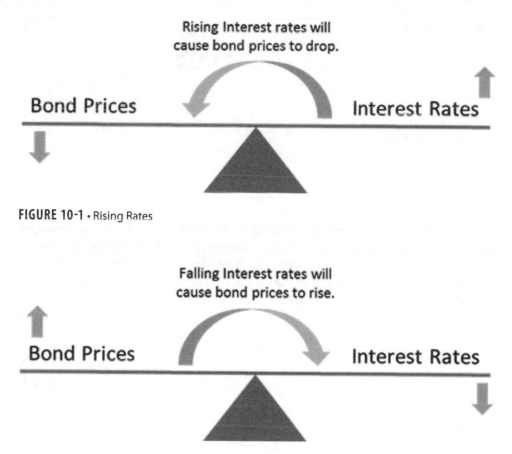

FIGURE 10-1 • Rising Rates

FIGURE 10-2 • Falling Rates

In general, the longer that a bondholder has to wait to get their money, the more the bond price will be affected by a change in interest rates.

- **Coupon Rate.** High coupon rates help the bond buyer to get some of their money early. High-coupon bonds are less affected by changes in interest rates than low-coupon (or zero-coupon) bonds.
- **Maturity.** Bonds with nearby maturities give bondholders their money back earlier than longer term bonds. Short-term bonds are less affected by interest rate changes than long-term bonds.

To compare the effect of interest rate changes on bonds with different coupons and maturities, bond investors generally look at the weighted average maturity of cash flows. This is commonly called a *Macaulay Duration* after Frederick Macaulay who introduced the concept, and is shown in Equation (10.5). (See Figure 10-7.)

Macualay Duration

$$Duration = \frac{\sum_{t=1}^{n} \frac{t * C}{(1 + i)^t} + \frac{n * F}{(1 + i)^t}}{P} \qquad (10.5)$$

where

C = annual coupon payments
P = current bond price
F = Face Value (par value)
n = years to maturity
t = used to count between 1 and n
i = current interest rates

A slightly modified version of duration is extensively used in risk management to calculate the amount of price change caused by a change in interest rates. This modified formula, shown in Equation (10.6), demonstrates how much the price of a bond will change for a 1% change in yield. Modified duration is commonly used by investors wishing to describe the price volatility of a particular bond relative to interest rates.

Modified Duration

$$Modified\ Duration = \frac{Macaulay\ Duration}{(1 + \frac{YTM}{n})} \qquad (10.6)$$

where

YTM = yield to maturity
n = years to maturity

Key Concept

Prices and Interest Rates

Bonds lose value (prices fall) when interest rates rise. Rising interest rates are generally bad for bondholders. Falling interest rates are generally good for bondholders.

- **Duration.** The weighted average maturity of cash flows. Bonds where cash flows will occur far in the future (high duration bonds) are more affected by interest rate movements than bonds with nearby cash flows (low duration bonds).
- **Modified Duration.** The amount of money that a bondholder would make or lose with a 1% shift in interest rates.

Bond Ratings

Bonds are not certain investments—there is a very real possibility that the issuer of a bond will go bankrupt before they can fulfill their obligations to the bondholders. As a result, to incentivize people to loan them money, issuers that are considered bad credit risks may have to pay substantially higher coupon payments.

To make it easier for investors to understand the risks of buying a particular type of bond, there are a variety of credit rating agencies that publish credit ratings for various issuers. Not all bonds are rated by each ratings agency. The bond issuer has to request a bond offering be rated and has to pay the ratings agency to rate the issue. This is generally done to establish the issuer's credit-worthiness and willingness to protect the interest of its bondholders. Unrated bond issues are not necessarily low credit quality—they might be too small to justify the expense of rating.

Credit ratings are primarily concerned with the risk of nonpayment (default risk). Investors should keep in mind that while default risk is an extremely important risk, it is only one of several risks facing bond investors. Inflation, illiquidity, and price fluctuations can all cause bond investors to lose substantial amounts of money in ways unrelated to defaults.

Credit ratings will be periodically reviewed and updated. This can have a dramatic effect on a price of a bond. Credit ratings of Baa/BBB– or higher are considered investment-grade bonds that are suitable for most investors. Bonds with lower credit ratings are considered *high-yield bonds* (*junk bonds*) and involve more substantial risks. Many investment funds like pension plans will have limits on the credit quality of bonds that they will hold in their portfolios. As a result, a rise or drop in credit rating can result in a large sell-off or substantially increased interest from potential investors (see Table 10-1).

Key Concept

Bond Ratings

The coupon rates for bonds will typically be proportional to the credit risk of the issuer.

- **Investment Grade.** Bonds rated Baa/BBB– or higher are considered investment grade.
- **High Yield (Junk Bonds).** Bonds rated lower than Baa/BBB– are considered speculative investments that may involve a high degree of risk that makes them unsuitable for some investors

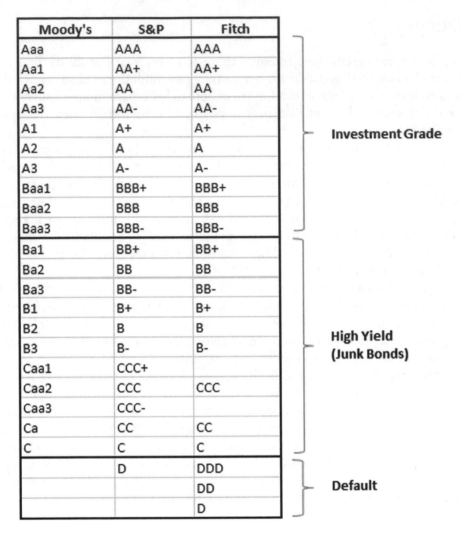

Moody's	S&P	Fitch	
Aaa	AAA	AAA	
Aa1	AA+	AA+	
Aa2	AA	AA	
Aa3	AA-	AA-	
A1	A+	A+	**Investment Grade**
A2	A	A	
A3	A-	A-	
Baa1	BBB+	BBB+	
Baa2	BBB	BBB	
Baa3	BBB-	BBB-	
Ba1	BB+	BB+	
Ba2	BB	BB	
Ba3	BB-	BB-	
B1	B+	B+	
B2	B	B	
B3	B-	B-	**High Yield (Junk Bonds)**
Caa1	CCC+		
Caa2	CCC	CCC	
Caa3	CCC-		
Ca	CC	CC	
C	C	C	
	D	DDD	
		DD	**Default**
		D	

TABLE 10-1 · Bond Ratings

Secured and Unsecured Bonds

The two main types of corporate bonds are secured bonds and unsecured bonds. Both types of bonds are backed by the full faith and credit of the issuer. However, secured bonds have the additional security of being backed with specific assets that are used as collateral.

Unsecured corporate bonds are secured only by the corporation's good faith and credit. These unsecured securities are also called *notes* or *debentures*. In the event of a bankruptcy, unsecured bondholders will be paid after the secured bondholders, along with other general creditors and before stockholders. When companies issue subordinated debt, subordinated bondholders will receive payments after the senior bondholders and other general creditors of the company but before stockholders.

Corporations also have the option of issuing secured bonds. These bonds will typically offer lower coupon payments to bondholders but have a higher degree of security. In the event of a bankruptcy, the trustee will liquidate the collateral on behalf of the bondholders using the proceeds to first pay the bonds secured by that collateral. If any money is left over, then the general creditors will be paid.

- **Mortgage Bonds.** Mortgage bonds are backed by a lien on a specific piece of property.
- **Equipment Trust Certificates.** In these types of bonds, a trustee will hold legal title to the equipment until the bonds are paid off. These are commonly used to finance transportation equipment like oil tankers or railroads.
- **Collateral Trust Bonds.** Collateral trust bonds are secured by a portfolio of third-party securities owned by the issuer. These are placed in escrow (under the control of a trustee) as collateral for the bond.

The collateral used to repay collateralized bondholders is linked to a specific piece of collateral. If that specific collateral does not cover the money needed to pay the bondholders, the collateralized bondholders become general creditors of the company. The order of payment in event of a bankruptcy is shown in Table 10-2.

Priority	Description
1	Wages
2	Taxes
3	Secured Bonds (collateralized bonds)
4	Unsecured Senior Debt (general creditors, debentures, trading partners, etc.)
5	Unsecured Subordinated Debt
6	Preferred Stock
7	Common Stock

TABLE 10-2 · Liquidation Rights

Key Concept

Secured and Unsecured Bonds

In order to lower the coupon payments that need to be paid to bondholders, companies will often secure their bonds with specific assets. Both secured and unsecured bonds are backed by the full faith and credit of the issuer—secured bonds have an extra level of protection.

- **Secured Bonds.** Secured bonds have specific collateral pledged to repay the bonds in event of a default.
- **Unsecured Bonds (Debentures).** Unsecured bonds are general credit obligations of a corporation and are the most common type of corporate bond.

Convertible Bonds

To provide investors more incentive to purchase their bonds or to lower the coupon rates that they need to pay, companies may issue bonds that are convertible into common stock. Convertible bonds allow bondholders to convert their bonds into shares of stock at a predefined ratio. This is often an attractive feature for bondholders because it will allow them to benefit from a rise in stock prices while still having more downside protection than preferred stockholders.

When a convertible bond is first issued, a conversion price is written into the contract. The number of shares that a bondholder will receive by converting their bonds into cash can be calculated by dividing the par value of the bond by the conversion price, as shown in Equation (10.7).

$$Conversion\ Ratio = \frac{Par\ Value\ of\ Bond}{Conversion\ Price} \tag{10.7}$$

The decision to convert bonds into common stock will largely depend on the stock price. To a lesser extent it will depend on upcoming dividend payments and coupon payments. Stock splits and stock dividends generally don't have an economic effect on convertible bonds—the conversion price of the bond will change proportionally with the split or stock dividend. For example, with a 2-for-1 split, the conversion price of a convertible bond would be cut in half. The dollar value of stock that could be obtained by converting the bond would remain the same.

Key Concept

Convertible Bonds

In order to lower the coupon payments that need to be paid to bondholders, companies may include a feature in the bond that allows it to be converted into shares.

Callable/Putable Bonds

Bonds can be written with features that allow either the issuer or the bondholder to redeem the bond at a predefined price prior the bond's maturity date. In most cases, there is a period of time after the bond is issued before the bond can be redeemed.

- **Callable Bond.** The issuer has the right to redeem the bond at a pre-defined price (usually at a premium to the par value of the bond). Callable bonds typically pay bondholders a higher coupon rate than noncallable bonds in exchange for giving the issuer the option to redeem the bonds early.

- **Putable Bond.** The bondholder has the right to redeem the bond at a predefined price (usually at a discount to the par value of the bond) prior to the maturity of the bond. Putable bonds typically have a lower coupon rate than non-putable bonds.

In practice, bonds are typically not bought and sold when a call or put provision is exercised—they are canceled with a corresponding payment from the issuer to the bondholder. Embedded call and put features in bonds are commonly valued using a generalized Black–Scholes type of model described in Chapter 7.

Key Concept

Callable/Putable Bonds

Bonds can contain embedded options that allow either the issuer or the bond-holder to redeem the bond early at a predetermined price. Various features can modify how likely a bond option is to be exercised.

- **Call.** The issuer has the option to redeem the bond (to call it back from the bondholder). A callable bond will typically offer the bondholder a higher coupon payment than a standard bond. This right can be valuable, and the issuer typically has to pay a higher yield on these bonds
- **Put.** The bondholder has the right to redeem (put) the bond back to the issuer. This right to force early redemption is valuable, so the bondholder typically has to accept a lower yield on these bonds.
- **Premium.** Redemption of callable and putable bonds is at a predefined price that may be at a premium to par value (common for callable bonds) or a discount to par value (common for putable bonds).

QUIZ

1. **Which type of bond will typically have the highest coupon payments? Assume all bonds have the same issuer and maturity date?**
   A. A zero-coupon bond
   B. A callable bond
   C. A putable bond
   D. A convertible bond

   Correct Answer: B

   Explanation: A callable bond will typically have higher coupon payments than putable or convertible bonds. Convertible and putable bonds will both give extra rights to the bondholder, which tends to lower the coupon payment. A callable bond gives extra rights to the issuer (the ability to call the bond back). A zero-coupon bond will have zero coupon payments. While it is possible to have a callable zero-coupon bond, it will result in the bond being issued at a larger than normal discount to par value. A putable bond will typically have a lower coupon rate than an unsecured corporate bond.

2. **What is the nominal yield on a 6% bond maturing in 10 years, if current interest rates have risen 2%?**
   A. 4%
   B. 6%
   C. 8%
   D. Insufficient Information

   Correct Answer: B

   Explanation: The nominal yield is equal to the coupon rate (6% in this case). The information that interest rates have risen is unnecessary to answer the question and included to make the question more difficult.

3. **Belinda, an analyst at an investment bank, has been asked by the head of trading to select a universe of high yield bonds for a comparative analysis. How should she limit her selections?**
   A. Bonds that have a credit rating of Ba1/BB+ and below
   B. Bonds that have a credit rating of B1/B+ and below
   C. Bonds that are trading at less than par value
   D. Bonds that are trading above par value

   Correct Answer: A

Explanation: The distinction of high yield depends on credit rating rather than a comparison to par value. High yield bonds have credit ratings of Ba1/BB+ and below. Investment-grade bonds have ratings higher than Ba1/BB+.

4. **If a corporation has a collateral trust bond on assets that have recently become worthless, what happens to the bond?**

   A. Unless there is a clause that replaces the collateral, the bonds become unsecured bonds backed by full faith and credit of the company.

   B. The company can default on the bonds without repercussions.

   C. The bonds will become worthless.

   D. The bonds will begin trading at a discount to par value.

   Correct Answer: A

   Explanation: All bonds issued by a company are backed by the full faith and credit of a company. Similar to defaulting on an unsecured bond, defaulting on a secured bond whose collateral is worthless will result in a default and possible bankruptcy proceedings. The bonds are unlikely to become worthless. There is insufficient information to determine whether the bonds would trade at a discount to their par value.

5. **A debenture is a(n):**

   A. Investment-grade bond

   B. Unsecured corporate bond

   C. Collateralized bond

   D. High-yield bond

   Correct Answer: B

   Explanation: A debenture is an unsecured corporate bond. Debentures are described as investment grade if their credit rating is above Baa/BBB– and high-yield or junk bonds if their credit rating is lower than that.

Questions 6 & 7 use the following information.
Austin, a private investor, decides to purchase a 10% bond maturing in 10 years for 96 with a par value of $1,000.

6. **How much money did Austin spend to purchase the bond?**

   A. $9.60

   B. $96

   C. $960

   D. $1,000

   Correct Answer: C

Explanation: Bonds are quoted as a percentage of par value, so a 96 price would be $960 (96% of $1,000).

7. **How much money will Austin receive on the maturity date if he holds the bond to maturity?**
   A. $1,000
   B. $1,050
   C. $1,060
   D. $1,100

Correct Answer: B

Explanation: At maturity, the bond will pay its face value ($1,000) plus the last coupon payment ($50). Bonds typically pay semiannual coupon payments, so a 10% bond will pay 5% twice a year. The last coupon payment will be 5% times the face value of $1,000 ($50).

8. **Who makes the decision on when to redeem a callable bond?**
   A. The bondholder
   B. The issuer
   C. The government
   D. The responsible party varies from bond to bond

Correct Answer: B

Explanation: A callable bond gives the issuer to option to call (redeem) the bond back from the bondholder.

9. **AngelaCo has issued a variety of bonds which differ only by coupon rate and maturity date. Which bond will suffer the sharpest decline in value with a rise in interest rates?**
   A. A 2% bond maturing in 5 years
   B. A zero-coupon bond maturing in 5 years
   C. A 2% bond maturing in 10 years
   D. A zero-coupon bond maturing in 10 years

Correct Answer: D

Explanation: Long maturity bonds with low coupon rates will be the most affected by interest rates. They will lose more money when interest rates rise and make more money when interest rates fall.

10. **How many shares would a bondholder receive for converting a $1,000 par value 10% bond with a conversion price of $50?**

    A. 1 share

    B. 10 shares

    C. 20 shares

    D. 50 shares

    Correct Answer: C

    Explanation: The bond could be converted into 20 shares ($1,000 par value / $50 conversion price = 20 shares).

Part III

Final Exam

Final Exam

1. Truman, a geologist working for an oil exploration company, has discovered a large oil sands deposit in a remote area. He has identified a lack of nearby water sources, skilled workers, and nearby pipelines as potential obstacles. What is likely to be the biggest constraint in the development of this reserve?
   A. Lack of pipelines
   B. Lack of water
   C. Lack of skilled workers
   D. None of these answers

2. If a shareholder has 100 shares of stock in a company that has 1,000 authorized shares, 500 issued shares, and 100 shares in treasury stock, what portion of the company is owned by the shareholder?
   A. 10%
   B. 20%
   C. 25%
   D. 50%

3. Edmund owns 10 put options on IBM stock.
   A. Edmund has an exposure that is long IBM stock and long volatility.
   B. Edmund has an exposure that is short IBM stock and long volatility.
   C. There is insufficient information to determine whether Edmund has long or short exposure to IBM stock but he is definitely long volatility.
   D. Edmund has an exposure that is long IBM stock and there is insufficient information to determine whether he is long or short volatility.

4. What term is used to describe a location where natural gas is injected into a pipeline?
   A. Receipt point
   B. Delivery point
   C. Natural gas hub
   D. Citygate

5. Who makes the decision on when to redeem a putable bond?
   A. The bondholder
   B. The issuer
   C. The government
   D. The responsible party varies from bond to bond

6. A large oil field has proven reserves of 2.6 billion barrels of oil and 17 trillion cubic feet of gas. Last year, the field produced about 250,000 barrels of oil and 1.6 billion cubic feet of gas per day. What is the producing gas-oil ratio in ft^3/BBL?
   A. 4,900
   B. 6,100
   C. 6,400
   D. 6,538

7. Haseeb, a private investor, has recently purchased $50,000 of corporate bonds. What will happen to the value of Haseeb's portfolio if interest rates decline?
   A. It will decline in value.
   B. It will increase in value.
   C. It will remain the same.
   D. Insufficient information.

8. Shale gas is discovered near an LNG liquefaction terminal. As a result, the raw material coming into the terminal will contain an especially high volume of condensate and natural gas liquids. How will this affect the revenue of the LNG terminal?
   A. Profits will decline because the NGLs must be removed and this will increase processing costs.
   B. There will be no effect on the profitability since LNG is sold on the basis of heat content.
   C. There will be no effect on profitability because the increased processing costs will be offset by the second revenue stream from NGLs.
   D. The presence of high quantities of NGLs will substantially improve the revenue of the facility.

9. Dan, an analyst at an investment bank, is advising senior management about a potential investment in a shale oil investment. There is confusion about the terms shale oil and shale gas. How should Dan describe how shale oil is produced?

   A. Superheated steam is injected to dissolve tar-like oil from shale rock.
   B. Shale rock, recovered using mining techniques, is crushed and heated to produce fuel.
   C. Shale rock is fractured using hydraulic fracking techniques to free hydrocarbons trapped inside.
   D. A well is drilled through shale rock to reach oil trapped underneath the impermeable rock.

10. Assuming that ethanol is 5% denser than gasoline, what percentage of E10 gasoline by volume consists of ethanol?

   A. 10.0% ethanol
   B. 10.4% ethanol
   C. 89.6% ethanol
   D. 90.0% ethanol

11. In the petroleum industry, what does a barrel of oil equivalent (BOE) measure?

   A. The energy content of crude oil from different locations
   B. The energy content of refined petroleum measured against a WTI or Brent benchmark
   C. The energy content of natural gas relative to that of crude oil in a reservoir
   D. The energy content of renewable fuels compared against a WTI or Brent crude benchmark

12. What does a bondholder receive for purchasing a bond?

   A. Voting rights that determine how a company is managed
   B. Ownership in the company
   C. Benefit of capital appreciation
   D. Interest payments

13. If price returns follow a random walk, volatility will scale with:

   A. The cube root of time
   B. The square root of time
   C. Time
   D. The square of time

14. If an energy holding company (HoldCo), whose sole asset is shares in a utility (UtilCo), has issued debt at both the holding company and the subsidiary level, what is the order of repayment in event of a bankruptcy ?

   I.   Senior debt issued by HoldCo
   II. Subordinated debt issued by HoldCo
   III. Senior debt issued by UtilCo
   IV. Subordinated debt issued by UtilCo

   In the following answers, the debt with the highest priority of repayment is listed first.
   A. III, I, II, IV
   B. III, IV, I, II
   C. IV, II, III, I
   D. IV, III, II, I

15. What is a reason that a large company might commit to buying 100% of its power for its data centers from renewable sources, even though it is not required to by law and buys enough RECs to meet its requirements?

   I.   The company is interested in ensuring a reliable supply of power.
   II. The company wishes to voluntarily pay higher costs for power to help fund the development of renewable energy.
   III. It is good advertising and will appeal to the company's client base.
   IV. The company is looking for the cheapest way to acquire power.

   A. Answers I and II
   B. Answers II and III
   C. Answers I and IV
   D. Answers I, II, and IV

16. Excluding time value of money, what instruments can be combined to create a synthetic long put?
   A. Long Future + Short Call
   B. Short Future + Long Call
   C. Long Future + Long Call
   D. Short Future + Short Call

17. Which of the following best describes the role of an ISO/RTO in an electric transmission network?
   A. The ISO/RTO is responsible for maintaining the transmission and distribution lines.
   B. The ISO/RTO controls the dispatch of generation units and coordinates the power grid.
   C. The ISO/RTO is the local governmental regulatory organization responsible for overseeing the power grid.
   D. An ISO/RTO is a private trade organization that lobbies for power grid reform.

18. **Which statement related to renewable energy is incorrect?**
    A. Renewable energy units often have uncertain capacity factors.
    B. Renewable energy sources are inexhaustible.
    C. Renewable energy resources are less useful than conventional, fossil fuel based units at balancing transmission congestion on a power grid.
    D. Renewable energy is commonly more expensive that using fossil fuels.

19. **What does the term arbitrage mean in the financial markets?**
    A. A risk-free opportunity for profit
    B. Detention of a cargo vessel past its scheduled time of departure
    C. An independent body chosen to judge or decide a disputed issue
    D. A market with limited trading opportunities

20. **If a corporation uses statutory voting rights for board of director elections, during an election for three directors, what is the maximum number of votes a shareholder who owns 100 shares can cast for the first director election?**
    A. 100
    B. 200
    C. 300
    D. Not enough information

21. **Approximately what percentage of samples will be within 2 standard deviations of the mean in a normal distribution?**
    A. 34%
    B. 68%
    C. 95%
    D. 99%

22. **Hydroelectric generation is an emission-free source of power that is highly reliable, and can be dispatched on short notice. What is the major reason preventing the construction of additional hydroelectric generation plants?**
    A. Environmental regulations limit construction of new hydroelectric generation.
    B. Financial subsidies for solar and wind generation units tend to be larger than for hydro units.
    C. Most sites suitable for hydroelectric generation already have existing generation units in place.
    D. Fossil fuel generation is less expensive than hydroelectric generation.

23. **What is the relationship between forward and spot prices in a contango market?**
    A. Forward prices are higher than spot prices.
    B. Forward prices are lower than spot prices.
    C. Forward and spot prices are linked by no-arbitrage concepts.
    D. Forward and spot prices follow a random walk process.

24. **Which of the following technologies uses a turbine to drive a generator and use the process of electromagnetic induction to generate electricity?**
    I.   Hydroelectric power
    II. Wind power
    III. Nuclear power
    IV. Fossil-fuel power

    A. I and II
    B. III and IV
    C. I, II, and III
    D. I, II, III, and IV

25. **What technology is used on most transmission grids?**
    A. Alternating current (AC) power that is scaled to higher and lower voltage using transformers
    B. Alternating current (AC) with variable wavelengths
    C. Direct current (DC) power arranged in a point-to-point network
    D. Direct Current (DC) power with a variable voltage based on grid location

26. **Biswajit, an auditor, is looking for the price for what a client describes as "red diesel." He should use the price for which product?**
    A. No. 2 Diesel Fuel
    B. Off-road diesel
    C. Ultra-low-sulfur diesel
    D. Premium-grade high-cetane diesel

27. **What is an Asian Option?**
    A. An option traded in Asia
    B. An option whose settlement price is based on the average price over some period of time
    C. An option which can be exercised at any time
    D. An option that can be exercised only on the expiration date

28. **Which type of crude oil is likely to be the most valuable?**
    A. 25 API gravity, 3.0% sulfur
    B. 25 API gravity, 0.5% sulfur
    C. 30 API gravity, 3.0% sulfur
    D. 30 API gravity, 0.5% sulfur

29. **What type of financial instrument is the most junior security that a corporation will issue?**
    A. Common stock
    B. Preferred stock
    C. Subordinated bonds
    D. Senior bonds

30. What is the payoff when a $10 strike call option is exercised when the underlying price is $12?
    A. −$2.00
    B. +$0.00
    C. +$2.00
    D. +$8.00

31. What is/are the primary difference(s) between physical commodities and most other financial products?
    A. Physical products have an associated location.
    B. Physical products have different levels of quality.
    C. Physical products can be very difficult to deliver.
    D. All of the above.

32. If a corporation declares a 3-for-1 stock split on a stock worth $240, what would the price be on the ex-dividend date?
    A. $60
    B. $80
    C. $720
    D. $240

33. Using the weight/volume conversion table provided, calculate the number of barrels in 60 metric tons of 20 API gravity heavy crude oil.

Degree API	Specific Gravity	Conversions	
		(lb/US gal)	BBL / MT
15	0.9659	8.0532	6.5180
20	0.9340	7.7875	6.7405
25	0.9042	7.5386	6.9629
30	0.8762	7.3053	7.1854

    A. 6.7405 barrels
    B. 6.9629 barrels
    C. 202.2150 barrels
    D. 404.4300 barrels

34. What is the primary component of consumer-grade natural gas?
    A. Propane
    B. Methane
    C. Butane
    D. Pentane

35. What term would be used to describe a 39 API gravity crude oil - for example, a crude oil with the same viscosity as West Texas Intermediate?
    A. Sour
    B. Sweet
    C. Light
    D. Heavy

36. If widget fuel is currently trading at $105/gallon, what is the extrinsic value of a call option on 1,000 gallons of widget fuel with a strike of $103/gallon whose premium is $3.50/gallon?
    A. $1,500
    B. $3,500
    C. $5,500
    D. $7,000

37. What is the primary unknown variable needed to solve a Black–Scholes genre option formula?
    A. Valuation date
    B. Forward prices
    C. Expiration date
    D. Implied volatility

38. What is/are the primary reason(s) that an emerging market country would consider coal as a primary fuel for electrical generation?
    I.   Coal is low cost.
    II. A large amount of coal is available locally and wouldn't have to be imported.
    III. The technology to mine and generate power from coal is readily available.

    A. Only I
    B. I and II
    C. I and III
    D. All of the above

39. Anna, works for an investment bank which has the opportunity to fund construction of a lignite-fueled electricity generation plant. Which of the following news stories would most impact this investment?
    A. Rising cost of rail transportation.
    B. Proposed legislation to limit pollution.
    C. Falling petroleum prices.
    D. The facility is in a migration corridor for wild birds traveling to warmer climates for the winter.

40. **Which of the following statements correctly describes shale gas?**
    A. Gas produced by using a Fischer–Tropsch process to convert shale rock to gas
    B. Gas produced from a reservoir of porous, permeable rock capped by an impermeable layer of shale
    C. Gas produced by fracturing layers of impermeable shale containing pockets of trapped natural gas
    D. Gas produced by mining, pulverizing, and heating shale containing trapped natural gas

41. **Which is the correct definition of oil and gas reserves?**
    A. Reserves are defined as identified deposits that can be extracted profitably using present-day techniques and under present economic conditions.
    B. Oil and gas reserves are total volume of fuel present in a gas or oil field and unrelated to the potential economic profit that could be obtained from extracting the fuel.
    C. Oil and gas reserves are a quantity of fuel set aside by a government for national security purposes.
    D. Reserves are profits that aren't recognized as P&L but represent oil set aside by production companies to meet unexpected shortfalls in output of an oil well.

42. **Which of the following describes combined-cycle generation?**
    A. A generation unit that uses one or more combustion turbines to provide heat to a steam turbine.
    B. A generation unit that sells both heat (steam) and electricity
    C. A generation that has the option of using multiple types of fuel
    D. A generation unit that can both produce electricity and take electricity off the power grid and store it (acting like a battery)

43. **Which of the following is a common closed-form equation used to value commodity spread options?**
    A. Black-76
    B. Garman–Kohlhagen
    C. Kirk's approximation
    D. Merton's formula

44. **What are the primary ways that corporations raise capital?**
    I. Issuing stock (equity)
    II. Issuing bonds (debt)
    III. Applying for government subsidies
    IV. Investment tax credits

A. I and II
B. I, II, and III
C. I, II, and IV
D. I, II, III, and IV

45. Rob, an analyst working on a trading desk, has been asked by the head of risk management to calculate an Ornstein–Uhlenbeck volatility. Should he use a Black–Scholes implied volatility calculator to perform this calculation?
A. Yes
B. No

46. What is the spark spread for a 10 MMBtu/MWh natural gas steam turbine with variable operations and maintenance costs of $3/MWh if power prices are $60/MWh and fuel prices are $4/MMBtu?
A. $7/MWh
B. $12/MWh
C. $17/MWh
D. $20/MWh

47. What can convertible bonds be converted into?
A. Investment grade bonds
B. Unsecured corporate debentures
C. Common stock
D. Secured bonds

48. What type of trade does not involve physical delivery of a commodity?
A. Futures.
B. Forwards.
C. Commodity swaps.
D. All of the financial instruments listed involve physical delivery.

49. How much energy is produced by a 100 MW generation unit operating for 10 hours?
A. 10 MW per hour
B. 1000 MW hours
C. 100 MMBtu
D. Insufficient information has been provided to calculate a value

50. Andrew bought a 7% bond maturing in 5 years at 85. The yield to maturity will be:
A. Higher than 7%
B. Equal to 7%
C. Less than 7%
D. Insufficient information

51. **What term would be used to describe crude oil with 2.1% sulfur content?**
    A. Sweet
    B. Sour
    C. Light
    D. Heavy

52. **Choose the best answer. The term landman describes:**
    A. The owner of a piece of property
    B. A unit of measurement used to describe the value of a property
    C. A professional responsible for contacting land owners and negotiating oil and gas contracts
    D. A geologist specializing in identification of oil and gas reserves

53. **Which term refers to the process of separating a mixture into its components by boiling it and then condensing the resulting vapor?**
    A. Distillation
    B. Catalytic conversion
    C. Catalytic cracking
    D. Vacuum cleaning

54. **Nathan, a trader with a bank, is long 500 barrels of crude oil. If prices rise $3/BBL, what will happen?**
    A. Nathan will make money.
    B. Nathan will lose money.
    C. Nathan will neither make nor lose money.
    D. The results can't be determined from the information provided.

55. **What is the most valuable type of fuel?**
    A. Gaseous fuels
    B. Low viscosity liquid fuels
    C. High viscosity liquid fuels
    D. Solid fuels

56. **Organize the following types of natural gas storage facilities in order of least to most desirable performance characteristics:**
    A. Aquifer, salt cavern, depleted reservoir
    B. Salt cavern, depleted reservoir, aquifer
    C. Depleted reservoir, aquifer, salt cavern
    D. Aquifer, depleted reservoir, salt cavern

57. **What does the octane rating of gasoline measure?**
    A. The predictability of gasoline ignition
    B. The quantity of heat energy contained in the gasoline
    C. The percentage of actual gasoline in the mixture rather than additives
    D. The quality of the cleaning and anti-pollution additives in the gasoline

58. In the context of a power grid, which of the following statements related to the transmission and distribution of power is incorrect?
    A. Transmission describes long-distance power lines, distribution shorter distance lines.
    B. Distribution systems need to maintain unprofitable power lines.
    C. Transmission lines typically use higher voltages than distribution lines.
    D. Transmission uses AC power while distribution uses DC power.

59. Historically, what was the largest obstacle that prevented exploration and production companies from economically utilizing shale resources?
    A. Shale is an impermeable rock.
    B. Shale gas is a wet natural gas containing a substantial amount of heavier hydrocarbons.
    C. Shale resources are located in remote regions of the Arctic and Antarctic.
    D. Shale rock is too porous for traditional equipment to drill through.

60. Bitumen, a type of extremely viscous heavy oil, is abundant in an oil sand deposit. While it could be strip-mined and processed off-site, it could also be processed on-site using which technique?
    A. Converting it into a gas by combusting the oil
    B. Forcing it to the surface by vacuum sealing the area
    C. Converting it into liquid through a chemical reaction by injecting hydrogen into the ground
    D. Liquefying it by injecting superheated steam into the ground

61. A bond rating describes what type of risk facing bonds?
    A. Price risk
    B. Liquidity risks
    C. Default risk
    D. Interest and inflation risk

62. What definition best describes initial margin for a future contract?
    A. It is a down payment against future delivery.
    B. It is a good-faith deposit.
    C. It is the difference between the bid and ask price on the exchange.
    D. It is the net profit expected by the trader.

63. Fossil fuels are primarily composed of what common elements?
    A. Carbon and hydrogen
    B. Carbon and oxygen
    C. Hydrogen and oxygen
    D. Oxygen and nitrogen

64. For what type of commodity is the spot price least reflective of future price movements?
  A. Nonconsumable commodities
  B. Nonperishable commodities
  C. Perishable, consumable, nonstorable commodities
  D. Commonly traded commodities

65. Based on the refined product yields summarized in the table below, identify the complexity of each refinery assuming that they each use the same crude oil as a feedstock.

Refined Product	Refinery X	Refinery Y	Refinery Z
Gasoline	60%	45%	25%
No. 2 Diesel	30%	20%	10%
Other products	10%	35%	65%

  A. X = simple, Y = complex, Z = very complex
  B. X = complex, Y = very complex, Z = simple
  C. X = very complex, Y = complex, Z = simple
  D. X − complex, Y − simple, Z = very complex

66. Colin, a scheduler at a major energy company, wants to schedule a tanker to transport crude oil from the Persian Gulf to Italy. He would like to minimize his transport costs and wants to utilize the Suez Canal to avoid circling Africa. What is the best class of ship for him to consider?
  A. Coastal Tanker
  B. Panamax
  C. Suezmax
  D. Aframax

67. Ken is an electric power trader who manages a portfolio of tolling agreements summarized in the table provided. Assuming the spot price of electricity is USD $60/MWh, and all plants are dispatched at maximum capacity, what is the portfolio's total net profit during a given hour?

Unit	Plant Size	Heat Rate	Fuel Price	VOM
Nuclear	1,650 MW	9,800 Btu/KWh	$0.30 / MMBtu	$5/MWh
Natural Gas Peaker	1,000 MW	10,400 Btu/KWh	$3.00 / MMBtu	$3/MWh

  A. $250,800
  B. $111,699
  C. $285,899
  D. $330,121

68. Angela owns 500 acres of land in southern Texas that she uses as a vacation property. A geological survey of the property indicates the presence of hydrocarbons underneath the property. Angela and the landsman assigned to the account negotiate a standard one-eighth royalty payment. If, during the first year, the well produces 10,000 barrels of oil that is at an average USD $85/BBL price, what is the royalty payment?
   A. USD $1,250
   B. USD $106,250
   C. USD $125,000
   D. USD $743,750

69. Tom decides to purchase RECs as an investment and hold them until they expire. How much money will Tom make from his investment?
   A. Tom will lose everything he invested.
   B. The REC registry will publish a settlement price that determines the payoff.
   C. The regulator will publish a settlement price that determines the payoff.
   D. Tom will break even for zero net profit.

70. What is the term that describes a large volume of natural gas dissolved in underground crude oil reserves due to high pressure on the crude oil?
   A. Associated gas
   B. Petroleum gas
   C. Swamp gas
   D. Working gas

71. What is a Power Purchase Agreement (aka, a PPA)?
   A. A standardized contract to trade power transacted on an exchange
   B. A standardized contract to trade power transacted bilaterally
   C. A long-term contract, typically signed during at construction of a generation facility to purchase the output of the generation facility
   D. A general term for any nonstandard contract to buy and sell power

72. What are the underlying assets involved in a heat-rate option?
   A. Electricity and a fuel (like natural gas)
   B. Electricity at two different locations
   C. Crude oil and a refined product
   D. Natural gas at two different locations

73. Alexey manages a natural gas combustion turbine generation unit with a 10 MMBtu/MWh heat rate. The power price is $65/MWh, the natural gas price is $6/MMBtu, and the plant's variable operations and maintenance cost is $3/MWh. If Alexey has the option of selling either ancillary services

or participating in the day-ahead market, what is the minimum price he would accept to sell ancillary services rather than power into the day-ahead market?
A. $2
B. $3
C. $5
D. $7

74. What does the term *grade* refer to when describing a commodity?
A. The physical location of the commodity
B. The quality and specifications of the commodity
C. The difference in price of the commodity at its particular location relative to the futures delivery location
D. A rating assigned to the delivery agent indicating the likelihood of the agent being able to deliver the commodity.

75. Why would a heavy crude oil, like Mexico's Maya crude, be cheaper than lighter crude oils like Arab light crude?
A. Heavy crudes like Maya crude are more difficult to transport.
B. The supply of untapped Maya crude reserves is larger than the supply of Arab light reserves.
C. Middle Eastern crude oil is higher quality than crudes from other parts of the world.
D. Refineries need specialized equipment that is very expensive to process heavy crude oils.

76. Raw Natural Gas typically has what level of heat content?
A. 500 to 800 Btu/ft^3
B. 900 to 1,200 Btu/ ft^3
C. 1,200 to 1,500 Btu/ ft^3
D. 1,500 to 1,800 Btu/ ft^3

77. Using the supplied forward curve table, what is the price of the asset for November delivery as of September 25, 2012?

	Delivery Month		
Valuation Date	October 2012	November 2012	December 2012
9/25/2012	101	102	103
9/26/2012	101.5	102.5	104

A. 101
B. 102
C. 102.5
D. 104

78. Estimate the profitability per barrel of crude oil for a refinery that produces
2 barrels of gasoline and 1 barrel of diesel for every 3 barrels of crude oil.

Crude Oil: USD $70/BBL
Gasoline: 198 USC/gallon
Diesel: 185 USC/gallon

A. $11.34 per BBL crude
B. $17.15 per BBL crude
C. $34.02 per BBL crude
D. $511 per BBL crude

79. In an electrical market providing retail competition, what is a "Provider of
Last Resort"?
A. A company where the legislature has determined that the business
affects the public interest and needs to be regulated
B. A company that owns generation, transmission, and distribution assets
C. A for-profit company that does not own transmission or generation,
but contracts with utilities and generators on behalf of its client
D. A power provider who is obligated to sell consumers power if they
don't choose a supplier or their supplier goes out of business

80. What type of Black–Scholes formula is used to value options based on
commodity futures?
A. Black–Scholes
B. Merton
C. Black-76
D. Garman–Kohlhagen

81. Heat rate refers to what property of a power plant?
A. How quickly the unit can start operations
B. The average daily high temperature in the unit's service area
C. The temperature at which the unit operates
D. The efficiency at which a unit converts fuel into electricity

82. What is *not* an advantage of transporting crude oil to refineries located
near the ultimate consumers of the refined products?
A. Refined petroleum products are cheaper to ship than crude oil.
B. Local refineries are better able to alter their refining operations to
maximize their ability to produce products that meet regional
consumer demand.
C. Refineries near consumer areas are at a lower risk of being damaged
by war or seized by an unfriendly government than refineries near
producing regions.
D. Refineries near consumer areas allow the refinery to source the most
cost-effective crude oil and adapt when existing crude oil wells are
depleted.

83. In the context of a regulated power market, what is a rate base?
    A. A benchmark interest rate which is adjusted upwards for bad credit
    B. The minimum number of consumers needed to make a utility profitable
    C. The lowest price of power offered by a utility
    D. The value of property and assets on which a utility is allowed to earn a return

84. Approximately how much energy would a 100 MW fixed-panel solar generation facility produce during a year?
    A. Between 87,600 MWh and 175,200 MWh
    B. Between 262,800 MWh and 350,400 MWh
    C. Between 428,000 MWh and 525,600 MWh
    D. Between 613,200 MWh and 700,800 MWh

85. In the electricity market, which of the following best describes the term *capacity market*?
    A. A capacity market is a system designed to compensate underutilized generation units for their role in providing the power grid a safety margin of excess generation.
    B. A capacity market is a mechanism where generators can donate unused generation capacity to charity for a tax write-off.
    C. A capacity market is a way for generation owners to self-insure against an unexpected outage in their facility.
    D. A capacity market is a way for retail service providers to offload consumers delinquent on their monthly payments to the Provider of Last Resort.

86. Marc is an energy investor analyzing crude oil reserves for potential investment opportunities. A reservoir is described as having a P90 of 100 million barrels. What does that mean?
    A. There is a 90% chance the actual reserves of the field will be less than 100 million barrels.
    B. There is a 90% chance the actual reserves of the field will exceed 100 million barrels.
    C. There is a 90% chance the actual resources of the field will be less than 100 million barrels.
    D. There is a 90% chance the actual resources of the field will exceed 100 million barrels.

87. In the futures market, what is the abbreviation EFP short for?
    A. Exchange for Principal
    B. Exchange for Physical
    C. Expiration from Proration
    D. Exchange Fixed Price

88. In a typical interest rate environment, will the market price of a zero-coupon bond trade at a premium or discount to its par value?
    A. Discount.
    B. Premium.
    C. Insufficient information is provided.
    D. The par value for zero-coupon bonds is an accounting tool unrelated to its market price.

89. Which of the following statements is true about extra-heavy crude oils (crude oil with API gravity below 15)?
    A. Extra-heavy oil is considered coal rather than petroleum due to its high viscosity.
    B. Extra-heavy oils are not a commercially viable fuel.
    C. Extra-heavy oils can be economically processed in a simple refinery.
    D. Extra-heavy oil deposits are more numerous than traditionally developed light crude oil deposits.

90. What is the primary reason that many energy products exhibit seasonal cyclical shapes to their forward curve?
    A. Illiquid trading
    B. Limitations on the storage of a commodity
    C. Bilateral and exchange-based trading
    D. Consistent arbitrage opportunities in the market

91. If widget oil is currently trading at $25/gallon, which of the following options on widget oil is NOT in-the-money?
    A. Call at $15/gal
    B. Call at $20/gal
    C. Put at $25/gal
    D. Put at $30/gal

92. What term is commonly used as a synonym for an end user of natural gas?
    A. Citygate
    B. Firm transportation buyer
    C. Interruptible transportation buyer
    D. Burner tip

93. A refinery with a coking unit would be described as:
    A. A hydroskimming facility
    B. A complex or very complex refinery
    C. A vacuum distillation
    D. A simple refinery

94. What is the correct definition of a European option?
    A. An option that is traded in Europe
    B. An option that has positive intrinsic value
    C. An option that can only be exercised on the expiration date
    D. An option denominated in a foreign currency

95. In a deregulated market, what is the market clearing price of power if demand is 1,000 MW, there is no congestion on the power grid, and generators in the region price their generation as follows:

Unit 1: 800 MW at $20/MWh
Unit 2: 500 MW at $50/MWh
Unit 3: 200 MW at $60/MWh
Unit 4: 100 MW at $100/MWh

A. $20/MWh
B. $26/MWh
C. $36/MWh
D. $50/MWh

96. If the return of an asset follows a continuously compounded random walk, prices will have which of the following distributions?
A. A symmetric platykurtic distribution
B. An asymmetric platykurtic distribution
C. A normal distribution
D. A lognormal distribution

97. What is a spot transaction?
A. A transaction where an asset is exchanged for cash "on the spot"
B. A transaction that has higher than normal risk
C. A transaction subject to synchronous purchase and trade rules
D. A transaction that occurs just prior to the end of the day

98. A bond with a Baa/BBB rating is considered a(n)
A. Investment-grade bond
B. Zero-coupon bond
C. Premium bond
D. High-yield bond

99. Tom, a stock investor, knows that XYZ stock is issuing a $2 dividend. What will happen if he buys the stock just before the closing trade on the record date and sells it on the opening trade of the ex-dividend date?
A. He will make a $2 profit.
B. He will lose money due to trading expenses that he might incur and the need to pay taxes on the $2 dividend.
C. He will break even.
D. Insufficient information.

100. What is the difference between No. 2 Heating Oil and No.2 Diesel Fuel?
A. There is no difference, they are identical.
B. Heating oil contains higher levels of sulfur and is not approved for on-highway use.
C. Heating oil has a higher cetane rating than diesel fuel.
D. Both B and C.

Final Exam Answers and Explanations

1.   B. An oil sand deposit typically requires large amounts of water. Many oil sand mines use as much water as a large city. Pipelines can be built and workers brought on site. However, a lack of water is difficult to overcome.

2.   C. The number of outstanding shares (issued shares less treasury stock) determines the total amount of shares owned by shareholders. In this case, 500 shares are issued, of which 100 were repurchased by the company. There are 400 shares outstanding. As a result, a shareholder that owns 100 shares will own 25% of the company.

3.   B. Put options benefit when the underlying price declines in value. As a result, Edmund has a short position in the underlying commodity. However, an option always increases in value as volatility increases.

4.   A. A receipt point is a location where natural gas is injected into a pipeline. Natural gas hub and citygate are terms meant to confuse the reader as these are common receipt and delivery points. However, hubs and citygates don't need to be injection points—they could be only distribution locations.

5.   A. A putable bond gives the bondholder the option to put (redeem) the bond back to the issuer.

6.   C. The definition of producing gas-oil ratio requires gas production (in cubic feet) to be divided by oil production (in barrels). The gas-oil ratio = $(1,600,000,000 \text{ ft}^3)/(250,000 \text{ BBL}) = 6400 \text{ ft}^3/\text{BBL}$.

7.   B. As interest rates decline, the value of existing bonds increases.

8.   D. NGLs can provide a second revenue stream for any type of natural gas development project. NGL products are generally more valuable than methane and, in the case of a field that is particularly rich in NGLs, could provide more revenue than the natural gas business.

9.   B. Shale oil is produced by mining, pulverizing, and heating shale rock. The other descriptions describe more common oil production techniques.

10.   A. By definition, E10 gasoline is 10% ethanol by volume. The "assuming that ethanol is 5% more dense" is misdirection designed to confuse the reader.

11.   C. BOE compares the amount of natural gas to oil within a reservoir by using the heat content of each as a conversion factor.

12.   D. A bondholder receives interest payments. A bondholder is not a partial owner of a company, does not benefit from the company becoming more valuable, and does not get a say in how the company is managed.

13.   B. Volatility with a random walk process will scale with the square root of time. This is a well-known constant that should be memorized.

14.   B. The HoldCo debt is structurally subordinate to the UtilCo debt. The HoldCo bondholders will get paid after the UtilCo bondholders. In both cases, the senior bondholders will be paid before the subordinated bondholders. The structural subordination makes UtilCo subordinated debt senior to the HoldCo senior debt.

15.   B. Answer II and III are reasons that are commonly used to purchase RECs when there isn't a regulatory requirement to do so. Answer I is incorrect partly because renewable sources of energy are usually less reliable than nonrenewable sources. However, that's somewhat misleading since RECs decouple the creation of RECs from electricity. The data center might actually be using power generated from a coal facility while the renewable provider sends power to someone else. The reason for that is because once electrons hit the power grid, they are indistinguishable and interchangeable. As long as the power grid can meet the power requirements of the data center, there should be no reliability concerns. Answer IV is incorrect since renewable power is generally more expensive than other alternatives. Otherwise, everyone

would already be using renewable energy sources and there would be no reason to commit to paying higher costs for it. In general, a company will purchase power off the electrical grid.

16.   **B.** A short future plus a long call can be combined to form a synthetic long put. One way to help remember this relationship is that both calls and puts benefit from volatility (they are long volatility).

17.   **B.** Answer B is the correct answer. An ISO/RTO is a type of power grid operator. Answer A describes a type of utility (called a T&D or a wire company) that is responsible for transmission and distribution of electricity. Answer C describes a local regulatory body which is commonly a public utility commission or public service commission.

18.   **B.** All of the answers except for B are correct. Renewable does not mean inexhaustible. Renewable energy sources can be exhausted or substantially diminished if not maintained. For example, man-made climate change can dry up rivers and change rain and wind patterns. Overplanting may damage crop yields, and dust storms could erode solar generation efficiency. Renewable energy is generally more expensive than energy from fossil fuel generation. Renewable units also have uncertain capacity factors due to constrained fuel supplies (biofuels) or reliance on an outside energy source (like hydro, solar, or wind).

19.   **A.** Answer B is the definition for the term demurrage. Answer C is the definition for the term arbiter. Answer D is the definition for an illiquid market.

20.   **A.** With statutory voting rights, a shareholder who owns 100 shares would get 100 votes to be used in each election.

21.   **C.** The answer is approximately 95%. Normal distributions are encountered sufficiently often that the 68/95/99% of samples corresponding to 1/2/3 standard deviations from the mean should be memorized.

22.   **C.** Although all these factors can limit construction, the biggest factor is that there are few places available to build hydroelectric generation units. Many of the best sites to locate hydroelectric generation are already in use or would require major disruptions to nearby communities.

23.   **A.** In a contango market, forward prices are higher than spot prices. In the energy markets, forward and spot prices are not necessarily linked by no-arbitrage. For example, superheated steam to heat an apartment building is far more valuable in the winter than the summer. A warm building in winter is good, but it may be highly undesirable in the middle of the summer. In fact, the spot commodity (steam in January) may not even be considered to be the same product as the forward commodity (steam in August).

24.   D. All of the answers provided in the question are correct. Photovoltaic solar power and batteries are common examples of generation that is not based on electromagnetic induction.

25.   A. Almost all modern power grids use AC power because the voltage can easily be scaled up and down using transformers. This allows a constant voltage across the power grid.

26.   B. High-sulfur diesel approved for non-highway use is dyed red to distinguish it from on-highway (low sulfur) diesel fuel. The most common uses for high-sulfur diesel are to fuel farm equipment or as a home heating fuel.

27.   B. An Asian option is an option whose payoff is calculated using the average price of the underlying over some period of time rather than the price on the expiration date. Answer C describes an American option. Answer D describes a European option.

28.   D. Higher API gravity is associated with lighter crude oils. Lower sulfur is associated with sweet crude oils. Light sweet crude is typically the most valuable crude oil.

29.   A. Since common stockholders are the last in line to get paid during a bankruptcy, common stock is considered the most junior type of security.

30.   C. When a call option is exercised, the payoff is Max(0, underlying price − strike price). In this case, $12 − $10 = $2. This payoff is the same as the intrinsic value.

31.   D. All of the above describe issues that are important to physical commodities.

32.   B. In a 3-for-1 split, each share turns into 3 shares. As a result, the ex-dividend price is one-third of the pre-dividend price. $240/3 = $80.

33.   D. (60 MT) * (6.7405 BBL/MT) = 404.43 barrels of crude oil

34.   B. Consumer-grade natural gas is composed primarily of methane and is considered dry natural gas.

35.   C. Crude oil with an API gravity between 38 and 45 degrees is considered a light crude. While WTI is a sweet crude, answer B is incorrect since the question is asking about crude oils with an API gravity similar to WTI crude, and provides no information on the sulfur content.

36.   A. The call option is $2 in the money (the intrinsic value is $2). The remaining value is extrinsic value ($3.50 − $2 = $1.50/gallon). $1.50/gallon * 1000 gallons = $1,500.

37. D. Implied volatility is the primary unknown quantity. The valuation date is the date when the option is being valued (commonly the current day). The expiration date is specified as part of the contract. Forward prices can usually be obtained from trading markets.

38. D. All of the reasons would be considered when determining whether to use coal or another fuel as the basis of an electrical grid.

39. B. Lignite emits substantial amounts of pollution when combusted. Legislation to limit pollution might prevent the plant from operating or require substantial upgrades to the facility. Rising transport costs is incorrect since lignite is typically not transported long distances. Falling petroleum prices is incorrect since oil is not a major fuel used to generate electricity. Wind farms, not coal-fired electrical generation, are impacted by bird migration routes.

40. C. Shale gas refers to gas produced by hydraulic fracturing of impermeable shale rock containing trapped pockets of natural gas.

41. A. Answer A is the correct definition for reserves. Answer B describes oil and gas resources. Answers C and D are trick answers. They are both appropriate uses for the term reserve as used in "strategic oil reserve" or "financial reserve," however they do not correctly define the petroleum industry term *oil and gas reserves*.

42. A. Answer a is correct. A combined cycle generation plant combines both combustion turbines and steam turbines. This question could easily be modified to ask about any of a variety of vocabulary words.

43. C. Kirk's approximation is a well-known formula used to value commodity spread options. While it's not the only approach to valuing spread options, and it has many critics, it is one of the more well-known and widely used approaches.

44. A. The two primary ways for corporations to raise capital are debt financing (issuing bonds) and equity financing (issuing stock). Grants and tax credits are important to some companies (particularly small companies) but are not the primary ways that most corporations raise capital.

45. B. The volatility using one set of assumptions (that prices follow a random walk) should not be used for a different set of assumptions (that prices are mean reverting).

46. C. This question requires the memorization of the spark spread formula. A spark spread is equal to Power Price − Heat Rate* Fuel Price − VOM. Putting in values, $60 − 10 * $4 $3 = $17.

47   C. Convertible bonds can usually be converted into common stock.

48.   C. Commodity swaps are cash settled—futures and forwards are physically settled.

49.   B. Energy is measured in megawatt-hours (megawatts multiplied by hours). In other words a unit of power (rate of work) multiplied by a unit of time. Units of MW per hour (megawatts divided by hours) might describe how quickly a generator can turn on, but it doesn't describe energy produced.

50.   A. Since the bond was purchased at a discount, the yield to maturity will be greater than both the nominal yield (coupon rate) and the current yield.

51.   B. Crude oil with a sulfur content of more than 0.5% sulfur is typically classified as sour, while oil with less than 0.5% sulfur is considered sweet. There is some variation in the border between sweet and sour, but 2.1% is well into the sour range. The terms light and heavy refer to density of oil rather than its sulfur content.

52.   C. The definition of a landman is a professional who negotiates with landowners for oil, gas, and other rights to their property.

53.   A. Distillation (vacuum distillation if done in a vacuum) is the process of separating a mixture into its components by boiling it and then condensing the resulting vapor.

54.   A. A trader with a long position benefits from a rise in prices. In this case, Nathan will make $1,500 dollars (500 BBL × $3/BBL profit).

55.   B. Low viscosity liquid fuels are typically the most valuable type of fuel due to their high energy density and engineering properties.

56.   D. Aquifers have the least desirable performance characteristics, depleted reservoirs are in the middle, and salt caverns have the most desirable performance characteristics.

57.   A. Octane measures the predictability of how the fuel combusts. Higher octane gasoline allows engines to be built with tighter tolerance thresholds. Higher octane gasoline often contains additives to keep engines clean and other additives are often mixed into gasoline to raise its octane rating. However, octane rating is a separate concept from additives.

58.   D. Both transmission and distribution systems typically use AC power. Modern distribution systems almost always use AC power. Long distance DC power lines are occasionally used for transmission underneath large bodies of water or where the transmission line doesn't need to branch or interconnect with other lines. However, that wasn't an option given as a choice.

59.   A. Shale is a porous, impermeable rock. Shale rock's porosity allows it to contain hydrocarbons. However, because shale is not permeable, it was hard to get those hydrocarbons out of the rock. While Answer B is true statement, it does not describe an obstacle—the heavy hydrocarbons in shale gas are very valuable and provide much of the economic incentive to develop shale resources. Answers C and D are incorrect. Shale reserves are located throughout the world, and high porosity does not prevent drilling.

60.   D. Heavy oil deposits are commonly processed on-site by injecting superheated steam into the ground. Combusting the oil would destroy the oil and prevent it from being processed. The other techniques are fictional.

61.   C. Bond ratings describe how likely an issuer is to default on their payments.

62.   B. Margin is a good-faith deposit. It involves collateral like cash or securities which are pledged to pay off the obligation incurred by signing a futures contract.

63.   A. Fossil fuels are hydrocarbons and composed of chains of carbon and hydrogen.

64.   C. In an extreme example, perishable, consumable, nonstorable commodities (like electricity) at one time of day (2 p.m.) may not be considered the same commodity at a different time of day (midnight). In these cases, spot prices are not at all indicative of future prices. However, for other commodities like natural gas, the relationship is less clear. Storage is possible, but limited, and new production is needed to replace the fuel consumed during use.

65.   C. More complex refineries can produce a higher quantity of gasoline and diesel fuel than less complex refineries.

66.   C. Of the choices offered, a Suezmax tanker is the best choice. A ULCC tanker may be a better choice if it didn't have to offload any products to traverse the canal. However, that requires information that wasn't included in the question and it wasn't offered as a choice.

67.   B. Answer B is correct. One trick in the problem is that heat rates in Btu/KWh must be converted into MMBtu/MWh by dividing by 1,000. The formula for determining the portfolio's net profit is: Net profit (Spark Spread) = Volume × (Power Price − Heat Rate × Fuel Price − VOM)

- The nuclear plant profit is 1,650 MW × ($60 − 9.8 × $0.30 − $5) = $85,899
- The natural gas plant profit is 1,000 MW × ($60 − 10.4 × $3 − $3) = $25,800
- Adding the two together gives a net profit of $111,699.

68.   B. The oil well produced $850,000 of oil during the year. One-eighth of the total (12.5%) is $106,250.

69.   A. RECs have no intrinsic value—they are only useful to meet a regulatory requirement. If Tom has no regulatory requirement to purchase RECs (or he has already met his requirement), holding additional RECs will do him no good. He should try and sell them to someone that needs them before the RECs expire worthless.

70.   A. Answer A is correct. Although natural gas is sometimes referred to as a petroleum gas, the gas dissolved in underground crude oil reserves is known as associated gas. Answers C and D are not related to the question.

71.   C. A PPA is a long-term agreement to purchase the output of the facility. PPAs are typically not traded. Instead, they are linked to specific generation units and will pass to the new owners if the units are ever sold. As a warning, the abbreviation PPA is used in other financial contexts with a different meaning. For example, a Purchase Price Agreement is also commonly abbreviated as a PPA.

72.   A. A heat-rate option gives the owner of the option the ability to convert a fuel, like natural gas, into electricity.

73.   A. Selling power into the day-ahead market, Andy could lock in a $2 profit by selling power at $65 when his cost is $63 (10 MMBtu/ MWh * $6/MMBtu + $3). He should accept no less than $2 for selling ancillary services. Because a gas turbine can turn on quickly, another choice for operating the unit might be to sell into the real-time market. However, that was not provided as an option here. If operating in the real time market were offered as an operating choice, the ancillary service price that Andy should accept would be the higher of the expected profit of selling into the day-ahead or real-time markets.

74.   B. The term *grade* describes the quality and physical specifications of a commodity. Answer A refers to a delivery location, and answer C refers to a basis price.

75.   D. Heavy crudes need specialized equipment, like cracking and coking units, to be fully processed. This equipment is extremely expensive and not installed at every refinery. The other answers are mostly misdirection. Middle Eastern crude oil is typically not considered a premium crude. Heavier crude is no more or less difficult to transport than light crude, and an untapped supply of crude has limited effect on current market prices.

76.   **B.** Most raw natural gas has a heat content that ranges between 900 and 1,200 Btu per cubic foot. Associated gas (gas found in oil wells) will typically have a higher Btu content because the gas will contain some of the heavier components found in the crude oil. Gas with a high CO_2 content will have a lower Btu content.

77.   **B.** A forward price is a price for delivery on a specific date (the expiration date) as of some valuation date. In the graph shown, the valuation date is shown in the first column and the delivery dates are across the top row.

78.   **A.** It is necessary to convert units of U.S. cents (USC) into U.S. dollars (USD) and barrels to gallons. There are 42 gallons per U.S. barrel.
   - Cost of input for 3 barrels: 3 barrels * $70 = $210 dollars / 3 barrels input
   - Value of outputs: 2 barrels of gasoline * $1.98/gallons *42 gallons + 1 barrel of diesel * $1.85/gallons * 42 gallons = $244.02 / 3 barrels input
   - Profit per barrel = ($244.02 −$210) / 3 barrels = $11.34 / barrel

79.   **D.** A provider of last resort is a retail provider in a deregulated market which is obligated to supply power to consumers if another provider is unable to meet its obligations.

80.   **C.** The Black–Scholes genre formula used to price options based on commodity futures is the Black-76 formula.

81.   **D.** Heat rate describes efficiency of conversion. The numerator and denominator are both units of energy. As a result, it can be converted into a variety of units showing amount of energy, or even shown as a unitless ratio.

82.   **A.** Answer A is incorrect since transport costs are similar for crude and refined products. All of the other answers are correct.

83.   **D.** A rate base is the accumulated property and assets of a utility (like a power line), which it has acquired on the behalf of consumers. The public service commission determines which costs can be recovered. For example, a utility might build a power line to serve consumers. The utility will then be able to charge consumers slightly higher rates to repay those construction costs.

84.   **A.** This question requires knowing that a fixed-panel solar facility typically has a capacity factor of 13% to 20% and that there are approximately 8,760 hours in a year (365 days * 24 hours). The number of hours multiplied by the capacity factor and the nameplate capacity of the facility can calculate the generation output of the unit. In the U.S., solar units in the desert southwest will be towards the high end of the range (20% capacity factor), while units in less optimal environments (like the Canadian border) will be towards the lower edge of that range.

85.   A. A capacity market is an auction-based system designed to compensate less utilized or unutilized generation units for providing a safety margin for the power grid

86.   B. P90 indicates that there is a 90% probability that the actual reserves will exceed 100 million barrels.

87.   B. EFP is an abbreviation for Exchange for Physical. An EFP is a way to get a delivery of a physical product using a futures contract away from the exchange settlement location.

88.   A. Zero-coupon bonds will typically trade at a discount to their par value since they don't pay any coupons.

89.   D. Approximately four times as many heavy crude deposits exist compared to traditional light crude deposits. Heavy crude is a commercially viable fuel that needs to be processed in a complex refinery.

90.   B. Nonstorability is the main reason for cyclical forward curves. While arbitrage opportunities might exist in a seasonal curve, arbitrage opportunities are not the reason why many energy curves show seasonality.

91.   C. A put written at $25/gallons on an underlying whose price is $25/gallons is at-the-money. All of the other options would be in-the-money.

92.   D. The term burner tip refers to a consumer, or end user, of natural gas.

93.   B. A coking unit is an expensive, complicated piece of equipment that is found in complex and very complex refineries.

94.   C. The terms American and European describe the rules on when an option can be exercised. A European option can only be exercised on the expiration date.

95.   D. If 1,000 MW of power is being used, Unit 1 will be dispatched at full capacity and Unit 2 will be partially dispatched. The market clearing price of power is determined by the most expensive generator that is currently operating (Unit 2). As a result, the market clearing price for power is $50. A variant of this problem can ask the profitability of each unit. Assuming that the plants are selling power at production cost, Unit 1 would be making $24,000/hour (800 MW times $30/MWh profit) and Unit 2 would have zero profit.

96.   D. If returns follow a random walk, then returns will be normally distributed. However, this question asks for the distribution of prices rather than the distribution of returns. Since returns are calculated by taking the natural logarithm of prices, this will make the distribution of prices lognormally distributed.

97.   A. A spot transaction is one that occurs "on the spot." Even so, it typically takes at least two days for the all the paperwork to finish and the money to be transferred.

98.   A. Bonds with a Baa/BBB rating or higher are considered investment-grade bonds suitable for most investors.

99.   B. The price of the stock will be reduced by the amount of the dividend on the ex-dividend date. As a result, there is little benefit trying to capture the dividend. Dividends are taxable, and trading does involve some cost, so this will likely be a net loss for Tom.

100.   B. Although chemically similar, Diesel typically has lower sulfur and a higher cetane rating than heating oil. This makes Answer A and C incorrect.

Endnotes

Chapter 1

1. There are often multiple names for both fuels and categories of fuels. In addition to regional variations, each industry has often developed its own terminology.

2. Petroleum is another term that means a variety of things to different people. From Latin, it means "rock oil" or "oil from rock," and in this book it refers to liquid hydrocarbons. In some textbooks, it may be used as a general term for all fossil fuels.

3. Sometimes called *hydrocarbon reserves*.

4. The statutory definition of a gas well and oil well in Texas and Pennsylvania.

5. These numbers are approximate, since crude oil and gas produced by a well are mixtures and don't have a consistent makeup.
   Source: Energy Information Agency, *Annual Energy Review, 1999*.

6. The formula for API Gravity can be expressed as:
   API = (141.5 / SG) − 131.5
   where
   API = Degrees API Gravity
   SG = Specific Gravity (at 60°F or 288.7 K)

7. The conversion factors needed to do this calculation:
   2204.62262 pounds per metric ton
   8.3378 lbs of pure water per gallon at 60°F
   6.205547 BBL of pure water per MT at 60°F

The density of water varies about $+/-0.5\%$ between 32°F/0°C and 100°F/37.8°C

8. Forward and spot prices will be defined in more detail in Chapter 6. Spot prices are a transaction "on the spot" involving an exchange of cash for a physical commodity. Forward transactions are a binding contract to exchange cash and a physical commodity at some point in the future.

9. From CME/NYMEX product specifications for WTI futures contracts.

10. Methyl Tertiary Butyl Ether (MTBE) is an additive that is used to increase the octane rating of gasoline.

11. Cetane numbers measure the ignition quality of the fuel. This number is roughly comparable to the octane number used to describe various types of gasoline.

12. This table gives approximate conversion factors. There are regional and formulation variations that will affect all of these numbers. For example CARBOB (California RBOB gasoline) will have a slightly different composition than RBOB (standard reformulated gasoline). Their densities in this table are approximate numbers not specific to any single formulation.

Chapter 2

1. In a theoretical sense, the value of interruptible transport should be zero if every market participant maximized their own profit (i.e., behaved according to the economic definition of rational).

2. The regulatory jurisdiction of pipelines can vary. For example, in the United States, pipelines that cross state boundaries fall under federal jurisdiction (the national government), while intrastate pipelines (those completely within a single state) would fall under state or local regulations.

Chapter 4

1. In some cases, there is not a clear-cut distinction between the buyer and seller. For example, two traders may agree to exchange one product for another at some point in the future. In these cases, language in the contract will describe the respective obligations of each party.

2. Arbitrage is the possibility of making a profit without taking any risk.

3. Margin is discussed in more detail in the section on futures trading. Traders who transact on an exchange will either receive or need to make a daily payment, called a margin, depending on whether prices go up or down. Since every trade requires both a buyer and a seller, the exchange will act as a

middleman to route these payments from traders who need to pay to those that are receiving money.

Chapter 5

1. In economic literature, there are a variety of financial definitions for efficient markets. However, all of the efficient market hypotheses agree that it is difficult to make arbitrage profits in financial markets. This is sufficient to make traded prices in liquid markets a reliable indicator of fair prices.

2. Liquidity refers to the ease at which a commodity can be converted into cash. Illiquid markets are ones where little or no trading is possible.

3. Historically, the U.S. Treasury rate was used as a risk-free rate. However, most large financial institutions have moved to using the LIBOR rate as the risk-free benchmark.

4. Nominal means "named."

Chapter 6

1. The exact mechanism for pricing will be discussed in the Futures Margining section later in the chapter.

2. In other financial markets, like the foreign exchange and fixed income markets, the term *swap* describes a very different type of financial instrument. While these instruments are not discussed in this book, the term commodity swap is used in this book to distinguish commodity swaps from fixed-income or foreign exchange swaps.

Chapter 7

1. Options on stocks and bonds with have a similar relationship. The primary difference is that these instruments can pay dividends or coupon payments and future cash flows will need to be present valued.

Chapter 8

1. A more complete discussion on the valuation of Asian options can be found in more advanced books on option formulas like Esper Haug's *The Complete Guide to Option Pricing Formulas*, 2nd edition, McGraw-Hill, 2006.

2. The distribution resulting from the ratio of two lognormal distributions is actually a Cauchy distribution. A Cauchy distribution is approximately normal when the two lognormal distributions are highly correlated.

3. This is a complicated, but well-solved, problem in mathematics that is generally described as a Cauchy–Lorentz distribution.

Chapter 10

1. Note: The term *basis* in this sense (a yield) means something completely different than the term *basis* used in the physical commodity market (a price resulting from a location difference).

Index